ENERGY, RISK & COMPETITIVE ADVANTAGE:

The Information Imperative

ENERGY, RISK & COMPETITIVE ADVANTAGE:
The Information Imperative

Scott Randall

Disclaimer

The recommendations, advice, descriptions, and the methods in this book are presented solely for educational purposes. The author and publisher assume no liability whatsoever for any loss or damage that results from the use of any of the material in this book. Use of the material in this book is solely at the risk of the user.

Copyright © 2008 by
PennWell Corporation
1421 South Sheridan Road
Tulsa, Oklahoma 74112-6600 USA

800.752.9764
+1.918.831.9421
sales@pennwell.com
www.pennwellbooks.com
www.pennwell.com

Marketing Manager: Julie Simmons
National Account Executive: Barbara McGee

Director: Mary McGee
Managing Editor: Marla Patterson
Production Manager: Sheila Brock
Production Editor: Tony Quinn
Cover/Book Design: Sheila Brock and Alan McCuller
Book Layout: Alan McCuller

Library of Congress Cataloging-in-Publication Data

Randall, Scott, 1958-
  Energy, risk, and competitive advantage : the information imperative / Scott Randall.
     p. cm.
  Includes bibliographical references and index.
  ISBN-13: 978-1-59370-134-5
  1. Energy industries--Information technology--Security measures. 2. Energy industries--Information technology--Management. 3. Energy industries--Risk management. I. Title.
  HD9502.A2R36 2008
  333.79068'4--dc22
                                                          2007050316

Printed in the United States of America

1 2 3 4 5   13 12 11 10 09 08

To my wife Kristi. Your encouragement and support inspired me to get up before dawn and write.

Foreword

In early 2003 when we first began to develop courses and perform consulting in the field of enterprise risk, Scott and I corresponded and then had the opportunity to work together, first in a training program for Petroleos de Venezuela in Puerto La Cruz, and later in London and Aberdeen. Over the years we've shared an interest in strategy and the portfolio effects of integrated corporate risks. Out of this mutual interest, we began to develop analytical tools and techniques that came out of other fields of study, but were perfectly well suited for application to operational risk problems. The accounting and financial services industry in the US had begun at that time to develop the COSO II Framework, and this, combined with the earlier released Turnbull Commission/Combined Code here in the UK, formed a conceptual basis for the then emerging discipline of Enterprise Risk Management. What the frameworks lacked however was a certain breadth of tools and specific application to the energy industry. Scott began to realize that it wasn't just the tools that were missing, but the very basis for sound decisions, *valid input data*. One night on the airplane together Scott began to describe to me how this fundamental basis for risk management seemed to be lost in the shuffle of the finger pointing that resulted from the Enron scandal and ensuing Sarbanes-Oxley legislation. Furthermore, he was resolved that evening to begin to compile the framework for what would now become an authoritative reference on the topic of *Information Integrity* for purposes of energy risk management. I am very glad to see this come to fruition precisely at a time when the stakeholders are demanding greater information due diligence, but don't have the tools that this book provides to truly follow through on those demands. Anyone from chief financial officer to bond rating analyst will benefit from this aid to "pulling back the corporate veil" of spurious external information.

David Wood, PhD; author, lecturer and founder of DWA, Lincoln, UK

Contents

3   Information Integrity Implementation—Tools, Techniques, and Examples 57

Preface

Sound governance requires reasonable assurance that the assets of the corporation are safeguarded and that stakeholder value is being created. The concept of reasonable assurance is fundamental to the auditing of internal controls over financial statements. However, making sure the financial recording and reporting process is robust is not the same as making sure the inputs to these processes are reliable. Thus, an analogous standard to reasonable assurance should be applied to the integrity of information that feeds every material aspect of a company's operations. In this sense, ensuring information integrity goes beyond merely financial statement compliance and strikes squarely at the heart of the emerging field of Enterprise Risk Management.

The goal of Enterprise Risk Management (ERM) is to reduce the band of uncertainty for both the probability and impact of occurrence of events representing threats and/or opportunities to growth stakeholder value, consistent with an organization's pre-established risk appetite. This is quite a mouthful, but what it means is that we have confidence that we are taking the appropriate risks to ensure an adequate return. Reduction of uncertainty relies upon more information in the form of new, validated data. In the absence of gathered information obtained through a process of market research for example, Monte Carlo sampling techniques can be used to simulate the outcomes, thus acting as a kind of proxy for validated data. There is a place for Monte Carlo techniques in quantitative risk analysis, but if the overall goal is important enough (i.e., investor confidence, market projections, sales forecasting), simulation is probably not sufficient to ensure that you have a robust process. Taking this "simulation short cut" is not adequate since it means that, although you are willing to postulate a range of uncertainty and a distribution around an event, you are admitting that you don't really understand the drivers behind those events. It is ludicrous to assume that reasonable assurance of either corporate governance or risk management can be achieved if the inputs, or the information upon which decisions are made, are fallacious or their drivers are not well understood. Therefore, the integrity of the information, assured by the proper gathering, validating and processing of this information is paramount to establishing good strong management and thus ensuring good corporate governance.

Furthermore, ERM by its nature is more than simply sub-optimizing the risk taking activities at each level or division of the organization. Instead ERM is a strategic level activity, drawing it out of the realm of "that's the line manager's job" and putting it squarely into the boardroom. Finally, because ERM is applied at the strategic level, it is a portfolio view of the threats and opportunities facing an organization. Thus the correlations between different threats and opportunities must be considered if the risks are to be effectively managed. The concept of information integrity then becomes much more important, and at the same time more complex, when taken in the context of strong ERM.

Much effort has been spent by software vendors and consultants on developing the concept of *data integrity*. Generally, the focus of this data integrity exercise is on how the controls over the information system can keep the data clean and organized once it has entered the system. In other words, data integrity concerns have dealt primarily with how the hardware and software can make sure that data is not altered or corrupted once it is inside the system. In this respect, data integrity is analogous to the auditing of internal controls over financial statements: it deals with the systems over the inputs and outputs, but does not concern itself with the integrity of the inputs themselves. Very little attention has been paid to the serious issue of information integrity, or the validity of that data before it is entered into the system. It is not enough to know what is in the black box we call the corporate information system; we should know what feeds the black box as well. Questions such as, "what level of due diligence has been performed in gathering the data?" and, "how well has this input data been 'scrubbed' down?" are serious risk management (and thus corporate governance) questions that boards, analysts, and investors should be asking today. How do we know that adequate care has been taken in gathering information—particularly from external sources? What can we do to ensure that this information, once gathered, is valid for use as an input to our management process? Ideally, stakeholders, particularly boards of directors and the analyst and investor community, should be able to apply "checks" on what feeds the black box-both in terms of process and substance. Management in turn should be confident enough with what goes into the black box that they can stake their careers on the way this information has been gathered and processed.

What is best practice for these black box inputs? To answer this question, we look to industrial market research and strategic planning—appropriating tools, techniques, and methodologies from these fields and applying them to the Enterprise Risk Management process. How this is done is the subject of this book.

Introduction

The topic of information integrity has haunted me for over 20 years. During this time, a few questions have nagged at me all the while: In this electronic era of data overload, what information should we keep track of? How can we make sense of it all? And most importantly, how can we use information to gain competitive advantage?

After years in the engineering and construction industry, I switched my focus to industrial market research and business strategy. I began to realize that there are tools and techniques such as surveys, secondary data gathering methods, and simple databases that market researchers use to collect and analyze data. If properly leveraged, these are very powerful when applied to the investigation of a new product or service. Equally powerful is the bounty of additional tools for analyzing data and information that came out of the quality movement in the early 1990s. But gathering and analyzing data is not enough. There must be a way to put the results of the analysis into action. Thus, techniques from a third field, strategic planning, provide some ways to link the goals of the company with reliable information toward action. Finally, as things are constantly changing, it is essential to keep on top of new developments. Systematic monitoring, sometimes called *environmental scanning*, is required to stay aware of changes in events by having your radar on and consistently reading certain publications, watching events, and talking with people.

Market research and quality management tools and techniques are often for a specific purpose. Strategic planning is for putting the results into action, and environmental scanning is for monitoring. However, each of these in isolation is devoid of a context or a structure, or an ongoing reason for its application. The growing field of enterprise risk management provides not only the reason (i.e., assurance), but a structure or framework within which to use these tools and techniques. But after all this, the question still remains, Why bother? The answer lies in that old quest for competitive advantage. Thus, this book is not specifically about enterprise risk management, market research, quality management, or strategic planning, although each is dealt with. Instead, it is about competitive advantage in the energy business, and how it can be gained using a cross-disciplinary integration of tools, techniques, and structure that yields reliable information.

Why should we focus on the energy industry? It is because the lack of information integrity in the energy industry is an important problem. Energy affects nearly everyone on the planet, and the energy industry is huge, global, and capital intensive, making it subject to enormous risks. Commodity price volatility provides a certain dynamism, while the geopolitical dimension provides the sizzle. Energy, whether it is traditional electric power, oil and gas production, or alternate technologies, is truly a dynamic and risky business. It can also be argued that at this point in the industry's history, there is a crisis of confidence. This is why the application of information integrity techniques at energy companies is such an important and valuable topic now.

The objective of the book is to provide tools for two groups: those providing oversight and those performing the work. The information due diligence pyramid (fig. I–1) shows how both groups apply the principles in this book. For those in an oversight capacity, their function should be to ask the right questions. But what are those questions? The protocol, or governance guidelines described in this book, provide a succinct question list for overseers.

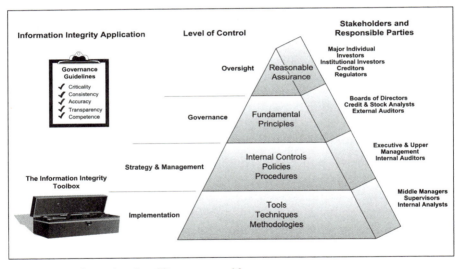

Fig. I–1. The information due diligence pyramid

For those actually performing the work, their function is to know how to do the job. What tools could be used to reliably gather and interpret information? The toolbox presented in chapters 3, 4, and 5, although certainly not exhaustive, provides a good foundation for the three-stage process of ensuring information integrity: discovery, assessment, and disposition.

As mentioned, the end state is sustained competitive advantage, a term practically coined by the renowned marketing expert, Michael Porter. For many years Mr. Porter has advocated a structured way of looking at information and an industry's participants through his five forces. I have taken Porter's model and adapted it to some of the realities of the 21st-century energy industry to arrive at a new model. At its core, this model depends on reliable information from stakeholders as the basis for achieving competitive advantage. Thus, competitive advantage for today's global energy merchant comes from strategy based on a systematic risk management process, trained business managers, and application of proven tools. In turn, this yields a cost advantage and/or enhanced differentiation by balancing stakeholder requirements.

Finally, instead of simply providing the *how* and the *why*, I have included a story to illustrate how information integrity management might be applied at a fictional oil and gas company, San Felipe Resources (SFR). Through a series of vignettes, the characters at SFR actually use some of the tools to avert a disaster. This vignette approach makes the book more than simply a handbook of techniques and provides a bit of relief to the discussion of concepts and the description of tools.

Fundamentals for Reasonable Assurance

Information integrity and corporate risk management—the two are inseparable

Corporate scandals, followed by increased regulation and corporate scrutiny over recent years, have created a new regulatory and competitive landscape for the energy industry. To deal with the challenges of this new environment, the first step is to take a fresh look at how well we understand the drivers of our future success, and ask some difficult questions: How confident are we about our market assumptions? Could they stand up to outside scrutiny by auditors and investors? Do we really understand the forces shaping our business over the coming years, or are we relying on old information, which may not even have been accurate when it was gathered? Are we comfortable that we have better information than our competitors to feed our forecasting models? What these questions have in common is a concern about the *integrity* or validity of information that supports our corporate-wide risk management.

Valid information is the backbone of any modeling effort. Whether it is for asset valuation, budgeting, or risk management, poor information yields poor analysis in any application. For example, an ad hoc system for gathering market intelligence yields poor forecasts and risk estimates, no matter how sophisticated the statistical techniques or how powerful the computing power. In this case, the quality of the model inputs is directly dependent upon the rigor of the market intelligence system. In today's new environment, if the market data gathering method is ad hoc, or not systematic, it will no longer stand up to the scrutiny of auditors, regulators, and shareholders.

Yet, many energy companies give validated market intelligence short shrift. Often, they rely on well-intentioned commercial staff who may be physically present in the market but have no market research or data management skills. In contrast, energy companies at times rely on consultants, who may have market research skills but do not provide the continuity between assignments to make this information truly valuable over the long term. In the worst cases, they rely on inexperienced in-house business analysts who are neither physically located in the market to develop (or guess) these critical inputs, nor have the required market or strategy skills. In any case, this makes the outputs of the forecasting models unreliable and calls into question the soundness of decisions taken by the company's upper management.

Today more than ever, debt rating agencies, regulators, auditors, and shareholders are demanding transparency and documentation of what is behind the model. Debt rating agencies, regulators, and board members are concerned about not being seen to adequately fulfill their oversight roles. Auditors are being held to more specific requirements for not only seeing the systems and data, but validating and documenting data sources and assumptions. These are the "show me" days. Neither corporate executives nor risk managers can afford to retreat back to playing financial Nintendo, tweaking their earnings models without really proving their understanding of the drivers of their business.

In this new era of corporate governance, an *information integrity framework* for market intelligence supporting corporate risk management should adhere to five fundamental principles:

- *Criticality.* A clear understanding of the relative sensitivity (and materiality) of each category of external information on the outcome of the analysis—whether it is a reserves report or an acquisition decision.

- *Accuracy.* A measure of closeness to either a directional or an absolute truth. This encompasses concepts such as timeliness of the information. The degree of accuracy of the information allows a decision maker to determine how much confidence he or she can place on the result.

- *Consistency.* This deals with precision and implies that a systematic process is employed. It is analogous to the scientific requirement for repeatability of experimental results.

- *Transparency.* Putting aside the risk of malfeasance, which has received so much press in recent years, transparency is simply adequate documentation, references to an accepted third-party standard or source, and use of an information system such as an electronic database to capture and securely store the information.

- *Competence.* Information collection must be performed by people who are competent in data gathering and interpretation techniques relevant to the type of information being gathered. The following is a further elaboration of these points.

Competently gathered, locally sourced market research

Reliable market intelligence relies on sound market research techniques. Professional market researchers in every field systematically use both primary data collection techniques (i.e., surveys, personal interviews, and observations) and secondary (or published) information to gather accurate information. It is probably not surprising that some of the best market research is performed by consumer products companies, such as Cadbury Schweppes and Coca-Cola. At these global food giants, such ideas and new products are extensively researched using sophisticated surveying techniques and conjoint analyses to determine revenue projections for the next blockbuster gourmet beverage product. What is surprising is that there is often a lack of even the most rudimentary of these market data collection techniques and tools used among nonmanufacturing industrial firms (such as those in the energy industry). It is not that the talent is not in the industry, or the techniques are unknown, it is that they are not being used effectively.

Furthermore, data should not only be collected systematically, but it should be carefully organized to be truly useful. To look for patterns and trends, market researchers have ways of tracking and making sense of this volume of market data in ways that others cannot. In this respect, the use of simple, desktop computer databases such as Microsoft Access are some of the most powerful tools individual researchers can employ to both store market information and slice and dice it for analysis. By using these simple tools, they can perform analyses of both "snapshot" and time series qualitative and quantitative information. Yet, it is surprising how infrequently desktop database tools are used to collect and analyze market data. Again, as with the techniques and understanding, this technology is readily available; it is just not widely used. Companies that use these simple data gathering tools and techniques to systematically update their critical data sets are those that will survive the current energy industry crisis of confidence. As investors, analysts, and regulators have seen in 2004 and in the first quarter of this year, it is often what is behind a company's reported results that is most important when evaluating future financial success. Raw data can often be misleading if its source is not known.

Locally sourced and validated data is critical. There can be a big difference between data that is simply reported and taken at face value and data that has been directly gathered and validated in the field by competent professionals. The quality of the directly gathered data is nearly always superior. In one example at a major energy company, I saw that there was a consistent difference between two sources for worldwide petroleum products production data between 1997 and 2001, as shown in figure 1–1 below. Upon closer inspection, we found that one data set was gathered and validated using direct personal interviews, while the other relied on "reported" production figures. Consistently, the unvalidated volumes were 5%–8% below the validated data. If the invalid data had been used to feed our worldwide supply/demand model over that period, there would have been significant errors in our forecasts. Fortunately, we were able to backtest the two data sets and thus rely on the more accurate data set.

In the years 2001–2003, concern over the quality of "reported" pricing data to publications led to scandals in the energy industry involving commodity traders at Enron and other energy trading companies. Poor quality data supporting price indices led to legal investigations (and convictions) of the traders involved in supplying the data. It also resulted in the establishment of a new standards working group for credible energy market price indices by the Committee of Chief Risk Officers, the association of utility and merchant power risk officers. People are now beginning to take the integrity of data seriously, but unless market intelligence systems are in place, reliable market data cannot actually be ensured.

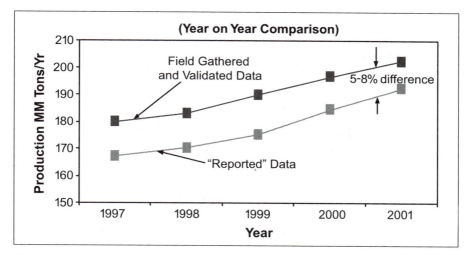

Fig. 1–1. Two sources of petroleum product data

Criticality is key: understanding what is important as well as the sensitivity of market model inputs

As mentioned, one of the key issues is that of the quality of data. Another is an understanding of the relative sensitivity of each piece of data on the final analysis. Every piece of data on a particular topic may be helpful, but it is often not practical to update and validate everything. In this era of data overload, it is more important than ever to "keep the main things, the main things" and not spend critical time gathering and analyzing noncritical data.

To illustrate this point, a typical stochastic modeling program I have used to simulate small hydro-dominated electric system behavior for four to six years can require as many as 10,000 discrete pieces of data. Most of this data is required to allow the program to close on an optimal solution, and therefore it must be loaded into the model. Yet, with most of these data points, their individual significance to the outcome of the analysis is not very high. On the other hand, there are approximately 80–100 pieces (or at most, 1% of the total data set) of highly sensitive data. A 2%–3% change in this critical data truly influences the final results.

In this case, it is important to focus the market intelligence on getting this 1%–2% of significant data right, rather than trying to optimize the entire data set. However, to know which 1% of the data to focus upon is the key. The sensitivity analysis requires a model. To perform the analysis, the entire data set feeding this model first must be inventoried, organized into categories, and sampled. Simulations are then run with each major category of data that could affect the results using the model. As can be imagined, this is a tedious process. However, it is crucial, since it lays the groundwork for not only efficient data gathering, but also practical and manageable scenario analyses.

Good and poor quality data sources and the ability to discriminate between them

The quality of data is not always readily apparent. It is often assumed that government data is reliable and that quantitative data is more authoritative than qualitative data or intuition. This assumption is quite suspect. The truth is, some government data is politically biased or just plain wrong, while other data gathered by government entities is excellent. In the energy industry, some nongovernmental, but publicly available, data is very good, and it is becoming available in a format that is convenient for feeding into a market intelligence database. For example, the California ISO's OASIS site is a source of very good public data on that state's electric system pricing. The data is even available to download from its Web site in XML format, allowing for automatic import into spreadsheets and databases. In fact, leading energy consultants such as PIRA, the New York–based consultancy, have taken advantage of this good quality data and created a direct data feed into their in-house analytical databases. Similarly, some publishers and consultants such as Henwood and RDI Consulting are beginning to sell very good, detailed powerplant data sets. But how can good data be distinguished from poor data without the advantage of hindsight? In other words, how can the wheat be separated from the chaff?

One way is to validate the data by either checking against third-party sources, personally performing spot checks of the data directly from the source, or backtesting the data against historical figures that are known to be accurate. The first step in checking data should be to question the motives and the true factual substantiation behind those providing the information. Where there might be an incentive toward manipulation of data (as in the case of government-generated economic projections, for example), the data should be treated with suspicion. The recent investor analyst scandal on Wall Street, and the ensuing uproar over conflicts of interest on the part of the investor analysts, should not have been news to anyone. It was well known that analysts were (and continue to be) heavily biased sources of market information. This is because their incentive structure is often tied to not just the retail brokerage, but the institutional sales and investment banking arms of their employers.[1] Follow the money in order to understand the motivation to manipulate the research.

Some of the most unreliable sources of data within companies often come from in-house "experts," with their qualitative, and often unsubstantiated, opinions. Are they truly experts, with well-substantiated, factual support for their pronouncements, or do they merely bully everyone into not disagreeing with them? More than one projection that has led a company to ruin has come from the in-house "sage," who by virtue of his political power, longevity in the organization, or force of personality dictates that "it" could never happen—and then it does! Strategic decisions based on systematically gathered market data can help avoid this in-house bias.

A regular, ongoing market intelligence gathering system, with a trend tracking capability

At many energy companies, a market intelligence gathering system is needed, not just an ad hoc collection of data. The goal is to turn data into information, and information into intelligent decision making. Often trend data is as important as spot data when developing inputs, since spot data can exhibit temporary anomalies that give the wrong indications. This data-over-time, or time series, analysis is critical to give context and perspective on an issue. Much has been made of using quantitative time series data for projecting trends; however, how often is qualitative data gathered and analyzed over time to project trends? Even in the absence of numbers, trends can be systematically collected and tracked. One approach used by researchers for spotting trends using qualitative data is to actually count the number of citations of a particular topic being reported by the trade journals over a period of time. A variation of this, *headline scanning* over time, can be very useful in identifying trends early and then drilling down to the details to determine what these trends actually mean for the business.

Of course, quantitative trend analysis is useful, but often it should be viewed from the perspective of developing indicators or surrogate measures to track risk. For example, in the area of counterparty credit analysis in a publication by the International Federation of Accountants, Canadian financial expert Raymond Darke mentioned that "the astute CFO will...be interested in the bond market itself where bond prices provide real-time feedback of the assessment of the credit situation for individual companies."[2] Again, the real value does not result from spot observations, but from analysis of data over time to look for trends. In this case, one could gauge whether the market senses more credit risk prior to an actual ratings downgrade by tracking the bond spreads of individual publicly traded companies over time. These spreads would then be compared with the range of spreads of identically rated companies.

In a similar way, could the emerging single stock futures market on the American Stock Exchange someday allow for an estimate in the expectation of the company's financial health based upon its stock futures price?

Spot data gathering often leads to poor decision making. Market information and data gathering need to be an integral part of someone's job, not just the sporadic data foraging of an analyst or salesperson. Only with a systematic market intelligence system can the proper perspective turn data into information.

A well-documented data register that is searchable, secure, and auditable

Back-of-the-envelope calculations just will not cut it anymore, even if they are performed with the aid of an electronic spreadsheet. Typical corporate analysts will have hundreds of documents scattered among different applications, repeating much of the same data in a different format. These analysts will misuse a spreadsheet for extensive text storage or use a Word document as a drawing template. This can and often is a data organization nightmare, and it provides very little in the way of an audit trail should someone need to come back and recreate the work. Use the right tool for the right task. As mentioned previously, for data storage, a database application should be used to create a data warehouse. A data warehouse allows a "single source of truth" system, extolled by leading edge information technology companies such as Oracle Corp. executive Fred Studer, who spoke at a conference on corporate governance in New York at the end of 2003.[3] Complex calculations should be done in calculation applications such as Excel, and reports should be formatted in word processing applications. Data registers, on the other hand, should be databases, which feed these other workhorse applications depending on the task required. Diagrammatically, the data warehouse or register concept is shown in figure 1–2.

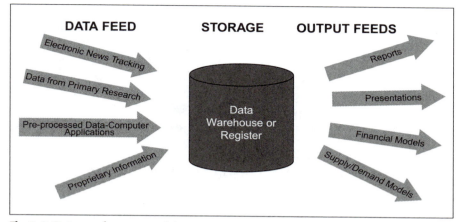

Fig. 1–2. Data warehouse or register

In the field of risk management, a data warehouse such as this would be called a *risk register*. To truly be effective, this risk register should not only store the results of risk workshops, but the information supporting the risk drivers as well. These results could include market research data, research from econometric models, and other proprietary information. The *expanded risk register* concept will be explored in more detail later in this book under the discussion of information transparency.

The key to compliance with new requirements from regulators may force more rigors into the market intelligence process by requiring CEOs and CFOs to quarterly certify that all activities that materially affect financial figures are performed diligently. For example, Section 404 of the Sarbanes-Oxley Act discusses quarterly certification by executives of their company's "internal controls over financial reporting." The SEC has now gone further with regulations such as 17 CFR Sections 210, 228, 229, 240, 249, 270, and 274 defining internal controls to include the safeguarding of assets. Regulation of pro-forma information is also a very hot topic at the SEC. In fact, the former SEC chairman Arthur Levitt strongly advocates more rigorous oversight of pro-forma disclosures, calling the current level of regulation the "pro-forma pretense."[4] I expect both the final interpretation of Section 404 and the regulation of pro-forma information to go beyond just auditing journal entry procedures and to include examination of whether a revenue projection is adequately substantiated. This will lead to a questioning by auditors of the quality of the systems, the controls for gathering market intelligence, and the integrity of the market data itself.

The new regulatory and competitive environment over the coming years will require more blood, sweat, and tears from corporate executives and risk managers than at any time during the heady days of the late 1990s. To survive, we must take a fresh look at how well we understand the drivers of our future success and ask some difficult questions about the integrity of our market data and the systems, techniques, and technology we use to gather it. Ensuring that this information infrastructure is in place should be a minimum standard for corporate governance demanded by stakeholders.

Sound corporate governance and reasonable assurance

Sound governance requires *reasonable assurance* that the assets of the corporation are safeguarded and that stakeholder value is being created. As a result of the rush of auditing relating to corporate financial reporting compliance, the idea of reasonable assurance is a key concept in auditing of internal controls over financial statements. However, making sure the financial recording and reporting process is robust is not the same as making sure the inputs to these processes are robust. Therefore to ensure good governance, a concept analogous to reasonable assurance should be applied not just to the financial reporting process but also to the integrity of information that feeds every material aspect of a company's operations. In this sense, ensuring information integrity goes beyond financial statement compliance and strikes squarely at the heart of the emerging field of enterprise risk management.

The goal of enterprise risk management (ERM) is to reduce the band of uncertainty for both the probability and impact of occurrence of events representing threats and/or opportunities to growth of stakeholder value, consistent with an organization's preestablished risk appetite. This is quite a mouthful, but what it means is that there is confidence that the appropriate risks are being taken to ensure an adequate return. Reduction of uncertainty depends upon additional information in the form of new, validated data. In the absence of gathered information obtained through a process of market research, for example, Monte Carlo sampling techniques can be used to simulate the outcomes—thus acting as a kind of proxy for validated data. But simulations are not a silver bullet. There is a place for Monte Carlo techniques in quantitative risk analysis, but if the overall goal is important enough (i.e., investor confidence, market projections, or sales forecasting), simulation is probably not sufficient to ensure a robust process. Taking this "simulation short cut" is not adequate, since it means that although a range of uncertainty and a distribution around an event can be postulated, the drivers behind those events are not really understood. It is ludicrous to assume that reasonable assurance of either corporate governance or risk management can be achieved if the inputs, or the information upon which decisions are made, are fallacious or their drivers are not well understood. Therefore, the integrity of the information, assured by the proper gathering, validating, and processing of this information, is paramount to establishing strong management and thus ensuring good corporate governance.

Furthermore, ERM by its nature is more than simply suboptimizing the risk taking activities at each level or division of the organization. Instead ERM is a strategic-level activity, drawing it out of the realm of "that's the line manager's job" and putting it squarely into the boardroom. Finally, because ERM is applied at the strategic level, it is a portfolio view of the threats and opportunities facing an organization. Consequently, the correlations between different threats and opportunities must be considered if the risks are to be effectively managed. Thus the concept of information integrity becomes much more important (and at the same time, more complex) when taken in the context of strong ERM.

Much effort has been spent by software vendors and consultants on developing the concept of *data integrity*. Generally, the focus of this data integrity exercise is on how the controls over the information system can keep the data clean and organized once it has entered the system. In other words, data integrity concerns have dealt primarily with how the hardware and software can make sure that data is not altered or corrupted once it is inside the system. In this respect, data integrity is analogous to the auditing of internal controls over financial statements. It deals with the systems over the inputs and outputs, but does not concern itself with the integrity of the inputs themselves. Very little attention has been paid to the serious issue of information integrity, or the validity of that data before it is entered into the system. It is not enough to know what is in the so-called black box of the corporate information system; we should know what feeds the black box as well. Questions such as, "What level of due diligence has been performed in gathering the data?" and "How well has this input data been 'scrubbed' down?" are serious risk management (and thus corporate governance) questions that boards, analysts, and investors should be asking today. How do we know that adequate care has been taken in gathering information, particularly from external sources? What can we do to ensure that this information, once gathered, is valid for use as an input to our management process?

Ideally, stakeholders, particularly boards of directors and the analyst and investor community, should be able to apply "checks" on what feeds the black box of the corporate information system, both in terms of process and substance. Management, in turn, should be confident enough with what goes into the black box that they can stake their careers on the way this information has been gathered and processed.

What is best practice for these black box inputs? To answer this question, we look to the various fields of industrial market research, strategic planning, traditional risk management, and quality management, and also to appropriate tools, techniques, and methodologies from these fields, applying them to the ERM process. The tools, techniques, and methodologies describe how this should be done. A more important question is, Why should it be done?

Thus both the *how* as well as the *why* of reliable information is the subject of this book.

References

1. Investment banking, but which way is up? 2003. *The Economist*. The Economist Newspaper Limited. January 25. pp. 67–68.

2. Darke, R. 2002. Capital structure risk and bond rating agencies. In *Managing Risk to Enhance Stakeholder Value*. New York: International Federation of Accountants and the Chartered Institute of Management Accountants.

3. Studer, F. 2003. Developing an implementation strategy for the new rules. Vice President, ERP, Oracle Corporation. Thunderbird Global Business Forum on Corporate Governance. The Princeton Club, New York, NY. January 16.

4. Levitt, A. 2002. *Take on the Street: What Wall Street and Corporate America Don't Want You to Know, What You Can Do to Fight Back*. New York: Pantheon Books. pp. 157–158.

The Rise of Enterprise Risk Management and the Information Imperative

2

An imperative suggests both a mandate and a sense of urgency. In the corporate world today, I see a confluence of trends. These trends include corporate scandals leading to increased regulation, mergers as a strategy for control over raw materials, and industry introspection resulting in a longer term business management approach. What these have in common is an increased level of competitive rivalry among industry participants. In turn, this new rivalry has created both the mandate and sense of urgency leading to an *imperative* that links information to enterprise risk management. To understand how to deal with this new imperative, it is useful to trace the roots of enterprise risk management.

Beginning in the 1980s, the total quality movement (TQM) began to develop, creating a renewed interest in business tools and techniques for improving quality and productivity. These were based on the principles of such thought leaders in the quality movement as Juran, Deming, and Crosby. The 1990s ushered in a refinement of these techniques and the worldwide codification and establishment of standards such as the ISO 9000, Malcolm Baldrige and the International Quality and International Safety Rating Systems (IQRS, ISRS). But the 1990s were also "go-go" years, and it seemed that no one could lose money in the stock market. This business optimism led to the freewheeling business culture between 1996 and 2001. For the energy industry, this culture led to the explosive growth of two major, interconnected subindustries: merchant power generation and energy commodities trading and marketing. Hand in glove with the growth, some of the country's most publicized corporate accounting scandals occurred, first at Enron, HealthSouth, and Worldcom, and later at Dynegy, Reliant, and Shell.[1] Thus the energy industry played a key role in bringing about a regulatory backlash: the Sarbanes-Oxley Act of 2002.

One of the most significant issues that public companies faced in the post-Enron era was how to comply with Sections 302 and 404 of the Sarbanes-Oxley Act (or "Sarbox"). That often-quoted piece of legislation requires attestation of the veracity of financial statements by senior officials of publicly traded companies. Often called the "accounting auditor's full employment act," Sarbox has led to intense scrutiny by auditors of internal processes dealing with financial statements. In the case of Sections 302 and 404 compliance, the audits deal very specifically with attaining "reasonable assurance" that there are adequate internal controls over the preparation and communication of financial statements. Again, a careful reading of the act implies that information integrity must be included within the scope of this auditing process. Therefore, one could ask how Sarbox auditors can be reasonably assured that information that could be material to the preparation of financial statements has been adequately controlled. In the early years of Sarbox compliance, i.e., 2003 and 2004, the SEC did not make clear how to attain this reasonable assurance. Thus, faced with criminal penalties for noncompliance, executives at large public companies fully employed armies of accountants to endlessly document financial and nonfinancial processes and procedures in an attempt to cover all their bases. Many lament the hours of needless profiling and documentation of processes simply because people did not know how much was enough to comply with the law.

However, even with this waste, there is a silver lining to Sarbox compliance. The process of compliance may have been financially painful for public companies, and there has been much written about these "wasted costs," but one side benefit is that it has forced deeper thinking into nonfraud-related risk management. In fact, the industry uproar over costs of Sarbox compliance and its ensuing regulations, standards, and best practices have led the SEC to determine that the way to comply with the law cannot be prescribed. Instead, every company is encouraged to follow a "top-down, risk-based" approach. Thus, it is a bit ironic that the process of corporate compliance with Sarbox has led to a general acceptance that risk is broader than fraud.

Consequently, there has been a slow shift of public company emphasis from control of financial statement risks to this intense concern about business risks. Furthermore, this concern reaches well beyond fraud control to include mismanagement, negligence, and incompetence. At this point, it may be helpful to take a fresh look at the terminology. In the context of Sarbox compliance, older accounting terms such *materiality* and *significant assumptions* have demanded more precise definitions. In accordance with the new SEC guidance, these old terms must be reconciled with the concept of a risk-based approach. The final layer of the risk discovery process is the role that validated external information plays in providing reasonable assurance over management of business risks. This last point strikes at the very heart of the issue: regulatory compliance is not the end state, and it might not even be a significant issue in two or three years. Business risks, on the other hand, will continue to be on every stakeholder's radar screen. The time is ripe for adoption by corporations of the emerging field of enterprise risk management (ERM), with its insistence on a broad view of all the company's risks.

ERM is a stark contrast to the departmental approach to corporate risk management traditionally characterized as either an insurance or a health, safety, and environmental function. More recently, along with the development of the commodity trading and marketing departments, the energy and financial services industries have developed risk management groups for controlling financial risks related to buying, selling, and holding derivative instruments. In energy companies today, an integration of risk functions into a corporate-level discipline called ERM, spanning all the activities of an organization materially affecting stakeholder value, is beginning to be seen.

In a way, the rise in ERM is the reincarnation of the TQM movement, appropriating many of the tools from that previous wave of business, but adding to it recent advances from the field of financial risk management. But ERM is significantly different from the TQM movement in a few important ways. First, the emphasis is not simply on an aggregation and reporting of risks, but on the correlation effect of significant or material risks and uncertainties within the entire corporate portfolio of activities. Another key difference from TQM is that the ERM specifics or baseline criteria for how much risk a company can tolerate and how much it should accept under various scenarios should be established by the board of directors acting in its capacity as shareholder representatives. A further argument for ERM arises from economics and finance theory. If markets are composed of rational investors, and rational investors consider either of the two prevailing theoretical approaches to asset valuation (the capital asset pricing model (CAPM) or the arbitrage pricing theory [APT]), ERM should be of direct concern to the individual and institutional investor. Both approaches consider not only systematic risk factors in the market affecting the company (i.e., those risks that affect everyone), but another factor generally denoted as ε, or the epsilon component, which represents the company's *idiosyncratic*, or nonsystematic, risk. This epsilon is a proxy for how well an individual company manages its systematic risk. Modern finance theoreticians may not agree with this assessment because they think that rational investors and institutions will diversify their risks, making the idiosyncratic issue inherent in their decision. However, here is where the theory differs from reality. Investors do not have perfect information about an individual company's nonsystematic risk because the companies themselves have poor information about their risks. It can be argued that ERM actually *supersedes* quality, health, safety, and environment, profitability, market share, and reputation issues because it defines and governs how each of these corporate categories will be managed. How is this so? To understand the answer, it is necessary to look at what ERM is and the role that information integrity plays.

The goal of ERM is to reduce the band of uncertainty for both the probability and impact of events representing threats to and/or opportunities for growth in stakeholder value. To make this goal realistic and relevant to the organization, it must be consistent with an organization's preestablished risk appetite. In other words, if we are the board of directors, we want to have confidence that our agents (the company's managers) are taking the appropriate risks to ensure an adequate return. This raises an important question with regard to information: How can we have this confidence if the information inputs to our system are questionable? At the crux of this question is how much you believe in the data received from others. I maintain that this depends on your level of trust in the motives involved, the level of due diligence applied, the competence of the data provider, and the possible consequences of erroneous data.

According to the Washington Post in its series on the Enron crisis, Jeff Skilling, purportedly mentioned that the best advice he had ever received was, "if it doesn't make any sense, don't believe it."[2] In 2001, as with the Wizard of Oz, many people in the energy industry were afraid or unwilling to pull back the Enron curtain. However, there is ample evidence that then, as now, it is naive not to do so.

Poor information integrity in the energy industry: two examples of failing to pull back the curtain

Price index scandals. The electric and natural gas price index scandal of 2002 in the energy trading and marketing business, and the petroleum reserves scandal of 2004, are two examples of poor quality control of external information by third parties receiving information from energy companies.

In 2002, five companies, Dynegy, AEP, Williams, CMS, and El Paso, admitted to the Federal Energy Regulatory Commission (FERC) that their traders had provided false data in 2000 and 2001 to the Platts publications, *Inside FERC* and *Gas Daily*. These publications blindly accepted this data as valid and created and published "price indices" or price references upon which other gas and electricity traders based future trading decisions. Complicating the issue was the specter of Enron and its intentionally fraudulent behavior, which at times used its own electronic trading platform, EnronOnline, and its actual trading activities to misrepresent and manipulate the gas and electric prices in California. There were three natural consequences of this false price index scandal. First, many companies improperly valued their forward contracts and other price sensitive instruments that relied on this information. Price transparency and liquidity underpin the theoretical basis for many market risk control and valuation models, from *value at risk* to the *Black-Scholes option valuation*. Because the assumption of a minimum level of liquidity and transparency was bogus, the valuations themselves were questionable. Second, today's spot prices in part determine tomorrow's prices—thus bogus reporting affected the next day's trading activity, and markets were manipulated. Finally, confidence in the entire gas trading system was undermined. No one believed what they saw on the screen was representative of the market fundamentals, and there was a breakdown in the trust in the efficiency of the markets. In short, unreliable information created a crisis of confidence in electric and gas company trading operations.[3]

It can be concluded from the FERC findings that the poor internal processes at natural gas companies and Platts regarding the reliability of external information allowed criminal behavior to flourish. As a result, Californians paid more for electricity and natural gas. The result of the FERC investigation, the ensuing criminal charges, and the history of careless data validation is that Platts and the industry have developed standardized procedures and best practices for this area of external data validation. These have been further codified by an industry group called the Committee of Chief Risk Officers (CCRO) in their February 2003 white paper, *Best Practices for Energy Price Indices*, which the FERC endorses.[4]

This raises an important question: How could Platts, a publisher that prides itself on accurate and reliable information, violate this most basic principle of external information, i.e., "garbage in, garbage out"? If this lack of circumspection could happen at the country's largest natural gas companies and at a respected publisher, could unreliable external information be an industry-wide problem? Events in the oil and gas industry in the year following the FERC report suggest that the lack of circumspection regarding external information continues to be an industry problem.

Oil and gas reserves. Because it forms the basis of cash flow projections, a company's oil and gas reserves data is used by stock analysts, investment bankers, and other investors to value companies. Granted, oil and gas reserves are estimates. Thus the evidence and records behind reserves estimates are not as well substantiated as historical costs or documented transactions supporting audited financial statements. It is for this reason that reserves data is reported in the "unaudited" portion of a company's financial statement. Even so, some oil and gas companies voluntarily choose to employ an outside auditor for their reserves data in order to provide additional assurance (or "certainty") to management and investors as to the reliability of these estimates. However, many of world's largest oil and gas companies still choose to self-certify their reserves. It is up to investors to believe them depending on their level of trust in the companies' truthfulness, their technical competence, or their diligence in preparing these estimates. In 2004 and 2005, there was a major reserves scandal involving the largest players in the oil and gas industry. This leads one to ask: why should anyone believe reserves numbers that are not certified by a third party?

The most egregious case of faulty reserves estimates and disclosure in recent history occurred in 2004 when Royal Dutch Shell admitted not once, but on five successive occasions that its reserves estimates were overstated. By the beginning of 2006, Shell had been forced to reduce its estimates of proved reserves by 6 billion barrels of oil equivalent (boe). It fired three of its top executives, suffered a credit rating downgrade, and paid fines totaling $151.5 million to securities regulators in the United States and the United Kingdom. Furthermore, the U.S. Department of Justice conducted a criminal probe, and there will continue to be shareholder lawsuits against the company for many years to come. The damage to Shell's reputation as a truthful corporate citizen may take years to repair.[5]

Like the price index scandal, this was not simply the working of one individual company, nor was it totally a result of malfeasance. It included elements of negligence and incompetence as well. El Paso Energy also revised reserves estimates in 2005 by a staggering 41% and was forced to restate earnings back to 1999.[6] The saga continued in 2006 as Respol YPF, one of the largest multinational energy companies in Latin America, and Harvest Natural Resources, a small U.S. producer in Venezuela, both used "unanticipated" political and regulatory changes as an excuse to downgrade their reserves estimates. The significance of these later year events should not be underestimated, considering the rise in oil and gas prices from 2003 to 2006. Based upon the way proven (as opposed to probable and possible) reserves are estimated, without any expenditures or new discoveries by the oil companies, a rise in petroleum prices should automatically add reserves, not reduce them. For these companies to dismiss political and economic events such as the above as "things happen" is a cynical way of admitting that they have poor market intelligence and do not know how or do not care to bother to perform scenario analyses.[7]

The question is, where were the stock analysts on these reserve write-offs? Did they again get caught unawares by the supposedly solid information published by these energy companies? For the case of these two companies operating in Latin America, dramatic political and regulatory changes are a constant occurrence. Planning for them should be routine for any company working in the region. Yet it is surprising how often I have witnessed a resistance or avoidance by energy industry operations teams to face these nontechnical "elephants in the room" during a project risk workshop. In this case, it is the duty of the workshop facilitator to organize the agenda so that these difficult issues are addressed and to insist that someone during the workshop accept responsibility for their management. I am afraid that too often these issues are swept under the carpet. In a high oil and gas price environment, when everyone is making lots of money, the eventual consequence of this mismanagement is not often perceived by the shareholders. With respect to reserves estimates, I suspect that the dramatic increase in oil and gas prices in the years 2004 to 2007 covered over a myriad of sins stemming from a lack of validated information and systematic market research.

An even larger question arises: If this is occurring at the publicly traded energy firms, how do we treat information from the parastatal oil companies that have much less transparency regarding their reserves information? Matthew Simmons, an energy industry investment banker, dealt with this very subject in his book, *Twilight in the Desert: The Coming Saudi Oil Shock and the World Economy.*[8]

What Mr. Simmons maintains is that if we analyze Saudi Arabia's field-by-field production and geological data published in the technical papers by the Society of Petroleum Engineers (SPE), and we raise a few reasonable questions about future production rates, there is very little likelihood that Saudi Arabia's reserves estimates are true. He claims that not only Saudi reserves, but also current production amounts are exaggerated by Saudi Aramco, the kingdom's parastatal oil company. If Mr. Simmons is correct, the implications are truly staggering. Saudi Aramco is one of the three largest suppliers of crude oil in the world. It produces in excess of 9 million barrels per day out of a total of approximately 83–85 million barrels per day (although these estimates themselves are questionable). Worldwide supply and demand forecasting models used by the commercials and the speculators alike in the commodities markets rely on these estimates to maintain some semblance of stability in oil prices. Inexpensive crude oil is so fundamental to the workings of the world economy that misrepresentation of Saudi reserves has an impact beyond its effect on Aramco's reputation and credit rating. This poor circumspection of external data could cause a world economic crisis.

Destroying Value: Part I of the *Why* behind Information Integrity

Having established the historical context for the information imperative, it may be useful to look at how information integrity is specifically linked to the drivers of negative shareholder value. One example will be examined where highly external information intensive drivers (or *value killers*) contributed to the collapse of not just one company, but an entire industry. In a strategic sense, these are the "threats" in a SWOT (strengths, weaknesses, opportunities, and threats) analysis.

The concept of external information intensity (EII). External (as opposed to internally generated) information is gathered in a variety of ways by people throughout the corporation to support management decisions. To understand how pervasive external data is to the workings of a company would require an exhaustive analysis of every process in a company that has contact with clients, competitors, suppliers—in short, the world outside the company's physical premises. Sales gathers competitor and pricing data, credit gathers counterparty data, finance and treasury gather interest rate data, and engineering and operations gather technology data, to name just a few areas where external information is used. External information is nearly everywhere. To understand its importance to a company, it is necessary first to try to get a feel for where external information (versus internal information) is critical to the functioning of a business.

After this screening analysis of where internal versus external information is used, a second cut should be performed. This would identify the degrees of dependence that a business process relies upon for externally versus internally generated information. One way to identify the impact or the importance of external information in a specific situation or process is to perform an analysis using criteria for testing the degree of dependence of various *elements* of a process on external information. Thus it is useful to develop a simple filter that asks, "To what degree does a description of the process or requirement cite or infer the gathering and analysis of external information?" Table 2–1 illustrates a 1 to 4 rating scale I have developed for determining what could be called the *external information intensity index* or the EII index for a process or set of requirements.

Table 2–1. External information intensity index

EII Index	Intensity Level	Description
1	Limited	Element strongly infers (but does not specifically cite) the *periodic* gathering or analysis of external information.
2	Moderate	Element cites one of the following words: information, events, factors, data, assumptions, or model(ling), and infers or states that this information is received from external sources.
3	High	Element cites one of the following words: information, events, factors, data, assumptions, or model(ling), and infers or states that this information is received from external sources.
4	Very High	External information and assumptions are essential to this element.

For purposes of analysis, the process would be carefully inspected, measured against one of the descriptions above, and assigned a rating. For example, commercial transactions are often highly external information intensive. One commercial transaction common in the energy business is the purchase or sale of natural gas. An illustration of this process (or *deal flow* diagram) is profiled in figure 2–1 with respect to each step's degree of external information intensity.

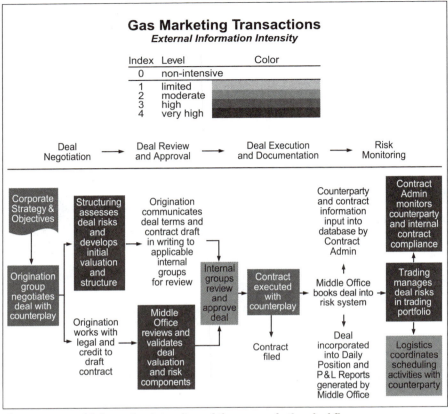

Fig. 2–1. External information intensity and the gas marketing deal flow

Note that slightly more than one-half of the steps in the gas marketing process are either highly or very highly external information intensive. Four of these steps (shaded dark) require market information such as pricing and economic trend data. Thus without valid external market or economic data, these deals would be poorly structured, either undervalued or overvalued, and only superficially monitored over the tenor of the contract. In this gas marketing process, the lack of valid information could be the driver behind a value killer for the transaction. In fact, it was precisely this carelessness that contributed to the collapse of the merchant energy industry in the United States, as described in more detail later in this chapter.

To understand the risk of poor external information on an organization, perhaps the value killers and their drivers should be analyzed and an information intensity index assigned to each value killer.

As mentioned, the goal of ERM is to reduce the band of uncertainty for both the probability and the impact of events representing threats and opportunities to growth in stakeholder value. One measure of stakeholder value for publicly traded companies is its share price. Thus, it would be reasonable to look at threats of a decline in share price as an ERM concern. In 2004, Deloitte Research performed just such a study of the stock price/value driver relationship.[9] The study considered the largest one-month declines in share price for the 1,000 largest international companies (based on market value) from 1994 to 2003 and carefully investigated the top 100 drivers for these declines. This was not a trivial endeavor. Among the 1,000 top companies in the study, almost one-half of them had lost more than 20% of their market value relative to the Morgan Stanley Capital International (MSCI) world stock index, at least once in the last decade, over a one-month period. Additionally, the value destruction was often long lasting. Roughly one-quarter of the companies had to wait more than a year before their share prices regained their original levels.

The report consolidated the losses into 29 different leading causes or drivers classified into four categories of risk: strategic, operational, financial, or external. To examine how external information might have played a role, I took the Deloitte results and applied our external information intensity criteria (limited, moderate, high, very high) to each of these value drivers. The results are shown in tables 2–2 and 2–3 below. As is evident, many value killers are either highly or moderately dependent upon accurate external information.

Table 2–2. Very high EII value drivers

Value Driver	Description	Category	External Information Intensity
Demand shortfalls	Insufficiently managing drops in demand either due to an industry-related event or firm-specific events	Strategic	Very high
Industry crisis	Problems arising from industry-wide supply, demand, regulatory, or other events	External	Very high
Country economic issues	Insufficiently addressing country-specific economic risks (currency, et al.)	External	Very high
Foreign economic issues	Insufficiently addressing foreign economic risk	External	Very high

Value Driver	Description	Category	External Information Intensity
Political issues	Insufficiently anticipating changes in government or policies	External	Very high
Legal risks	Insufficiently anticipating and ineffectively addressing legal issues	External	Very high
Partner losses	Unanticipated losses from partner weaknesses	External	Very high
Terrorism	Insufficiently anticipating and managing possible terrorism	External	Very high
Supplier losses	Unanticipated losses from the failure of suppliers to meet their commitments	External	Very high
Weather losses	Losses from weather-related events	External	Very high

Table 2–3. High and moderate EII value drivers

Value Driver	Description	Category	External Information Intensity
Customer losses/ problems	Insufficiently managing losses when specific valued customers have problems leading to falling demand or payments	Strategic	High
High input costs	Insufficiently forecasting and controlling the costs of inputs	Operational	High
Product/services competition	Ineffectively introducing innovative products into the marketplace	Strategic	Moderate
Regulation	Ineffectively planning for regulatory-driven compliance, demand and supply constraints	Strategic	Moderate
Capacity problems	Inadequate or too much capacity to handle demand	Operational	Moderate
M&A problems	Insufficiently valuing or merging two firms	Strategic	Limited
Noncompliance	Insufficient compliance with general industry norms, rules, and regulations	Operational	Limited

Value killer analysis conclusions

As can be expected, there are more external information intensive value drivers in the *external* and *strategic* categories than in the *financial* and *operational* categories. Additionally, the types of information required for the external and strategic drivers relate to an ability to foresee market events or to follow market trends (competitor, customer, or macroeconomic). These market events could fall into two categories: those considered "normal" or periodically recurring, and those that are truly unpredictable random events. Although seemingly obvious, the conclusion from this analysis (for the normally recurring events) is that market risk control through better gathering and use of market intelligence could be an important determinate of shareholder value. If this is true, for normally recurring market events, could better market intelligence through superior market research be a key differentiator between poor performing and better performing companies?

Another conclusion from the Deloitte data addresses the issue of truly unpredictable (random) market events with significant impact on shareholder value, i.e., the "low-frequency/high-impact" events. A statistician may call these *tail event* risks, because they fall into the outer reaches or tails of a normal (or bell-shaped) distribution. The statistical convention of fitting regular, naturally occurring, empirically gathered phenomenon (i.e., discretely distributed events) to a continuous bell-shaped distribution is a widely accepted practice in fields from sociology to finance. The extremes of this normal distribution mentioned above are termed the *tails* and are generally defined as the area beyond the 95% confidence interval. Statisticians also recognize that observed behavior conflicts with the way the height or "thickness" of the tails is represented by the theoretical normal distribution. It is often found that the tails of a distribution may be "fatter," or indicate a much more frequent occurrence of events, than would be statistically explainable simply by using the normal tails as a representation of what should happen. Therefore highly unlikely events, sometimes resulting in extreme consequences, are often poorly predicted using standard statistical methods. Figure 2–2 illustrates the normal distribution and these tail areas or *zones* as "fat tails."

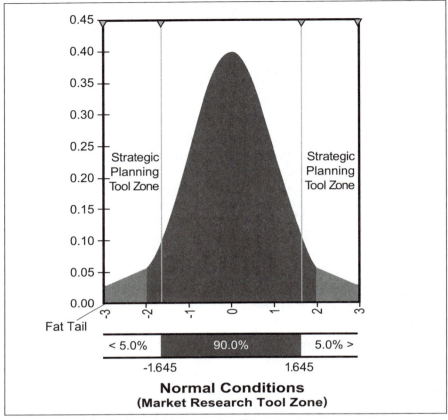

Fig. 2–2. Normal distribution and the zones for different tools

Fat tails are a big concern, since they represent unpredictable events that could have catastrophic consequences and thus are seemingly unmanageable. In fact, over the past 10 years, there has been increased study of how to predict a more realistic frequency, or thickness, for these tails. There also is increased concern among financial regulators. The international banking industry's *Basel II, International Convergence of Capital Measurement and Capital Standards, A Revised Framework* makes specific mention that financial institutions should ensure that analysis of fat tail losses meets its "soundness standard" accounting for events beyond 95% confidence interval of the distribution.[10] The current thinking from the field of financial risk management is that these tail event risks cannot be effectively managed using regular market monitoring, data gathering, and trend analysis. Neither can they be managed using standard value-at-risk calculations, which rely on assumptions of normality. Even "technical analysis," which considers patterns and the regular recurrence of historical events, cannot be relied upon for evaluating tail event risks. Instead, tail event risk management requires a different tool set, outside the bounds of normal statistical theory or technical analysis. Two possible avenues for answers to this dilemma are advanced mathematics or strategic planning. Much research has been done looking at the mathematics and developing advanced statistical models such as the famous GARCH (generalized autoregressive conditional heteroscedasticity) models, for example. Although they are much discussed in financial risk literature, advanced statistical/mathematical techniques such as GARCH are still not well understood or accepted techniques in mainstream business. This leaves strategic planning tools—and in particular, stress testing and scenario analysis—to deal with tail event risks. Both have been used extensively in military and corporate strategic planning circles. However, because strategic planning techniques are conceptually more understandable and intuitive than the mathematical approach, they are more likely to be accepted in broader risk management circles. What are some examples of value destruction through poor market intelligence and strategic planning? Read on for the sad tale of merchant power in America.

Value destruction in the U.S. merchant energy markets: a case study of poor external information. For a period of nearly 40 years after World War II, electric power generation, transmission, and distribution investor-owned utilities (IOUs) were among the few monopolies allowed by public utilities commissions in the United States. IOUs such as Commonwealth Edison, The Southern Company, Dominion Energy, and Duke Energy were highly regulated by each state's public utilities commission. In return, these IOUs were granted exclusive rights to generate, transmit, and distribute electric power to residential, commercial, and industrial consumers in their "franchise" territories. It seemed like a comfortable relationship for everyone. Consumers received safe, reliable electric service at a reasonable cost. The utilities provided steady employment for their communities and were allowed to invest in large-scale, expensive power generation technologies, such as nuclear power, while being shielded from the rough-and-tumble world of competition. Finally, from an investor's standpoint, the IOUs were a good complement to the technology stocks in their portfolios. These highly regulated, yet very financially stable, monoliths of the industrial age were considered the perfect stocks for "widows and orphans," given their history and outlook for steady (albeit low) returns growth.

However, by the 1980s to mid-1990s, industrial customer demands for more competitive energy pricing spurred changes to the regulatory environment. In addition, the status quo of the protected utility dominating the wholesale electric supply was being challenged by activist entrepreneurs and independent power developers who wanted a piece of the huge, growing U.S. electric power market. The federal government, as well as some public utilities commissions, were pressured to experiment with allowing limited "independent wholesale power" to serve industrial customers and other large commercial consumers.

From 1998 to 2002, many of the IOUs began to see these regulatory changes brewing in the United States regarding their franchises. At first the IOUs fought the trend, seeing only a threat to their protected businesses. But by 1998, most utilities considered that these changes might provide them with new marketing opportunities to sell power outside their territories. Concurrently, as parts of the U.S. electric power began to be "commoditized," a new market space developed—first between principals and their brokers, then over some of the country's commodities exchanges. For the IOUs, this wholesale power market added the allure of buying and selling electricity not just as a public service, but as an entrepreneurial business venture. By participating in this new trading and marketing business and owning the means of production, the IOUs saw an opportunity for them to break away from the "widows and orphans" stereotype and really impress Wall Street (and Main Street, by this time) with the promise of double-digit earnings growth. They would form new, unregulated subsidiaries to launch out into the territories of others and build "merchant" generating units that would sell power to the highest bidder. Furthermore, through this new business model, they would leverage the market power of these assets and metamorphose into wheelers and dealers, shedding their plain vanilla utility image forever!

This was the dream, but in a few short years, these companies had lost their shirts and were bailing out of the business. By the end of 2003, the oversupply of natural gas–fired merchant power plants in the United States led to the collapse of wholesale power prices. The merchant portfolios of the IOUs were suddenly worthless. By 2005, much of the 160 GW of new generation capacity they added to the U.S. inventory since 1998 was still uneconomical. These companies spent tens of billions of dollars building power plants that were not needed. What these old regulated monopolies did not realize was that although they had the means of production and the capital, they lacked the market savvy required to succeed in this new rough and tumble merchant power industry. How did this happen?

"Blame it on Enron" is still a common excuse for the collapse of the merchant power industry. The comic strip version is that Enron executives lied to investors, tricked the regulators, and cheated their customers, causing a lack of confidence in the benefits of electric power deregulation and a collapse in this fundamental driver of the merchant power business. However, as with most pat stories, this masks their true problem—a poor understanding of market fundamentals, particularly on the supply side, combined with a lack of robust strategic planning. For the merchant power industry, the cash flow forecast and the plant valuations were underpinned by a projection of *spark spreads,* or the difference between the cost of raw materials (fuel) and the value of the finished product (wholesale electricity). According to CERA, an industry market research firm, between 1999 and 2002, these spark spreads fell dramatically in every major region of the United States. Due to a combination of higher gas prices, slower-than-expected deregulation, and an oversupply of power plants, the value of nearly $50 billion of investment—much of which was concentrated in three overbuilt states, Texas (23 GW), Illinois (14 GW), and Georgia (11 GW)—was destroyed.

Even companies with large, stable core utility businesses such as Duke Energy and Entergy were hurt by their exposure to merchant plants. Duke is a prime example of this exuberance turned to disappointment. At one point in 2001, its stock price appreciation and short-term earnings painted a very rosy outlook for its investors. In meetings with shareholders, Duke's CEO, Rick Priory, said, "Today, investors are seeking companies with the growing and staying power to prevail. And no company is better prepared to reap those rewards than Duke Energy.... We deliver far more than lofty forecasts—we deliver the earnings and growth fundamentals that investors expect."[11] At that point, Duke's North America merchant energy group (DENA) had 13,500 MW of new generation under advanced development, and it expected to add 10 to 11 new energy facilities annually between 2002 and 2003. Yet its fortunes quickly turned. Between 2002 to 2004, DENA wrote off more than it had ever earned in merchant power—a total of more than $6 billion in destroyed value, mostly in noncash charges, compared with pretax profits of about $2.1 billion in 2000–2002. This did not even begin to quantify the loss in market capitalization it suffered.

But Duke was not Enron. This southern belle of propriety in the utilities business was not trying to hide losses or mislead investors. Their management, with a very few exceptions, were truly trying to do the right thing; they simply did not see it coming. After the dramatic fall in projected spark spreads and being forced to face the prospect of continued write-offs, Priory purportedly admitted in an internal executive staff meeting that "we got out in front of our headlamps." Evidently he wanted to communicate that somehow an economic hurricane, like one of those unpredictable forces of nature that so often beat mercilessly against the shores of the Carolinas, had hit. And when it did, it caused the merchant power business to develop more slowly than he had expected. In the aftermath, Duke was left with many power plants and little market.

It seems possible that the real story is that Duke, like many regulated utilities developing merchant power in the late 1990s, did not get out ahead of its headlamps, it just never bothered to turn them on. Because of their poor supply-and-demand fundamentals knowledge outside of their rate base, Duke's traders and developers (like many of their utility company peers) were driving in the dark. This short-sightedness was complemented by a flurry of market optimism and the misuse of *dual variable options models*, which relied on transparent, liquid trading markets to give correct pricing signals for valuation forecasting. The problem was that power trading markets were neither liquid nor transparent, particularly when dealing with long dated instruments. As a result, the entire merchant power market as underpinned by these assumptions of growth and deregulation collapsed in a few short years.

In the end, Duke was fortunate. After changing out its CEO and selling off its merchant power assets at fire sale prices, it was able to exit the merchant power business and remain solvent. But Duke was not alone, nor was it the hardest hit. There was a long list of merchant power companies such as NRG, Mirant, and Calpine that successively declared bankruptcy after 2002.

The merchant energy industry collapse vis-à-vis external information intensive value drivers. Revisiting the listing of value drivers with a significant external information intensive component, it can be noted that many of them (35%) were contributors to value destruction in the U.S. merchant power industry. Furthermore, very few (8%) of the low external information intensive value drivers were contributors to the merchant power industry collapse. In other words, there is a commonality of factors between what happened in the merchant power industry between 1998 and 2003 and what happened with the MSCI 1,000 companies over the period 1994 to 2003. This commonality is the link between external information and value destruction.

Competitive Advantage: Part II of the *Why* behind Information Integrity

The flip side of value destruction is value creation. The key to creating value is to have a sustained competitive advantage. In effect, just as value destruction is the *T* (for threats) in a SWOT analysis, value creation is the *O* (for opportunities). But how are opportunities created, and what exactly are the characteristics of sustained competitive advantage? To answer this, it is helpful to consider what one leading management expert has said about creating value.

In his seminal work published in the 1980s, management author Michael Porter stated that there five forces defining the attractiveness of an industry. Porter further described a successful strategy for an industry participant as resulting in lower costs and/or enhanced differentiation leading to competitive advantage. Furthermore, Porter proposed effective use of information technology as a strategic vehicle for securing this competitive advantage by the following:

- Fortifying the value chain of the company with information content

- Optimizing the linkages between "value activities"

Porter's thesis as described in a July 1985 article in the *Harvard Business Review* is diagrammatically summarized in figure 2–3.[12]

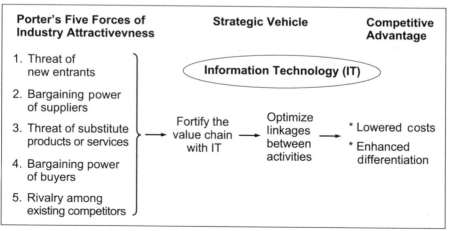

Fig. 2–3. Porter's five forces and competitive advantage

Over the years this framework has become an accepted way to think about strategy and competitive advantage, and most business schools now teach Porter's five forces as a fundamental marketing concept. Even so, there are three limitations for application of Porter's ideas to the energy industry today. First, Porter did not describe the tools, techniques, and methodologies needed to leverage information technology in the oil and gas industry. Second, his examples related more to industrial and consumer products companies than to wholesale commodity producers (such as oil and gas companies). Finally, Porter's discussion assumed reliable information would be used to feed the new computer hardware and software technology. I submit that contrary to the reality of the 1980s, today it is **reliability of information** that begs for improvement, not the hardware and software.

In spite of the limitations of the original model, Porter's concept of the value chain, the preeminence of the five forces, and the characteristics of competitive advantage continue to be relevant. Furthermore, the limitations can be overcome if Porter's "information technology" is replaced with "enterprise risk management using reliable information" as the strategic vehicle for competitive advantage and some approaches or tools are suggested for dealing with the forces. This modified model including both changes is represented diagrammatically in figure 2–4.

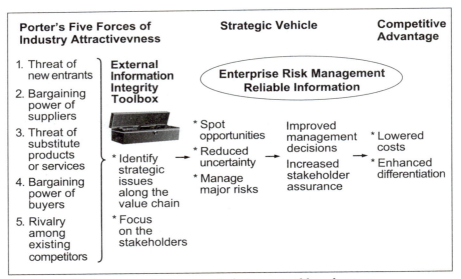

Fig. 2–4. Modified Porter model for energy industry competitive advantage

If the five forces are considered in the context of a multinational energy company, they can each have an impact on creating enterprise value, and they all rely on externally gathered information. Competitive advantage can be achieved through the application of approaches to better understand and take advantage of each of these five forces. Of the five, one force worth renewed attention in the energy industry is number 4, the "bargaining power of buyers." First, I would like to mention that the term *buyer* may be a bit misleading. When considering energy industry buyers, the definition should be broadened beyond the traditional notion of crude oil, natural gas, or electric power customers. The redefined "buyers" in the energy industry context are all those *interested* parties that producers and operators must somehow answer to. Considered in this way, the interested parties (or stakeholders) are equivalent to Porter's buyers. Table 2–4 compares how the bargaining power of buyers is leveraged in the Porter model versus what would be considered in today's analogous energy model.

Table 2–4. Comparison of traditional Porter model vs. energy model

	Porter Model	Energy Model
Force	Bargaining power of buyers	Power and sensitivity of stakeholders
Issue	Buyer needs vs. participant offering	Competing stakeholder requirements vs. participant performance
Goal	Diminish power of buyers	Balance and satisfy stakeholder requirements
Benefit	Enhanced differentiation relative to competitors	Enhanced differentiation relative to competitors
	Improved market share	Improved market capitalization
	Higher revenues or prices	Lower cost of capital
		Improved access to acreage
		Lower regulatory burdens
Result	Sustainable competitive advantage	Sustainable competitive advantage

Competitive advantage is obtained through the satisfaction and balancing of different stakeholder requirements. A systematic stakeholder analysis is one way to discover and understand these needs. Performing a stakeholder analysis is akin to conducting market research, but application of the results is a bit more complicated because there are often many conflicting sets of stakeholder requirements. For the energy industry, the list of possible stakeholders can span from regulators to board members to nongovernmental organizations (NGOs).

How could a better understanding of stakeholder requirements at oil and gas companies result in enhanced differentiation or lower costs? Imagine that you are a U.S. oil and gas exploration and production company and that an identified stakeholder is the national oil company (NOC) with whom you must partner to gain access to acreage in a developing country. This stakeholder will likely have requirements beyond oil production to its government. These may include social (or in the case of Venezuela, socialist) offsets for community development, training of local cooperatives, and building public infrastructure. As an investor-owned oil company (IOC), you may be much more competent than the host country government or the NOC at efficiently providing training of cooperatives and community groups or in building roads. If this superior ability is well-known by the host government, you may receive favorable treatment in the award of concessions or in the negotiation of royalties, resulting in a differentiated offering and providing you competitive advantage over other IOCs that had not done a careful stakeholder analysis. Of course, you must also be willing to allow the foreign government or your local partner to take the credit for a job well done with respect to community building. In another example, suppose the results of the stakeholder analysis indicate that bond rating agencies are both sensitive to your cash flow volatility and powerful enough to cause your cost of borrowing to increase should they signal a ratings downgrade. If the reliability of your cash flow projections were assured through effective risk management, this would probably provide your company with a cost advantage compared with those forced to borrow money with a worse credit rating.

Reliable information about stakeholder requirements is needed to achieve these benefits, and a stakeholder analysis is required to determine these requirements. In summary, the stakeholder analysis is a systematic process of discovering, validating, and assessing information about the stakeholders' requirements. In turn, the analysis provides the necessary grounding for an enterprise risk management program that yields tangible results in terms of lower costs or enhanced differentiation. This approach is so important that a step-by-step process for performing a stakeholder analysis is described later in this book.

The question that you may be asking is, "All this may be true, but does anyone really care?" I think they increasingly do. Given our previous analysis of the role of external information on 1,000 companies and the company value drivers, along with a review of the value destruction in the U.S. merchant energy industry, it seems that they should. And yet, we must ask ourselves whether anyone actually does consider the integrity of external information an important concern. To answer the question, it is useful to turn our attention to what members of the stakeholder community (i.e., investors, regulators, bond rating agencies, and practitioners of risk management best practice) are saying. These stakeholders are the people who live with the energy industry, rely on it for their livelihood, and are responsible for its oversight. Do they consider validated external information, particularly market information, an important issue? Are stakeholders demanding assurance of reliable information in the support of better management decisions? In other words, are the stakeholders restless? The evidence suggests that they are.

The stakeholders are restless: the drumbeat of new expectations. Something significantly different is seen today with respect to corporate governance and accountability relative to the pre-Sarbanes-Oxley period of the late 1990s. Stakeholders, or those who "have a dog in this fight" when it comes to corporate governance, are becoming more demanding regarding not only what, but how and why, certain corporate results are being delivered. This is partly a reaction to the scandals of the 2000–2004 period, but it is also a result of the increasing sophistication of investors and the rise in the broad dissemination of business news worldwide. Irrespective of the cause, there is growing scrutiny of a company's policies, procedures, and diligence by stakeholders in ensuring compliance when it comes to risk. As will soon be seen, an era of new stakeholder expectations has begun.

If a key aspect of ERM is growth in stakeholder value, then first it is important to understand who these stakeholders are and how they perceive the management of risk within the context of the companies, industries, and geographies where they are active. Certainly for publicly traded companies, shareholders are stakeholders. How the theoretical shareholder would evaluate the management of external information in light of a company's intrinsic or nonsystematic risk profile has already been discussed. However, to really get a feeling for the expectations of shareholders requires a finer read on how they see specific threats or opportunities. The following questions should be asked: Exactly where do shareholders see the greatest risks and uncertainties? In which category do they feel the greatest risks reside? How important to shareholders is the use of reliable external information in the areas of market risk, operational risk, credit risk, and strategic risk? Until expectations are determined regarding risk to at least this level of detail, it will be impossible to meet or exceed these expectations. Therefore, one influential shareholder group—the institutional investor—will be examined first to get a better insight into shareholder external information expectations.

If others who might have claims to a company's assets are considered, the company's debtors would certainly be another important stakeholder group. Therefore, as a proxy for the debtor's risk concerns, the credit rating agencies and an international banking oversight group will be considered next to discover how they evaluate business risks at companies. More specific to this topic is the important question, "Is reliable external information playing an increasingly important a role in their evaluation of the creditworthiness of companies and the governance of the world's central banks?"

Third, there are those directly charged with oversight and quality control—the auditors—who could be considered important stakeholders. Thus, next will be an examination of how financial statement and petroleum reserves auditors evaluate the importance of reliable external information, with a particular focus on their requirements in the energy industry.

Finally, there are the developers of standards and best practices. Although not directly responsible for results, they are accountable for the effectiveness of what they publish and thus could be considered a legitimate stakeholder group. Overall, the question that must be asked is, "How much do each of these groups really care about the reliability of external information?" Some trends in each group will be examined to discover whether the information imperative really exists.

The institutional investors

Institutional investors such as pension funds and various trusts and equity funds today move hundreds of millions of dollars of investment capital into individual stocks. Because of their market power, these fund managers have been able to wield significant influence on Wall Street and in the boardroom. What do they think of the importance of external information and how it relates to business risks? One insight might be drawn from a survey sponsored by Russell Reynolds Associates in 2005, *The Eighth Survey of International Institutional Investors: A World of Risk*.[13] For this study, more than 100 institutional investors from Canada, China, France, Germany, Japan, Mexico, the United Kingdom, and the United States were polled. The results highlight what they expect from board members in two areas: where they should place their priorities, and which risks they should be concerned with. To understand how these results might relate to the importance of external information, I performed an assessment of how dependent the most frequently cited priorities and serious risks are on external information.

First the results of the survey will be presented. The top five priorities that institutional investors expect of corporate board members where they invest are listed as follows in order of importance:

1. *Compliance is crucial.* In tandem with ethical business practices, the institutional investors polled believe compliance and *data reliability* are of paramount importance (96%).

2. *Management integrity.* Investors are concerned about the risks associated with improper and unethical business practices and for that reason are demanding higher standards of management and boardroom behavior (91%).

3. *Monitor market conditions.* Investors want directors to understand how shifting market conditions impact their industry (91%).

4. *Take the long view.* Investors say that the board needs to have a long-term growth perspective (90%).

5. *Financial prudence.* Investors do not want companies to overextend debt (83%). They want directors to be financially astute and, therefore, prefer to see board members with a strong financial background.

If these are examined to see which heavily depend upon external information, it is clear that two of the top five priorities (1 and 3 above; note critical wording is underlined) could be said to depend heavily on external information. It could also be argued that priority 4, "take the long view," implies, although it does not explicitly state, that board members must be aware of long-term trends as well as an emphasis on long-term vs. short-term financial results. In turn these could be said to support the performance of more rigorous strategic versus simply tactical planning.

The second outcome of the survey demonstrated which risks institutional investors were most concerned with. For the purposes of the survey, the types of business risk were broken down into five categories: market risk, management risk, operational risk, credit risk, and geopolitical risk. Respondents were also asked to identify specific aspects of risk within each category that they found important.

The survey concludes that across all business sectors, market risk is the highest area of concern for institutional investors in every geographic region worldwide. It also revealed that a change in economic conditions was the most frequently cited concern within market risk. Competitive threats were perceived as the second most frequently cited market risk for firms in North America, while changes in demand for the product was the second most often cited elsewhere in the world. Less frequently cited but still significant were the lack of risk management systems as a management risk, failure to comply with accounting regulations as an operational risk, and a credit rating downgrade as a credit risk. Other than for investors in Asia, geopolitical risk was not cited as frequently as market, management, operational, and credit risks.

Conclusion—institutional investors and external information. Finally, analysis is conducted concerning how external information intensive each of the survey's identified risks is. It is then apparent that one-half of the areas of risk that institutional investors thought were important were highly external information intensive and the other one-half were not. Again, market risk, as the most often cited concern of institutional investors, is undeniably highly external information intensive. Do institutional investors care about the reliability of external information? From the survey, it can be concluded that it is one of their chief concerns.

The credit rating agencies

The job of a credit agency is to measure the risk of default on the debts of companies and countries by analyzing indicators of a company's or country's financial liquidity. The product of this measurement and analysis is the agency credit ratings, which in turn have a direct impact on interest rates demanded by financial institutions to lend them money in the form of loans, bonds, notes, and other debt instruments.

The three major credit rating agencies, Moody's, Standard & Poor's, and Fitch, enjoy a privileged position of market power as a ratings service. Competition in the field is limited by the granting of the designation by the SEC as a Nationally Recognized Statistical Rating Organization (NSRO). Effectively, this gives the NSROs a type of franchise, and maintenance of this franchise is based upon a good reputation built over many years for objectivity and diligence in the assessment of a company's liquidity and susceptibility to default. However, in the wake of the collapse of Enron in 2001, this reputation for diligence was seriously impaired. The agencies had failed to warn lenders through a ratings downgrade or even putting Enron "on watch." The subsequent loss of confidence when Enron suddenly declared bankruptcy was not only expressed by lenders but by Enron trading partners, suppliers, and pensioners, who were all caught short by the collapse. In the wake of the collapse, the agencies felt suddenly vulnerable. Their privileged position as the authoritative arbiters of corporate liquidity and their exclusive franchise to emit ratings was being challenged. Thus in an effort to bolster confidence, since 2002, the agencies have poured significant effort into strengthening their capability in understanding not only what is shown on a company's financial statements, but how a company manages its business risks. One outgrowth of this effort is their development of new methodologies for assessing a company's ERM capabilities.

When a rating agency begins to apply its ERM assessment to public companies and does not like what it finds, it might consider putting that company on *credit watch*, which is one step before a downgrade. A credit downgrade by an agency can spell disaster for a company trying to raise money through issuance of debt or servicing existing debt with a ratings covenant or clause. When borrowing costs rise dramatically and a company cannot finance expansion, it sometimes must sell assets to meet cash flow or investment requirements. Thus it is no wonder that institutional investors in the Russell Reynolds survey cited a credit downgrade as one of the more serious risks that they expect board members to manage. When the board is concerned, executive management gets nervous.

Thus, taking ERM seriously and complying with the rating agency recommended practice could soon rise to the top of executive management's agenda. The following discussion reviews the enterprise risk assessment criteria of two credit rating agencies with respect to information integrity.

Moody's and Standard & Poor's. As part of its "Enhanced Analysis Initiative," in 2004 Moody's began to assess the quality of risk management practices at large global financial institutions and large corporations with significant economic exposures to financial, commodity, or energy price risk.

Moody's risk framework has four key domains: risk governance, risk management, risk analysis and quantification, and risk infrastructure and intelligence. From the standpoint of external information, the most pertinent section of their framework is risk infrastructure and intelligence. It is under this category that validation of models and data used is specifically cited.

Standard & Poor's has developed what they call the *PIM framework*, standing for policy, infrastructure, and methodology. The most relevant external information reference is within the methodology component, where there is a specific requirement for *assessment to ensure that there are processes in place to verify inputs to pricing models, assumptions made, and methods employed for verification*.[14]

Conclusions—the credit analysts and external information. At Moody's, the first risk management assessments performed under its Enhanced Analysis Initiative have been at companies from the four major segments of the financial industry: global broker-dealers and securities firms, large international universal banks, specialized financial institutions, and global insurers/reinsurers. I expect that the next round of assessments will be at oil and gas companies with active derivatives trading and marketing programs. It will be interesting to see how they fare.

Based on the way in which these two rating agencies are beginning to assess companies, it is clear they are adopting a "show me" rather than a "don't ask/don't tell" attitude toward the validity of input data and assumptions used for risk management modeling.

The international banking and finance community

The international financial community has for the past 10 years been at the forefront of the advances in financial risk management, and arguably, the leading edge of thinking in risk management in general. In the field of enterprise risk management, it was a group of financial experts who developed the COSO II framework for enterprise risk management.

One of the most widely respected financial risk management standard-setting bodies in the world is the Basel Committee on Banking Supervision under the direction of the International Bank of Settlements in Basel, Switzerland. As a result of a near collapse in 1973 of a German bank, due to failed international transactions, the committee was formed in 1975 by central bank governors of the Group of Ten countries. Today the committee is comprised of central bank representatives from the major countries of Europe and North America, as well as Japan, and it issues various standards and directives for the world's international banks. One of these standards is the so-called Basel II Accord, which specifies how to determine the amount of capital (i.e., the assets minus the liabilities) that a bank should keep on hand at any one time. As can be imagined, with a broad spectrum of possible risk appetites and regulatory regimes in different banks around the world, this is a massive project. Thus, the committee has spent significant time developing its risk-based framework for capital adequacy, including best practices for not only credit risk, but the area most relevant to our discussion: market risk. From the standpoint of the banking industry, market risk is defined as the risk of losses in on– or off–balance sheet positions, arising from movements in prices relating to interest rates, equities, foreign exchange, and commodities.

Bankers obviously see the key role that market risk plays in the stability of their industry. The question is, how important do they consider validated external information to be in the management of this market risk? It turns out that this is critical, since much of the market risk at banks is measured and monitored using internal models that are fed by external information. Under Part B of the 1996 Market Risk Amendment of the framework, extensive mention is made of how internal models are used to measure market risks. Furthermore, the amendment stipulates the minimum standard requires that the risk management system is conceptually sound and implemented with integrity. By integrity, the amendment further delineates a) the integrity of the management information system, b) *the verification of the consistency, timeliness, and reliability of data sources used to run internal models, including the independence of such data sources*, and c) the accuracy and appropriateness of volatility and correlation assumptions.

Conclusion—international bankers and external information. It can be concluded that these well-respected bankers not only recognize the importance of market risk, but prescribe standards relating to the essence of the information imperative for market risk management: validated external information.

Another interesting and relevant section to corporate enterprise risk management deals with operational risk. The Basel Committee on Banking Supervision defines *operational risk* as "the risk of loss resulting from inadequate or failed internal processes, people and systems, or from external events."[15] Of particular interest is the requirement within the framework for credible and consistent estimates of potential operational losses, and the use of "relevant external data, scenario analysis and factors affecting the external environment."[16]

Regarding relevant external data, this is specified as either public data and/or pooled industry data. Such external data is considered especially important regarding actual loss amounts, information on the scale of the business operations where the event occurred, information on the causes and circumstances of loss events, or other information that would help to assess the relevance of the loss event for other banks. A bank must have a systematic process for determining the situations for which external data must be used and the methodologies used to incorporate the data (e.g., scaling, qualitative adjustments, or improving scenario analysis). The conditions and practices for external data use must be regularly reviewed and documented and must be subject to periodic independent review.

Again, as with market risk, it cannot be clearer that these well-respected international bankers take validated external information very seriously when it comes to measuring and monitoring a bank's operational risk.

The financial statement auditors

Financial statement auditors are accountants whose core competence lies in inspecting both the process and the documentation behind information on four of a company's financial statements: the income statement, the balance sheet, the statement of cash flows, and the statement of changes in owner's equity. Anyone who has studied accounting remembers that historical cost records are the primary basis of support for the reliability of these financial statements. However, there are special cases where information supporting financial statements relies not only on historical cost records but involves a significant amount of judgment. Nowhere is this truer than in the establishment of the "fair market value" of assets. Because the fair market value process involves many assumptions and models, valuations on this basis are not as easily verified by auditors as are historical costs. Valuation of financial derivatives, particularly hydrocarbon commodities derivatives such as oil and natural gas futures, forwards, swaps, and options contracts, is an area of particular interest to the energy industry.

In the years leading up to and following the Enron debacle, fair market asset valuation came under intense scrutiny by regulators and investors because of energy industry scandals involving improperly inflating earnings based on the revaluation of derivatives. This practice played a key role in increasing the regulatory controls over energy firms with speculative trading and marketing divisions. However, lost somewhere in the media noise about greed and scandal was the existence of negligence and incompetence regarding both external information and the critical assumptions behind derivatives transactions. Some in the accounting profession did recognize that valuation practices should be tightened up. The American Institute of Certified Public Accountants (AICPA), for example, issued an auditing standard entitled, "Statement on Auditing Standards 101, Auditing Fair Value Measurements and Disclosures" in 2003 to deal with this subject.[17]

What does this standard say about how external information and assumptions are to be validated?

To answer this question, the most relevant section of the standard, "Testing Management's Significant Assumptions, the Valuation Model, and the Underlying Data," can be examined. In this section, it clearly states that the auditor is to evaluate whether management's *significant assumptions* are reasonable and reflect, or are not inconsistent with, *market information*. Additionally a determination of whether management used relevant information that was reasonably available at the time should be made, indicating a *timeliness* requirement. Furthermore, the standard states that the auditor is required to evaluate the source and reliability of evidence supporting management's assumptions, including consideration of the assumptions in light of historical and market information. The auditor's tests may include, for example, procedures such as verifying the source of the data, mathematical recomputation of inputs, and reviewing information for internal consistency. Finally, the auditor considers, for example, the expertise and experience of those persons determining the fair value measurements.

Conclusion—financial statement auditors and external information. The conclusion from this analysis of the fair value auditing standard is clear. Wherever fair value is used by a company to support financial statements, the integrity of external information is of paramount importance.

The petroleum reserves estimators and auditors

Due to the dramatic petroleum reserves restatements between 2003 and 2006 previously mentioned at Shell, El Paso, and Repsol among others, petroleum reserves estimating has become quite a popular topic in the energy industry press. However, petroleum reserves estimating and auditing is not a new concept, and there are well established firms that have developed techniques and specialize in auditing oil and gas company reserves. The Society of Petroleum Engineers has even published standards on the subject. To understand how important external information is to reserves estimating, it might be useful to look at how estimates are used.

An interesting aspect of petroleum reserves estimating is its dual function of serving as both a technical and financial source of oil and gas company information. Not only does the reserves estimate guide oil and gas company management and boards in terms of corporate strategy, budget and long term financial plans, but it plays an important role in the market values of the publicly quoted companies in the sector. From a financial compliance standpoint, the reserves estimate is a key determinate in the development of the "standardized measure" of discounted future cash flows projected to arise from production (SMOG) of proved reserves as required by the SEC for the preparation of oil and gas company financial statements. In a strange twist of legal interpretation however, these estimates and the resulting SMOG calculations are excluded from the requirements of Sarbanes-Oxley Section 404 internal controls auditing. Even so, because of their importance to the company management and the investing public, many experts believe this is one of the few areas in the oil and gas business that requires more international regulation. No where has this need been more clearly demonstrated than in the oil and gas reserves scandals of 2004 and 2005.

The reserves "de-booking" at Shell cited earlier have brought to light the incidence of fraudulent or careless reserves estimating. The larger issue however, is one of simple carelessness, willful negligence or incompetence as with El Paso, Harvest International and Repsol regarding external information. The most authoritative body on the estimating of petroleum reserves is the Society of Petroleum Engineers (SPE). In their reserves standard, "Pertaining to the Estimating and Auditing of Oil and Gas Reserve Information" there is a critical reserves estimating criteria mentioned: the sufficiency and reliability of the database. Furthermore, the standard states that the reserves estimate documentation should include the manner in which the assumptions were made and used and the source of the data used with regard to ownership interests, oil and gas production and other performance data, costs of operation and development, product prices, and agreements relating to current and future operations and sales of production. Clearly, according the SPE, the integrity of external information is important to the reserves estimate. According to one of the standard's authors and a leading authority on petroleum reserves auditing, Ryder Scott Company chairman emeritus Ron Harrell, the validation of market and economic information such as product prices and costs of operation and development as of the effective report date typically falls within the responsibility of the petroleum reserves evaluator and/or auditor but such economic data may also be subject to authentication by the financial auditor. Nevertheless, regardless of the auditor primarily responsible, the standard makes it clear that market and economic information are critical to the reserves estimates, and that care should be taken when gathering it.

Conclusion—external information and petroleum reserves estimates. Petroleum reserves estimates depend upon such a wide range of external information that it is difficult to see how the reliability of this information is not essential to oil and gas companies and their stakeholders. Although geological and other technical information is carefully developed, there is clearly a gap in where the ultimate responsibility lies for certifying the validity of market and economic information. Thus there is a vital step concerning this non-technical information that seems to be missing to ensure transparent valuation and market capitalization of oil and gas companies.

Best practices and emerging risk standards: COSO, EFQM, and the CCRO

The reincarnation of risk as a truly comprehensive and strategic corporate discipline requires new standards, tools, techniques, and methodologies. Consequently, since 2002, three industry-sponsored organizations have moved to the forefront in the establishment of these standards: The Committee of Sponsoring Organizations of the Treadway Commission (COSO), the European Foundation for Quality Management (EFQM), and the Committee of Chief Risk Officers (CCRO). Strictly speaking, it could be argued that they are not really stakeholders—they have no ownership role, no legal claims, and no regulatory authority. Instead, they provide information and guidelines for the other stakeholders to adhere to. However, a bit deeper look into the background behind each of these groups would reveal one curious commonality: they all represent corporate management's thoughts on how risk management should be self-regulated. Therefore, the following is a discussion of what each of these corporate management representatives feels about the importance of validated external information.

Committee of Sponsoring Organizations of the Treadway Commission (COSO). The *COSO Enterprise Risk Management—Integrated Framework and Application Techniques* was published in September 2004. This document has incorporated all the major steps of the risk management process and thus is a good representative of incorporating a new focus with a traditional process. Its perspective is that of U.S. financial and strategic risk management and regulatory compliance, and its pedigree is from the fields of accounting, finance, and audit. For example, the major contributors in its formation were the American Institute of Certified Public Accountants, the Institute of Management Accountants, the Institute of Internal Auditors, the American Accounting Association, the Financial Executives International, PricewaterhouseCoopers, and Protiviti. Because its contributors were accountants, its financial and compliance focus leads to a general weakness in the measurement of operational risk. Even so, in the United States, the COSO ERM framework is the most widely accepted approach for enterprise risk management.

The framework is divided into eight elements:

1. Internal environment

2. Objective setting

3. Event identification

4. Risk assessment

5. Risk response

6. Control activities

7. Information and communication

8. Monitoring

This division reflects the steps of classic risk management methodology first established by the Australia/New Zealand Standard AS/NZS 4360. Overall, the importance of external information is cited or inferred quite frequently throughout the framework, and with the exception of risk response and objective setting, valid external information is cited or inferred in each of the other COSO elements to varying degrees. After performing an external information intensity audit on the COSO framework, I determined that the three key areas for external information were risk identification, risk assessment, and information and communication. These three key areas accounted for 25 out of 32 (i.e., 79%) of all citations and inferences of external information among the framework's processes. In the risk assessment element, for example, when talking about qualitative risk assessment techniques, the framework states, "Qualitative techniques are highly dependent on the quality of the supporting data and assumptions, and are most relevant for exposures that have a known history and frequency of variability and allow reliable forecasting."[20] In the area of event identification, the framework states, "By monitoring data correlated to events, entities identify the existence of conditions that could give rise to an event. For example, financial institutions have long recognized the correlation between late loan payments and eventual loan default, and the positive effect of early intervention. Monitoring payment patterns enables the potential for default to be mitigated by timely action."[21] The number and detail of this type of citation throughout the framework demonstrate the clear link that the COSO authors see between ERM and reliable external information.

The European Foundation for Quality Management (EFQM). The *EFQM Risk Management Framework* is a compendium of risk management ideas and practices incorporating the EFQM "excellence model." Developed in 2004, its origin is European, with an operational risk and quality management orientation based on the preestablished EFQM excellence model. The framework was produced by the European Foundation for Quality Management, a European industrial cooperative in collaboration with Det Norske Veritas, a Norwegian risk management consultancy.

In criterion 1 of its framework, the EFQM states that one of corporate leadership's responsibilities is ensuring the environment is scanned for trends and discontinuities in trends and updating risk management activities to reflect changes. Furthermore, in criteria 4 and 5, it specifically mentions the following as important:

- Managing information and knowledge and capturing external knowledge to support risk management. Poor data gathering can jeopardize the value of the outcome (of the risk management activity).

- Conducting research to reduce uncertainties about the likelihood and consequences of risk.

- Using accurate and up-to-date information for risk assessments.

- Scanning for emerging risks and use of this information to make changes in advance of events.

There are numerous other areas in the framework where the importance of valid external information is not specifically cited but it is strongly inferred.

The Committee of Chief Risk Officers (CCRO). The CCRO is an energy industry advisory group composed of the chief risk officers of companies that are involved in both physical and financial energy trading and marketing. Its white papers on a variety of risk management topics form the basis for current best practice in the energy trading and marketing industry. Some of the issues covered by the CCRO white paper on governance go beyond what should be done to stipulate who is responsible for reliable external information. For example, in a paraphrase of the portions of the report dealing with external information and assumptions:

- The objective is to develop a full understanding of the market, including risks, and to ensure that due diligence has been performed before a company enters into new markets, trades in new commodities, or introduces new products (including assets, origination deal structures, and other offerings).

- The market risk group within a company's corporate risk management department is responsible for assuring information integrity by reviewing and validating valuation methodologies, curves and assumptions, and by performing backtesting.

- The front office (or the commercial group) is responsible for performing the research required to understand market rules, risks, barriers to entry, competition, customer needs, logistics, and other market factors in order to analyze the economics and develop a business plan or report. Special emphasis is placed on the wording "develop new business after extensive research" and documenting this information in a market business plan or risk analysis report.[22] The documentation includes industry background, entry and exit plans, and limits, among other things. Again, before the plan is approved, the middle office (or market risk group) should validate the appropriateness of market research, models, curves, and assumptions used to value new business and independently verify and quantify the various risks involved in accepting the new business activity.

Ensuring reliable external information is mentioned or inferred so often in the CCRO white paper that there is no doubt that they consider it a critical area of governance and controls for energy trading and marketing.

Conclusion—best practices and emerging risk standards: COSO, EFQM, and the CCRO. Based on the number and ways that reliable external information is mentioned in various emerging risk standards and best practices, it can be concluded that the corporate manager stakeholder group is in strong agreement with other stakeholders. Reliable external information is an imperative for effective business risk management.

Having established the change in stakeholder expectations, the following must be considered: How can we measure reliability, and how can we ensure that we have attained it?

Reliable External Information: A Conceptual Framework

Up to this point, we have reviewed a number of trends. We have looked at how stakeholder value can be created and destroyed by fraud, negligence, and incompetence in the gathering and use of external information. We have also seen that the important corporate actors (the stakeholders) have made recent pronouncements that they consider reliable external information critical. Furthermore, they expect and have actually specified their requirements for external information gathering and use. As a result, we can conclude that corporations now have both a mandate and a sense of urgency when it comes to risk. There is an information imperative regarding reliable external information.

The next question is, what does reliability look like? This seems like a very basic question that certainly should have been answered years ago. After all, we use information of all types and are constantly making judgments as to how reliable it is before we use it as the basis for a decision. But are there any standards for external information reliability? After all, mechanical and industrial engineers have definitions, criteria, and standards for reliability of equipment and systems based on concepts such as mean time to failure (MTTF) and mean time to repair (MTTR). What are the concepts behind reliability of external information? More interestingly, what tests are there to determine whether external information is reliable enough for a specific application, or in other words, fit for a purpose? Surprisingly, I have found that there are no international standards or best practices behind the reliability of external information. So after searching the literature, speaking with a number of engineers and information specialists, and thinking carefully about this issue, I have developed five fundamentals of reliable external information. These five fundamentals are: criticality, accuracy, consistency, transparency, and competence.

1. Criticality. This involves a precise understanding of the relative sensitivity (and materiality) of each category of external information on the outcome of the analysis. Since it is usually not an efficient use of resources nor is it practical to perform exhaustive market and economic research on every possible category of external information, we need to figure out which pieces of data most influence the analysis. We then focus our investigative efforts on that information. This seems obvious, but often because there is no systematic process for ensuring external information reliability, there is even less, if any, structured process for determining criticality. By extension, for financial statement risk, how is materiality, or the degree to which an individual process is critical to the overall financial statement, determined? Sadly, the accounting profession and even the SEC have left this up to the judgment of each accountant, thus introducing a variance of opinions into the process, making *materiality* a very subjective term. As mentioned, usually materiality assessments are based on deterministic judgments by accountants concerning some threshold above which a loss is considered "material." However, any method that relies on a deterministic judgment does not really comply with the spirit of Section 404 auditing, which the SEC has determined should be a "top-down, risk-based approach" toward assessing which processes contributing to the company's financial statements are material. (A more structured and truly risk-based approach to materiality involving fault tree analysis followed by use of a quantitative simulation tool will be described in more detail later.)

2. Accuracy. This is a measure of the closeness to truth, either directionally or in an absolute sense. Notice that because things change with time, accuracy must include the timeliness of the information. Accuracy is essential for reliability, because the degree of accuracy of each piece of critical data allows a decision maker to determine how much confidence he or she can place on the result. However, accuracy is not sufficient for reliability, because a single estimate may not be repeatable, and accuracy is often only able to be determined after the fact, using various backtesting methods. Some of these after-the-fact techniques are described in the Bank for International Settlements (i.e., Basel II) *Amendment to the Capital Accord to Incorporate Market Risks.* For example, a methodology for calculating an appropriate error metric, and then comparing the error to a simple decision rule (or random selection) of benchmark performance, will be described in later chapters.

3. Consistency. This deals with precision and implies that a systematic (as opposed to an ad hoc) process is employed. It is analogous to the scientific requirement for repeatability of experimental results. For market information, a remedy for inconsistent, out-of-context external information is a regular, ongoing market intelligence gathering system with a trend tracking capability. This is to gather enough data so that individual points are able to be viewed as part of either a cluster or a data cloud, as a statistical outlier, or as part of a distribution. The same practice of locating data points within a larger context is used by petroleum reserves auditors to determine the sufficiency of their geologic data, which is one of the tests to arrive at *reasonable certainty.* Reasonable certainty is a key concept in the SPE petroleum reserves estimating and auditing standard.

4. Transparency. Putting aside the risk of malfeasance and intentional falsification of records as previously mentioned, transparency can be ensured through adequate documentation, references to an accepted third-party standard or source, and use of an information system such as an electronic database to capture and securely store the information. To be truly transparent, this information system should consist of a well-documented data warehouse that is searchable, secure, and auditable. The documentation in the information system should contain as much of the original or source data as possible, tagged with references in order to allow drill down, tracing back, and validation if required by auditors.

5. Competence. Information collection must be performed by people who are competent in data gathering and interpretation techniques relevant to the type of information being gathered. Although this seems obvious, considering the variety of different types of external information gathered and analyzed by a company and how poorly gathered information could affect the analysis, the qualifications of those gathering the data are critical. No one would allow collection of medical data from laboratory tests to be performed by a nonspecialist. In the same sense, oil companies should not trust gathering and analyzing reserves data to someone other than a petroleum engineer who is competent in reserves estimation. Finally, market and economic information should be gathered and analyzed by trained market researchers and economists. Too often this critical first step, gathering the external market data, is left to general business analysts, engineers, salesmen, accountants, or anyone else who happens to be available but who has never had formal training in market research techniques or econometrics.

The objective of the following chapters is to describe techniques and tools that world-class companies—those that strive to be the best of the best—can use to achieve reasonable assurance of the reliability of external information.

References

1. U.S. Securities and Exchange Commission, Litigation Release No. 17744 / September 25, 2002, "SEC Settles Securities Fraud Case with Dynegy Inc. Involving SPEs and Round-Trip Energy Trades." http://www.sec.gov/litigation/litreleases/lr17744.htm; U.S. Securities and Exchange Commission, Litigation Release No. 19119 / March 3, 2005, "SEC names Tamela Pallas, former officer of Reliant Resources, in accounting fraud case involving over one billion dollars in round trip energy trades." http://www.sec.gov/litigation/litreleases/lr19119.htm; U.S. Securities and Exchange Commission, press release, Aug. 24, 2004. "Royal Dutch Petroleum Company and the "Shell" Transport and Trading Company, P.L.C. Pay $120 Million to Settle SEC Fraud Case Involving Massive Overstatement of Proved Hydrocarbon Reserves, Companies Simultaneously Settle a Market Abuse Case With the United Kingdom Financial Services Authority, Settlements Are the Result of a Comprehensive Joint Investigation Conducted by SEC and FSA." http://www.sec.gov/news/press/2004-116.htm

2. Behr, Witt, "Hidden Debts, Deals Scuttle Last Chance." *Washington Post.* August 1, 2002; Page A01.

3. Final Report on Price Manipulation in Western Markets—FERC, Fact Finding Investigation of Potential Manipulation of Electric and Natural Gas Prices, U.S. Dept. of Energy, Federal Eergy Regulatory Commission, March 2003, Docket PA02, p. ES-6.

4. Committee of Chief Risk Officers. 2003. *Best Practices for Energy Prices Indices.* White paper. (February 27).

5. Carr, M. and Coulter, T. Feb. 4, 2005. "Shell Cuts Oil and Gas Reserves for the Fifth Time." Bloomberg Energy Bulletin. http://www.energybulletin.net/4235.html

6. Fowler, T. "Following the rules of the Sarbanes-Oxley-Act has its defenders and detractors as companies shell out to comply, taking an accounting of reform." Jan. 29, 2006. *Houston Chronicle.*

7. Repsol YPF SA, Securities and Exchange Commission Form 20F, filed July 14, 2006, p. iv. Presentation of Certain Information. http://sec.edgar-online.com/2006/07/14/0001193 125-06-146964/Section20.asp; Harvest Natural Resources, Inc. Securities and Exchange Commission Form 10K, file Feb. 27, 2006, Item 1, Business, Executive Summary, p. 1. http://www.sec.gov/Archives/edgar/data/845289/000095013406003753/h33383e10vk.htm

8. Simmons, M. R. 2005. *Twilight in the Desert: The Coming Saudi Oil Shock and the World Economy.* Hoboken, NJ: John Wiley & Sons.

9. Deloitte Research. 2005. *Disarming the Value Killers: A Risk Management Study.* www.deloitte.com/dtt/cda/doc/content/DTT_DR_Vkillers_Feb05.pdf

10. *Banks for International Settlements, International Convergence of Capital Measurements and Capital standards, A Revised Framework.* Nov. 2005. Basel, Switzerland. ISBN 92-9131-669-5.11. Priory, R. 2001. Duke Energy CEO tells shareholders that company's growth strategy will keep delivering. Duke Energy press release. April 26. https://www.duke-energy.com/news/releases/2001/Apr/2001042601.html

12. Porter, M. E., and V. E. Millar. 1985. How information gives you competitive advantage. *Harvard Business Review.* (July).

13. Russell Reynolds Associates. 2005. *The Eighth Survey of International Institutional Investors: A World of Risk.* Russell Reynolds Associates.

14. Samanta, P. "Enterprise Risk Management and Risk Assessment." Nov. 18, 2005. *Ratings Direct*. New York: Standard & Poor's.

15. Basel Committee on Banking Supervision. *International Convergence of Capital Measurement and Capital Standards*. Section 644.

16. Basel Committee on Banking Supervision. *Basel II Accord*. Section 669. Part e. http://www.basel-ii-accord.com/BaselText/Basel664to683.htm

17. American Institute of Certified Public Accountants. 2003. *Statement on Auditing Standards 101, Auditing Fair Value Measurements and Disclosures*. (January). New York: AICPA.

18. Society of Petroleum Engineers. 2001. *Standard Pertaining to the Estimating and Auditing of Oil and Gas Reserve Information*. Sec. 5.1. (June). SPE. p. 6. http://www.spe.org/spe-site/spe/spe/industry/reserves/Estimating_and_Auditing_Standards_for_Reserves.pdf

19. Interview with D. Ronald Harrell, chairman, Ryder Scott Co. March 2, 2006.

20. Committee of Sponsoring Organizations of the Treadway Commission. *Enterprise Risk Management Framework—Executive Summary*. (Draft). p. 49. http://www.erm.coso.org/Coso/coserm.nsf/vwWebResources/PDF_Manuscript/$file/COSO_Manuscript.pdf

21. Ibid. p. 74.

22. Committee of Chief Risk Officers. 2002. Governance and Controls. Vol. 2. White paper. CCRO Organizational Independence and Governance Working Group. November 19. p. 18. http://scudderpublishing.com/publications/white_papers/CCRO%20Whitepaper%20%20Best%20Practices%20on%20Governance%20&%20Controls.pdf

Information Integrity Implementation— Tools, Techniques, and Examples

3

The integrity of a report depends in part on the integrity of the process of evidence construction; alert consumers of a report must seek some kind of assurance that the process was sensible and honest.

—John Ioannidis, August 2005

External Information Integrity and Enterprise Risk

The purpose of this book is to demonstrate how external information integrity (EII) and the enterprise risk management (ERM) process are so intimately linked that an organization cannot achieve competitive advantage through ERM without reliable external information. This seemingly obvious statement will be illustrated in detail throughout the book by following a three-stage EII process of *discovery, assessment,* and *disposition.* The EII process will be linked to both the enterprise risk process and the *modified Porter model of competitive advantage* as shown in figure 3–1.[1]

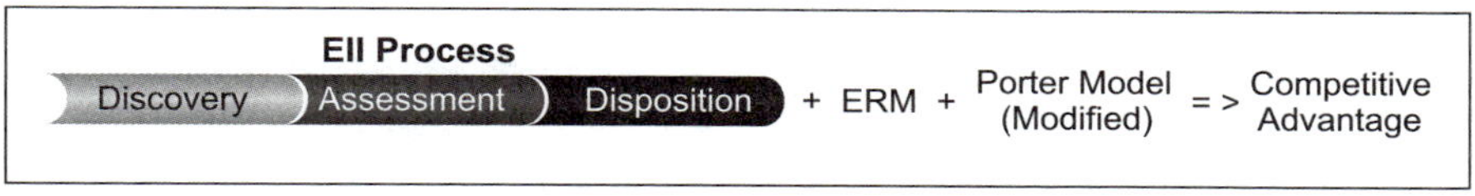

EII Process

| Discovery | Assessment | Disposition | + ERM + | Porter Model (Modified) | = > | Competitive Advantage |

Fig. 3–1. EII process

As an example of how information integrity maps onto the enterprise risk process, two risk management standards, the Australia/New Zealand (AS/NZ 4360) and the internationally recognized COSO ERM framework, can be considered. The steps or activities in the risk management standards can be examined to discover where external information integrity becomes important. Among the first holistic risk management standards was the Australia/New Zealand (AS/NZ 4360), whose first version was published in 1995, with subsequent 1999 and 2004 editions. Nearly 10 years after the first AS/NZ 4360 edition, and in the wake of the Enron scandal, the COSO *Enterprise Risk Management—Integrated Framework* was also developed and released by the Institute of International Auditors. The COSO framework borrowed heavily from Standard 4360, updating it with new measures relating to compliance and reporting. Although there are many possible risk management standards to consider, for simplicity, without deviating into an exhaustive standards comparison, these two will be considered as representative of the current state of the industry.[2]

Prior to publication of Standard 4360, much risk management centered solely on techniques for identification, assessment, and treatment of health and safety risks. In fact, many technical risk methodologies for applications such as fire and explosion analysis and pipeline leak detection continue to deal exclusively with identification and assessment. This two- or three-phase approach to risk management is also prevalent when performing financial and project risks using quantitative Monte Carlo simulations risk analysis. Thus when looking at specific business activities in isolation dealing with property, plant, and equipment risks, the historical practice has been to use the *risk identification*, *risk assessment*, *risk treatment* sequence.

However, the historical focus on merely these two or three activities is insufficient to effectively manage risks on a strategic or corporate level. This limited focus is inadequate because isolated business activities often start from the basis of a predefined model of a layout or a project involving property, plant, and equipment. Thus, they start with certain assumptions concerning organizational and business boundary conditions before launching into the risk management activities. In contrast, when dealing with corporate-level risk management, the situation is more complex. Corporate-level risk management does of course involve property, plant, and equipment, but it also includes people, processes, politics, and a myriad of other business considerations as well. The Australia/New Zealand Standard 4360 in 1995 attempted to deal with this added complexity by broadening the traditional risk management approach and adding new activities. These new activities explore and describe the "context" or environment within which the risk analysis is applied, as well as the methods by which risks are communicated and monitored. To give a better understanding of the added activities, a simplified outline of the steps included in the Australia/New Zealand standard is shown in figure 3–2.

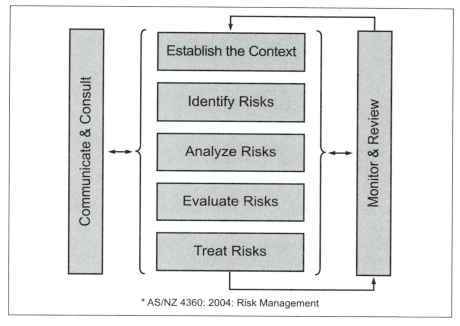

* AS/NZ 4360: 2004: Risk Management

Fig. 3–2. Australia/New Zealand risk standard

In fact, the additional activities of *establishing the context, evaluating risks, monitoring and review,* and *communication* are now recognized as being as important to the success of the corporate risk management effort as the original risk identification and assessment steps.

The COSO ERM framework contains similar steps, although its application is often associated with strategic planning and financial compliance rather than health and safety. A simplified diagram of the COSO ERM approach is shown as an activity block in figure 3–3.

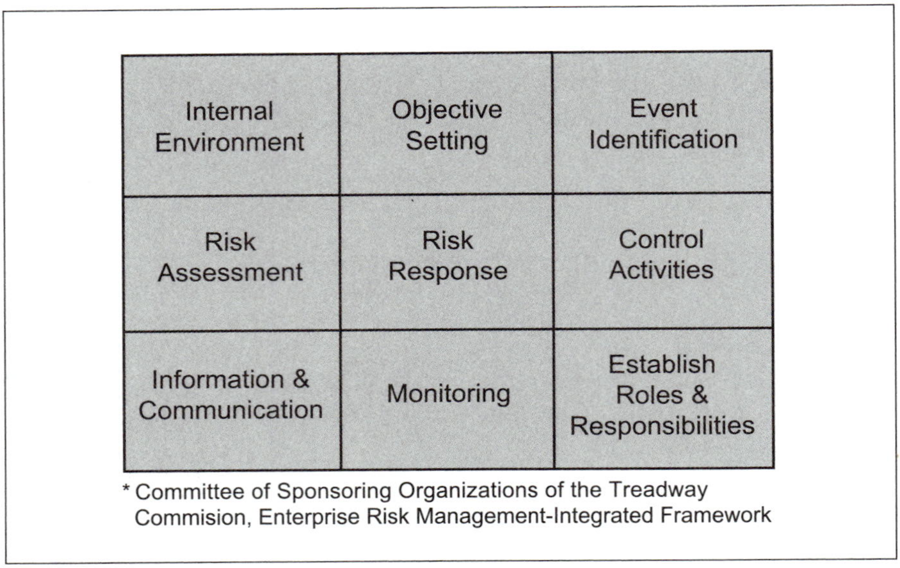

Internal Environment	Objective Setting	Event Identification
Risk Assessment	Risk Response	Control Activities
Information & Communication	Monitoring	Establish Roles & Responsibilities

* Committee of Sponsoring Organizations of the Treadway Commision, Enterprise Risk Management-Integrated Framework

Fig. 3–3. COSO ERM framework

In a general sense, the *internal environment* and *objective setting* steps in the COSO framework correspond to the *establish the context* step in Standard 4360, while COSO breaks out *risk response and control activities* from the category of *risk treatment* described in Standard 4360. An additional activity, *establish roles and responsibilities*, is also part of the COSO framework. However, careful inspection of both show that the two are quite similar in their approach. Given that the two frameworks (4360 and COSO ERM) are so similar, I will use the COSO activity blocks in figure 3–3 as the graphical representation of the enterprise risk approach throughout this book.

When the three phases of information are mapped onto the COSO ERM activity blocks, the diagram in figure 3–4 illustrates how the three EII phases and the ERM activities work together.

As indicated, there are two important activities of the COSO ERM framework where external information does not play a significant role. Since the purpose of this book is to explain how reliable external information supports the ERM process and not to explain how enterprise risk is to be implemented, this text will not address *control activities* or *establishment of roles and responsibilities*. Thus, having established a three-step external information integrity (EII) process that is analogous to two of the world's leading enterprise risk standards, a discussion of the first step in the EII process, *discovery*, will follow.

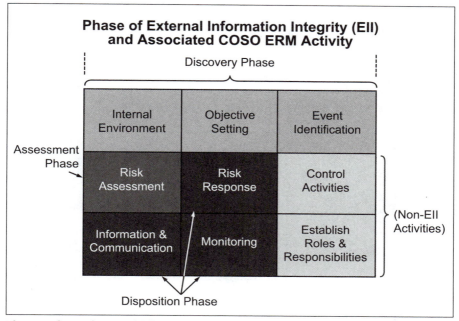

Phase of External Information Integrity (EII) and Associated COSO ERM Activity

Discovery Phase

Internal Environment	Objective Setting	Event Identification
Risk Assessment	Risk Response	Control Activities
Information & Communication	Monitoring	Establish Roles & Responsibilities

Assessment Phase

(Non-EII Activities)

Disposition Phase

Fig. 3–4. Phase of external information integrity and associated COSO ERM activity

Discovery

With ERM implementation, the question of where to begin sometimes arises because, as with any new or unfamiliar activity, it is not always apparent exactly where to start. When considering external information integrity within the context of enterprise risk, other questions arise, including: Should we immediately start gathering information? If so, what information should we gather, and why? Should we call a meeting? If so, what will we discuss? The information integrity discovery phase attempts to answer some of these questions with an approach that is both introspective as well as outward looking in nature. As with the first steps of the COSO ERM framework, the discovery step in the EII process considers activities associated with knowing yourself and knowing your environment. Throughout this chapter, we will profile various tools and techniques needed to effectively implement the discovery phase of EII.

As mentioned, discovery is both introspective as well as outward looking in nature. Thus, the COSO activities of internal environment, objective setting, and risk identification correspond to the EII discovery process as highlighted in figure 3–5.

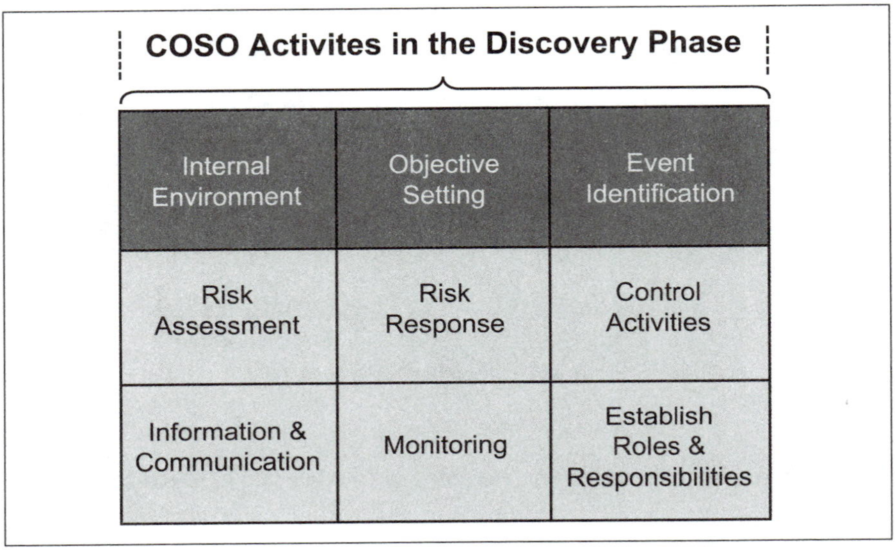

COSO Activites in the Discovery Phase

Internal Environment	Objective Setting	Event Identification
Risk Assessment	Risk Response	Control Activities
Information & Communication	Monitoring	Establish Roles & Responsibilities

Fig. 3–5. COSO activities in the discovery phase

However, since our focus is specifically information integrity, only those processes, tasks, or tools essential for information integrity will be considered in this book. This is a critical distinction because it is effective information integrity management *within* the risk management process that is fundamental to establishing a competitive advantage—not simply having an ERM process itself! Thus, the entirety of the COSO process with regard to internal environment, objective setting, and event identification will not be explored. Instead, specific illustrative tools relating to information integrity (and competitive advantage) while implementing ERM will be described. Additionally, although this is by no means an exhaustive treatment of risk management tools, those I have profiled provide a solid foundation for any analyst or manager to establish the context for purposes of information integrity management.

A general road map or outline of the discovery process illustrating the tools to be profiled is shown in figure 3–6.

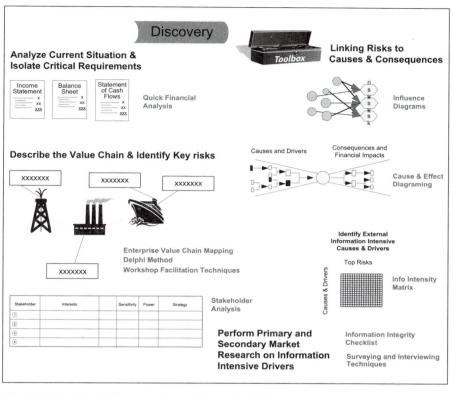

Fig. 3–6. Overview of discovery phase tools and activities

Upon inspecting each of these tools, we see that they can be characterized as information *gathering* as opposed to information *assessment* tools. Returning to our question concerning where to begin, the answer is, Know your customer and know yourself. We begin with the stakeholder analysis, follow with a quick financial analysis, and then develop a value chain map. These three tools provide the three-legged stool upon which the organizational context sits.

The stakeholder analysis is fundamental to setting the stage because it truly defines who the customers are and what their needs are, thereby establishing a sound basis for corporate objectives. The quick financial analysis is oriented toward understanding the drivers of the firm, particularly for a publicly traded company. A wealth of information beyond simply the numbers is found in a public company's financial statements, particularly when analyzing a company's U.S. Securities Exchange Commission (SEC) Form 10-K or Form 20-F. Even if it is a privately held or government-owned oil and gas firm and does not file with the SEC, a review of the annual report with financial results provides an important overview of where the company has been and where it might be heading. Finally, the company's value chain map is the third foundational tool of establishing the context by helping the analyst to understand how the activities, assets, and processes work together to produce results.

The other tools in the discovery step deal with refining the information and determining what is important. Determining what is important relates to the concept of *criticality*, one of the five fundamentals of information integrity as later described. Together with the best practices for market research, including the information integrity and the surveying and interviewing techniques, these fill out the entire complement of tools in the discovery toolbox.

To demonstrate how these tools work together, a series of vignettes is given at the end of the chapters showing how they are used at a fictional oil and gas company, San Felipe Resources. Risk managers who frequently feel like the underdogs will like this story. After plenty of hard work, the main character, Barry Craddock, is able to earn the respect and admiration of his boss and colleagues. The chapter finishes with observations about what the characters did well, what they could have done better, and what additional tools might be considered. In a similar way, the saga of San Felipe Resources continues through chapters 4 and 5 to illustrate how the assessment and disposition steps might play out in a real company.

First, however, we should examine the three tools in the discovery toolbox to see how each is used to accomplish the discovery process.

Discovery Toolbox

The following detailed description of the discovery tools is meant to be a step-by-step, "cookbook" approach toward implementation. This description should be in enough detail to aid any analyst or manager who is interested ensuring that due diligence has been performed in the pursuit of *adequate assurance* in the gathering of external information. The first of these will be the *quick financial analysis*. Since businesses by their nature have financial targets and metrics, a risk analyst who examines the financial statements of a company can get an amazingly deep appreciation of the "current situation" regarding enterprise risk and assurance.

The Quick Financial Analysis

The quick financial analysis is a process for discovery of corporate-level risks and uncertainties leading to financial consequences. The following tool describes the first step toward discovering these risks: establishment of the current situation and outlook using financial statements. A complete introduction to financial statement analysis is beyond the scope of this monograph. However, with the application of these techniques, the current situation of a company and a look at its risks from the perspective of the company's management can be quickly obtained. This analysis relies primarily on annual financial statements (SEC Form 10-K and Form 20-F) to provide a "snapshot" of a company's current financial situation as well as its goals and objectives.

For companies not listed on U.S. securities exchanges (such as national oil companies, start-up companies, and private companies), it may be more time-consuming to obtain this information, as they are not required to prepare and present standardized reports to the SEC. In these cases, interviews and an analysis of internal company documents would be required.

The phrase "quick look" was coined by Daniel Johnston, an oil and gas industry author from whose work the following discussion draws heavily. It will be concerned with three types of financial statements: the income statement, the balance sheet, and the statement of cash flows. By answering the questions that follow the description of each financial statement, the analyst can get a good indication of the size of the company.[3]

Discovery Tool 1: The Quick Financial Analysis

As mentioned, the quick financial analysis primarily relies upon annual financial statements (SEC Form 10-K and Form 20-F) to provide a snapshot of a company's current financial situation as well as its goals and objectives. There are four topics to consider in this type of high-level analysis:

1. The quick look

2. High-level financial ratios

3. Risk factors

4. Management's discussion and analysis

For companies not listed on U.S. securities exchanges (such as national oil companies, start-up companies, and private companies), it is more time-consuming to obtain this information. Standard credit reporting agencies such as Dun & Bradstreet can sometimes provide information, but this is often very suspect and should never be taken at face value. Therefore, for private companies, interviews and an analysis of internal company documents are the best way to get this information. If the analyst is analyzing his or her own company, the controller should be able to quickly pull financial statements from recent years.

The quick look

As stated earlier, the phrase "quick look" was coined by Daniel Johnston, an oil and gas industry author from whose work the following discussion draws heavily. It will be concerned with three types of financial statements: the income statement, the balance sheet, and the statement of cash flows. If the analyst answers the questions following the description of each statement, he or she will have a good indication of the size of the company.

A quick look at the income statement. The income statement records the transactional side of the business over a defined period of time: the buying and selling of goods and services and the expenses related to these transactional activities. It is where the company's profits and losses are documented most succinctly (fig. 3–7).

(Dollars in millions, except per share data) December 31,	200X	200X	200X
Revenues and other income:			
Sales and other operating revenues (including consumer excise taxes)	**$37,447**	$29,871	$24,973
Revenues from matching buy/sell transactions	**9,603**	7023	5,459
Sales to related parties	**1,066**	799	700
Income from equity method investments	**202**	129.2	22
Net gains on disposal of assets	**43**	27	126
Gain (loss) on ownership change in San Felipe Resources Company	**–**	1.6	
Other income – net	**29**	77	59
Total revenues and other income	**48,391**	37,930	31,339

Fig. 3–7. Income statement sample

(*Note:* The extract from the income statement shown is for illustrative purposes, showing only some of the line items from a typical energy company income statement.)

Quick income statement questions to ask:

How big is the company (revenues)? _____

How much are the earnings? _____

Net income _____

Earnings per share _____

How much is spent servicing debt? _____

How big are the extraordinary items relative to revenues? _____

A quick look at the balance sheet. The balance sheet is a record of the company's "net money in the bank" and represents an accounting for the value of all the company owns and all that it owes. Figure 3–8 is an example of some of the items on a typical oil and gas company balance sheet. (Again, the extract from the balance sheet is for illustrative purposes, showing only some of the line items from a typical energy company balance sheet.)

(Dollars in millions, except per share data) December 31,	200X	200X
Assets		
Current assets:		
Cash and cash equivalents	**$1,989**	$2,560
Receivables, less allowance for doubtful accounts	**2,642**	2,391
Receivables from South African Copper Ltd.	**15.2**	11
Receivables from related parties	**29**	56
Inventories	**2,311**	1516
Other current assets	**145**	203
Total current assets	**7,131**	6,738

Fig. 3–8. Sample balance sheet

Quick balance sheet questions to ask:

How big is the company (total assets)? _____

What is the book value (assets – liabilities)? _____

How much debt does the company have? _____

Is the company taking on or reducing debt? _____

Is the company growing (increase in assets)? _____

A quick look at the statement of cash flows. Since public company accounting systems are set up on a noncash basis, the cash flow statement is the result of an adjustment to the income statement to remove accruals and other noncash expenses. The results show how much actual cash is coming into and leaving the business over a period of time. Future cash flows are one of the key measures for determining a company's value. Thus, the historical amount of these cash flows can give an indication of the health of the business. Figure 3–9 is an extract from a cash flow statement.

(Dollars in millions)	200X	200X	200X
Increase (decrease) in cash and cash equivalents			
Operating activities			
Net income	**$ 2,304**	$ 958	$ 1,004
Adjustments to reconcile net income to net cash provided from operating activities:			
Cumulative effect of changes in accounting principles	**14**	–	(3)
Income from discontinued operations	–	(3)	(232)
Deferred income taxes	**(158)**	(55)	54

Fig. 3–9. Extract from cash flow statement

Cash flow question to ask:

How much cash flow is (or has recently been) generated? _____

High-level financial ratio calculations

A few calculations of financial ratios can give a summary-level picture of whether the business is profitable or not. Three interesting summary-level ratios that give an indication of the health of the business are shown in table 3–1.[4]

Table 3–1. High-level financial ratios

Ratio	Calculation	Quick Indicator of:
Return on Sales	Net Income/Revenues	Profitability
Quick Ratio	(Current assets minus inventories)/current liabilities	Liquidity
Reserve Replacement	Production/proven reserves added though exploration, development, and revisions over the period	Performance

Comparisons with competitors can be checked online through Web sites such as Yahoo! Finance. However, Yahoo! Finance is somewhat suspect since it is a repackager of information filed on EDGAR. Therefore, if this information is being used for serious analysis or strategy, it should be checked against the original SEC filings.

A very good, in-depth discussion of oil and gas company valuation and financial statement analysis is found in Daniel Johnston's book, *Oil Company Financial Analysis in Nontechnical Language*.[5]

Risk factors—standard financial statement disclosures

One way to understand the corporate-level risks is to analyze specific areas of the company's financial statements that will be likely to mention these risks. For example, a publicly listed company on any U.S. securities exchange will disclose in writing what it considers to be corporate-level risk factors in its annual financial statements. For U.S.-based companies, these are found in Form 10-K under Item 1A, "Risk Factors" and under Item 7A, "Quantitative and Qualitative Disclosures about Market Risk." In the same way, non-U.S. headquartered firms with listings on U.S. exchanges will list their risks in SEC Form 20-F, in Items 3 and 11.

Combing through Items 1A, 7A, 3, and 11 in the financial statements will provide useful insight into what upper management considers as its major risks. Then based on this list of risks, an analysis of the drivers behind these risks and the critical information needed to monitor these drivers can be discovered using cause and effect diagrams (described elsewhere in this text).

Management's discussion and analysis (MD&A)

The final section that is very useful for a summary-level company analysis is Item 7 of Form 10-K, "Management's Discussion and Analysis." This is where the company's activities are summarized by upper management, and it sometimes makes reference to the company's strategy, goals, targets, key performance indicators, and other metrics used for internal performance measurement. In turn, these measurements and activities form the basis (or background) for the financial and operating risk analysis.

With information from the quick look, high-level ratios, risk factors, and MD&A activities described above, the risk analyst now has all the information necessary to begin to put the externally gathered information into the proper context for enterprise risk management. Concerning the high-level activities, the next technique helps managers and analysts working inside companies to "see the big picture." It is a graphical approach to understanding the context within which an organization works and is called *enterprise value chain mapping.*

Enterprise Value Chain Mapping

Enterprise value chain mapping is a strategic segment process flow analysis and documentation performed on the highest level of an organization's activities. It combines Michael Porter's approach to analyzing the business "value chain" with process mapping techniques and financial analysis as illustrated in discussion of quick financial analysis. The result is an enterprise value chain map, which is a diagram of the organization's main value activities and their linkages.

Key questions to be asked when developing a value chain map are as follows:

- What is the main business?

- How is success measured?

- Which activities provide the most revenues?

- Which activities are the most profitable?

- What are the plans for growth?

- How can the business be displayed in a diagram?

Discovery Tool 2: Enterprise Value Chain Mapping

As mentioned, the enterprise value chain mapping is a strategic segment process flow analysis and documentation performed on the highest level of an organization's activities.

Enterprise risk management application

For enterprise risk management applications, this tool is most appropriate as a method to create a snapshot of the company, viewing its entire business as a system. Ideal value chain mapping applications for enterprise risk management fall into the following categories:

- As the graphic backdrop for a facilitated risk identification workshop

- To communicate the risk profile to the company's board, investors, or other stakeholders

- To achieve a consensus among all the people running the business about what is important

- As the starting point or baseline document for detailed process mapping for process improvement, quality system documentation (i.e., ISO 9001), or regulatory compliance (Sarbanes-Oxley, etc.)

A graphical view combined with textual notation has numerous advantages over a purely textual description of the business often found in public company Form 10-K filings (Item 2, "MD&A" section). According to C. G. Cobb in his excellent book, *Enterprise Process Mapping*, these advantages are as follows:[6]

- **Visual impact.** The overall process and the interrelationship of the activities in the process can be much more easily visualized and understood if they are displayed as process blocks and icons.

- **The appropriate level of detail is documented.** Processes can be shown at various levels of detail to fit different levels of interest. For example, senior managers might be interested in a top-level view of the core processes and how they work together. This high-level view is probably the most appropriate level for an enterprise risk brainstorming. On the other hand, people performing a specific process would be more interested in the step-by-step description of how it is actually done.

- **Connectivity.** The interrelationship of various processes can be more easily understood if links between icons are shown with lines or arrows. In electronic documents, hyperlinks can even be used to allow a more detailed "drilling down" into the process.

An organization can be modeled and mapped in different ways depending on the desired analysis. For example, if the object is to show how one activity feeds another in an integrated business system, an approach oriented more toward process flow might be desired. On the other hand, if the purpose is to illustrate the portfolio effect of different businesses, an operating segment approach might be better.

To illustrate these different approaches, examples of enterprise risk value chain maps for a national oil company, a heavy crude upgrading project company, and an investor-owned oil and gas company are given.

The national oil company petroleum supply and disposition illustrates a process flow diagram approach to the value chain. It shows how everything is driven by a central planning department and emphasizes the description of each activity and how one activity feeds the next (fig. 3–10).

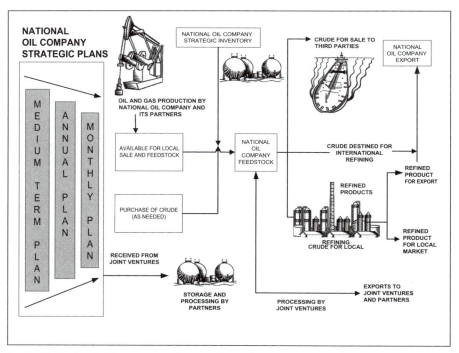

Fig. 3–10. National oil company sales, supply, and transport of petroleum

The heavy crude oil project company diagram below illustrates the flow of product through various major assets and highlights the involvement of partners and customers as part of the value chain (fig. 3–11).

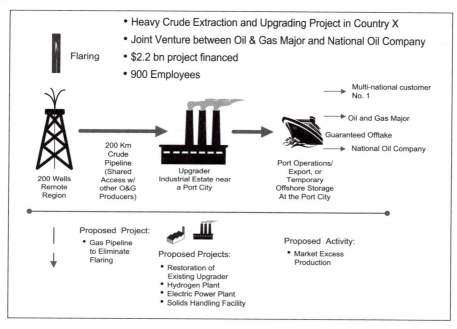

Fig. 3–11. Heavy crude oil project company

Figure 3–12 illustrates the operating segment approach to value chain mapping, focusing on how one investor-owned company is formally organized and how each segment contributes to the company's financial picture as part of a portfolio of businesses.

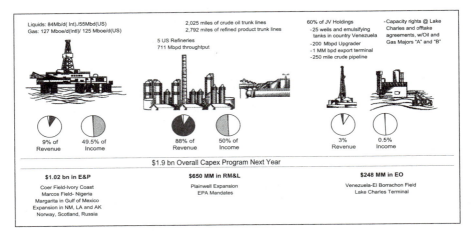

Liquids: 84Mb/d(Int)./55Mbd(US)
Gas: 127 Mboe/d(Intl)/ 125 Mboe/d(US)

2,025 miles of crude oil trunk lines
2,792 miles of refined product trunk lines

5 US Refineries
711 Mbpd throughput

60% of JV Holdings
- 25 wells and emulsifying tanks in country Venezuela
- 200 Mbpd Upgrader
- 1 MM bpd export terminal
- 250 mile crude pipeline

-Capacity rights @ Lake Charles and offtake agreements, w/Oil and Gas Majors "A" and "B"

9% of Revenue | 49.5% of Income

88% of Revenue | 50% of Income

3% Revenue | 0.5% Income

$1.9 bn Overall Capex Program Next Year

$1.02 bn in E&P

Coer Field-Ivory Coast
Marcos Field- Nigeria
Margarita in Gulf of Mexico
Expansion in NM, LA and AK
Norway, Scotland, Russia

$650 MM in RM&L

Plainwell Expansion
EPA Mandates

$248 MM in EO

Venezuela-El Borrachon Field
Lake Charles Terminal

Fig. 3–12. Investor-owned oil & gas company

The enterprise value chain mapping tool is not as useful as other analytic approaches in the following situations:

- When a quantitative model is needed to perform calculations, manipulate a database, or run quantitative stress testing, such as Monte Carlo simulations

- When step-by-step instructions are needed, requiring checklists and detailed descriptions

- When legal or regulatory documents require precise wording and textual descriptions

Process

The process for developing an enterprise value chain map is diagrammed in figure 3–13.

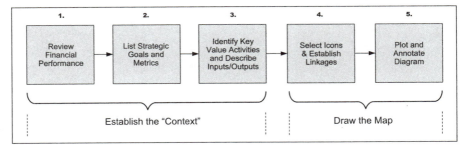

Fig. 3–13. Process for developing an enterprise value chain map

Some considerations and questions for application of this process to enterprise risk management are described in the following.

Establishing the "context." This involves understanding the background or "givens" of the business. Questions to be asked could include:

- How big is the company in terms of revenue, assets, cash flow, and proved reserves, and is the company growing in these areas?

- Over the past five years, what has been the company's history of financial performance in terms of level of debt and returns on sales, equity, and assets?

- What are the company's specific goals or targets in areas such as revenue growth, increased margins, credit rating, stock multipliers, new technology development and product launch, health, safety, and environmental performance, and corporate social responsibility?

- How is the company currently organized? What are the steps or activities involved in making money and achieving the company's goals? How are these activities connected?

(For more information on reviewing financial performance, see the section, "Discovery Tool 1: The Quick Financial Analysis" or the references at the end of this chapter.)

Draw the map. This involves making a picture of how the business works. Questions to be asked could include:

- What is the best way to graphically display the company's activities (process flow chart, block diagram, or influence diagram)?

- What are the best icons to use to communicate the business's main activities?

- What additional numbers or textual descriptions are needed to annotate the icons for purposes of risk identification and communication?

Microsoft Visio is an ideal software application for drawing enterprise value chain maps. This is because Visio is not only easy to use, but provides predrawn shapes, icons, and templates and has an electronic layering capability that allows the inclusion of hyperlinks and documents stored "behind" the graphics. For the purposes of risk identification, enterprise value chain mapping using Visio is a powerful way that risks can be captured and documented in a risk matrix linked to the value activities shown in the value chain map.

A more detailed discussion of the specifics of process mapping can be found in the references at the end of the chapter.

As mentioned earlier in this chapter, there are three tools used as the foundation for the organizational context: the quick financial analysis, enterprise value chain mapping, and the next tool, stakeholder analysis. Of these three, stakeholder analysis is one of the most strategic, since it answers the question, who are the internal and external customers, and what should be done to meet their needs? Yet, because this is a qualitative tool requiring management of multiple nontechnical uncertainties, it can be one of the most overlooked tools by the risk management team.

Stakeholder Analysis

A stakeholder analysis identifies and prioritizes the individuals or groups with an interest in an issue. It is analogous to a customer survey used for product development because its purpose is to systematically capture information about the issues facing different "customers" (called *stakeholders* here) and align the company's strategic direction with these interests. Because there are numerous stakeholders, their interests must be balanced or prioritized. By translating these prioritized interests into strategic objectives, the company's mission can be aligned by senior management with stakeholder interests. If a company does this consistently and more effectively than its competitors, it can achieve sustained competitive advantage. In the context of strategic risk management, reducing uncertainty around achievement of these objectives is an increased opportunity for competitive advantage, while increasing uncertainty is an increased threat.

Stakeholder analysis is part of the discovery phase of the information integrity process supporting enterprise risk management. Along with the quick financial analysis and the enterprise value chain mapping tools, a stakeholder analysis helps to establish the context within which a company operates.

Discovery Tool 3: Stakeholder Analysis

In the context of strategic risk management, reducing uncertainty around achievement of key objectives provides increased opportunity for competitive advantage. On the other hand, the increased possibility of failure to meet these same objectives is a threat to a company's competitive position. Nowhere is this more true that when the objectives relate to key stakeholder needs. In fact, the degree to which an oil and gas company successfully identifies and meets key stakeholder requirements may be one of the most defining factors of its success in the 21st century.

Enterprise risk management application

The stakeholder analysis contributes to accomplishment of the internal environment and objective-setting phases of the COSO II framework for enterprise risk management (fig. 3–14).

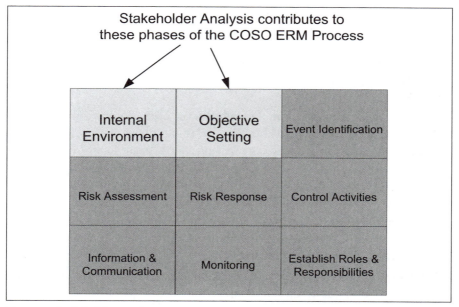

Fig. 3–14. Stakeholders and COSO II

As mentioned above, the tool's most effective application for enterprise risk management is to establish the basis for achieving a competitive advantage.

Process

Stakeholder analysis incorporates not only an inventory of stakeholders and an identification of their issues, but a transformation of the issues into a strategy and management plan, as shown in steps 7 and 8 of the process (fig. 3–15).

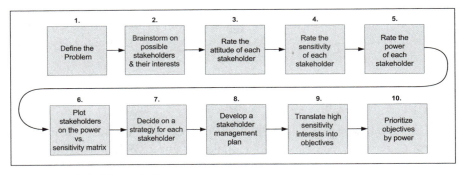

Fig. 3–15. Stakeholder analysis process

Furthermore, steps 9 and 10 translate the stakeholder issues into strategic objectives and are steps to focus the organizational goals and management's attention on the most important drivers of success. Some of the key considerations for implementation of a stakeholder analysis are described in the following.

Steps 1–5. Identify the stakeholders and their requirements. Typically this is performed by the strategic planning and executive management team in a workshop setting using some form of facilitated brainstorming. As with any workshop, a written agenda, a facilitator, and a well-defined problem (or opportunity) statement formulated **prior** to the meeting are three important success factors.

The elements to be captured during this workshop are a listing of the stakeholders and their respective interests, attitudes, sensitivities, and power, as described in the following.

Interests are the issues that each stakeholder has relative to the problem. For example, one identified stakeholder may be an NGO (for example, an environmental group) that may be concerned with CO_2 emissions from a new refinery or power plant. Another stakeholder could be a credit rating analyst, who is concerned with the level of liquidity as measured by the company's debt to equity ratio and the quality of future cash flows to service long-term notes.

Attitudes are the way the stakeholder is likely to feel about or react to the problem or opportunity. It has to do not only with their interests, but with their relationship to the company, and may involve a trust factor. For example, a regulator may be interested in promoting safe, sustainable development, but may have a low level of trust in the company. This regulator would probably have a negative attitude toward new projects the company was promoting, in spite of the safeguards put in place to protect public health and safety on the project. The attitude is either positive, negative, or noncommittal and could be indicated with an up, down, or double-headed arrow.

Sensitivity is a refinement of the stakeholder attitude that focuses on the degree to which the problem or opportunity affects their interests. For example, a board member may be interested in the appearance of a corporate governance breach. In the wake of the Enron scandals, they might thus be very sensitive to launching a new business venture that relies on the infamous *special purpose entity (SPE)* financing mechanism used by Enron. This sensitivity could be translated as low, medium, or high, depending upon the board member's aversion to the SPE structure.

Power has to do with a stakeholder's "gorilla factor." It measures the answers to the following questions: To what degree do you need the support of this stakeholder for the project to succeed? Could this stakeholder kill the proposal if he or she chose to do so? Notice that powerful stakeholders may or may not be engaged in the process. If they are not, this is a red flag. For example, a state governor's office may or may not be involved in the concept development of a project. Nevertheless, as has been seen with offshore LNG terminal developments in the United States, these governors can make all the difference to the project's success before it gets to the public hearing phase. If at all possible, these powerful stakeholders should somehow be engaged early in order to manage the threat of surprises when these interested parties are needed for approval.

A useful template for aggregating the results of a stakeholder analysis workshop as well as the fields used to document the results from each step in the process are indicated in figure 3–16.

		Step 2		Step 3	Step 4	Step 5	Step 7
Stakeholder	Interests			Attitude	Sensitivity	Power	Strategy
①							
②							
③							
④							

Fig. 3–16. Stakeholder analysis workshop template

Steps 1–5. Stakeholder analysis workshop template. As a result of having a problem definition (step 1) as a result of the workshop, the first two columns should be filled in with all the possible stakeholders (step 2 in the process). Then each identified stakeholder should be evaluated one by one on attitude, sensitivity, and power (steps 3, 4, and 5).

Steps 6–10. Turn the stakeholder information into action. Consider our previous examples of the environmental group (the NGO) as a powerful stakeholder, with its issue of a reduction in CO_2 emissions from oil refineries, its negative attitude toward our company, and its extreme sensitivity toward the expansion of one of our company's existing refineries. To determine what we should do with this stakeholder (who could sabotage our project), we might first establish a grid of their power versus their sensitivity relative to other stakeholders, then determine a strategy based upon where the NGO falls on the grid. An example of how this might be performed (i.e., steps 6 and 7 in our process) is illustrated on a preformatted 3 by 3 grid, with the circled numbers representing different stakeholders (fig. 3–17).

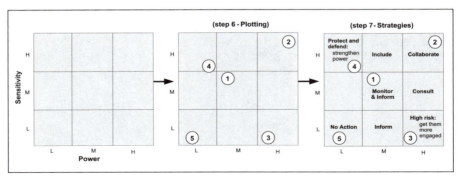

Fig. 3–17. Stakeholder strategy grids

In this case, the NGO might be the stakeholder shown as ② in the right-hand quadrant of the middle plot. Looking at the plot on the far right, the strategy for the upper right-hand quadrant where the NGO is located is to collaborate. Knowing that the NGO is concerned about carbon emissions, its concern could be translated into a strategic goal of reducing carbon emissions at the existing plant through carbon sequestration to compensate for the additional CO_2 production of the plant expansion. In this case, perhaps keeping total yearly carbon emissions at the refinery at its current level (say, 6 million tonnes/yr) would be the strategic objective for the company. The risk action or disposition would be to use various project and operational risk management tools and techniques to ensure that with an acceptable level of certainty, this target is achieved. In turn, this assurance to one of the key stakeholders allows the company to obtain its permit to expand the refinery with the blessing of the stakeholders. Finally, through differentiation of its offering in this way, the company achieves a strategic advantage relative to its competitors in the region.

Other considerations

Of course, the previous example is simplified. In an actual situation, there are many stakeholders, and requirements of each must be balanced. Additionally, the company may not actually know what the powerful stakeholder issues are, or even worse, what the stakeholder's attitude might be regarding the company, project, or initiative. This lack of knowledge is a strategic blind spot that must be removed using market research techniques such as personal interviews and surveys. (These techniques are described in the section, "Discovery Tool 7: Selected Surveying and Interviewing Techniques," later in this chapter.) Finally, the power/sensitivity dynamics of various stakeholders will change over time. Therefore, the company's objectives should be prioritized and the stakeholders monitored and reevaluated at least every quarter year in order to maintain competitive advantage.

If it is performed, documented, and acted upon, the process of a stakeholder analysis is an excellent tool for understanding internal and external customers and aligning the enterprise risk management activities around their requirements. Very few energy companies today perform stakeholder analysis with competitive advantage as the objective, and they do not seem to have a very thorough or systematic approach. In the future, those companies that recognize stakeholder management as a competitive weapon will begin to develop such an approach, while the others will be left behind.

It has been mentioned that using a workshop is an important way to discover and capture important information. What are the most effective ways to conduct a risk workshop? The following description provides a structured approach to this topic that can be adapted to nearly any facilitated group setting.

Selected Workshop Facilitation Techniques

Workshop facilitation for purposes of information integrity and risk identification requires a delicate balancing act between the three roles assumed by the facilitator: *organizer, neutral intermediary,* and *motivator.* As an organizer, the facilitator is responsible for structuring the workshop to the extent necessary to keep discussions on track and ensure results. As a neutral intermediary, the facilitator must catalyze discussion but refrain from providing value judgments or even giving a hint of endorsing or disapproving ideas. Finally, as the motivator, the facilitator must encourage participation by and cooperation between members of the group.

To successfully carry out each of these roles, specific techniques can be used to ensure that the workshop is a success. Among these are developing a structured agenda, capturing notes of the meeting, guiding discussion, and encouraging participation.

Discovery Tool 4: Workshop Facilitation Techniques

This discovery phase tool outlines a workshop facilitation process. However, to a certain degree, facilitation is an art, and the approach cannot be codified. Thus, the following discussion is meant to be a set of guidelines rather than the definitive handbook for workshop facilitators. Too often, workshops, discussion groups, and even staff meetings are managed in an ad hoc manner, leading to frustration, boredom, and wasted time for the participants. These guidelines are meant to provide some structure and a few facilitation tips to make information integrity and risk identification workshops more productive.[7]

The role of the organizer

As with any meeting, a failure to plan leaves success to chance. Nothing demonstrates poor meeting planning more vividly than the lack of a written agenda. Thus the first technique for a good workshop facilitator is putting together a clear, concise agenda. This should include, as a minimum, the following:

- Objective of the meeting

- Location and start and finish time of the meeting

- Participants

- Listing of each topic to be covered, with approximate time to be spent on that topic and the person(s) responsible for contributing to the topic

- Any reference materials as attachments

The written objective of the workshop helps the facilitator keep the discussions on track by providing a benchmark or "process check" aligning all the group members. An example of an agenda for a business risk workshop is shown in figure 3–18.

Insisting on and arranging for a dedicated *scribe* (or note taker) for the workshop or meeting is another requirement of the organizer's role. So much value is "left on the table" due to lack of meeting documentation of results and action items. Developing a written agenda and taking and distributing notes is so important to meeting success that when a meeting organizer skips these two items, attending the meeting is probably a waste of time.

Quarterly Business Risk Management Workshop

Date: March 30, 2006
Time: 7:30 am - 9:30 am
Venue: The Woodlands Conference Center
Attendee Groups: SFR Strategic Planning and E&P Group leads

Purpose: Provide the EO project team with a working knowledge of the risks and how to review and update risks and actions in San Felipe Resources' approved risk register and action tracking tool

Workshop Agenda

Time	Topics	Objective	Facilitator
7:30-7:45	• Introductions • Workshop overview	- Briefly introduce attendees - Review agenda & workshop purpose - Answer questions	Barry Craddock
7:45-8:00	• The SFR Risk Register and the Project Risk Process	- Explain how capturing and tracking EO risks in the SFR risk register is part of the overall risk management process for the project	Maria Elena Alvarez
8:00-8:15	• Overview of EO risk management plan	- Focus on the project Risk Matrix and discussion of very low, low, medium, high and very high rating scale.	Barry Craddock
8:45-9:15	• Hands- on SFR Risk Register Use	- Teaching attendees how to update and review existing risks and actions and enter new risks and actions	Carson Smith
9:15-9:30	• Recap • Action Items • Adjourn	- Ensure that assigned risks are clear	Barry Craddock Facilitator

Fig. 3–18. Quarterly business risk management workshop

In addition to the agenda and the minutes, the workshop environment and the tools for successful facilitation should be organized ahead of time. Nothing should be left to chance. If possible, the day before the workshop, the facilitator should visit the room where the workshop will take place and check to ensure that the layout and furniture is conducive to the free flow of ideas. The facilitator should visualize the flow of the agenda and consider what could go right and wrong, developing backup plans for things such as computer crashes and malfunctioning projectors. If the furniture is poorly organized (for example, row after row of tables, classroom style), the facilitator should try to rearrange the furniture the night before to allow people to see each other and feel more like a group. Tools for the workshop should also be prearranged and confirmed. Projectors and markers should be tested, handouts printed, and flipcharts and whiteboards verified and positioned appropriately. Anything can go wrong, but based on my experience, a nonworking laptop projector and not allowing enough time for traffic when traveling to the workshop venue are the most common causes of workshop delays. Nothing destroys the momentum of a workshop more quickly than having to scramble around to get organized after the participants have already arrived!

The role of the neutral catalyst

The workshop facilitator should stimulate productive, unrestricted workshop discussions by creating the right environment for free expression. If the topic is important enough to the participants, the facilitator may need to simply "prime the pump," and the discussions will flow.

One common error for experienced and novice facilitators alike is to get involved in the discussion. For a facilitator who is knowledgeable about the subject being discussed, **not** contributing ideas is one of the most important, but difficult, parts of his or her job. The facilitator must maintain a completely nonjudgmental demeanor or risk stifling ideas and losing authority. Positive or negative comments, noises, gestures, and even body language can signal disapproval and criticism and cause role confusion in the eyes of the group. When the facilitator contributes to the discussion, it sends the wrong signal by mixing the facilitator function with that of a content contributor and influencer. In summary, the facilitator must project the following message to the participants: "As a facilitator, I am organizer, catalyst, and motivator. I will not step into your shoes as a discussion participant."

The role of the motivator

The final role of the facilitator is as a motivator. This might require a bit of psychology, as the facilitator should have the ability to read the behaviors of different participants to better manage the group dynamics and keep the atmosphere of the workshop upbeat and stimulating. Experienced facilitators can also look for behavioral traits in individuals that signal personality types and can use them to put together more effective teams. Finally, the facilitator should act a bit like a cheerleader, while at the same time maintaining his or her authority as the neutral catalyst and organizer. When used properly (and sparingly), contests, games, and even lighthearted jokes are just a few of the techniques that can be helpful to turn a sleepy, boring meeting into a stimulating and friendly, competitive atmosphere. The facilitator must be creative, however, since some of the same stories and games have over the years been used too frequently. Care must be taken to avoid the same "ice-breaker" game as the last motivational speaker the company hired.

Other considerations. As mentioned previously, workshop facilitation is an art. To do it well requires creativity, practice, and experience. The best way to learn is to work alongside an experienced facilitator as a workshop scribe and over time assume more and more of the responsibility for directing a group.

Workshops are one of the most commonly used methods for eliciting ideas among groups in a corporate setting. They are also an embedded part of the risk management process as many companies. The question is, are they always the most appropriate ways to get objective, unbiased information from participants? No matter how carefully planned and expertly facilitated the workshop, there will always exist a certain group dynamic among the participants that may inhibit the free flow of ideas. The next discovery tool, the *Delphi method*, combines the best features of a brainstorming session with a minimal amount of potentially distracting group dynamics. It also allows participants to be actively involved in information exchange without participating at the same time or being physically located in the same geography. With the advances in electronic communications systems, the time is ripe to address the risk management issues of tomorrow using the Delphi method, a tool that was originally developed more than 40 years ago.

Delphi Method

The Delphi method is a tool for controlled debate among anonymous experts for the purpose of rationally considering the full range of informed opinions on a complex issue. The idea is that the result of a consensus building among experts (each anonymous to the others) is superior to the result from a single person or traditional group workshop where personalities, politics, and group dynamics interfere with rational debate. The methodology was developed during the 1960s by three researchers at the RAND Corporation, a California nonprofit think tank. However, its foundation (the thesis/antithesis/synthesis approach to scientific inquiry) dates back to 18th and early 19th century German philosophers. Diagrammatically, the concept behind the Delphi method can be illustrated as shown in figure 3–19.[8]

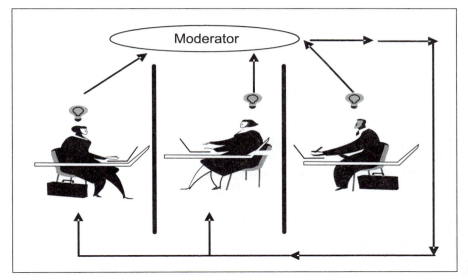

Fig. 3–19. Delphi method

Under certain conditions, the Delphi method can be one of the most effective ways to identify and classify risks.

As an enterprise risk management application, this tool is most appropriate as a method for identifying and classifying risks when key issues can be clearly articulated, they involve a high degree of uncertainty, and they require the judgment of experts because of their complexity.

Discovery Tool 5: Delphi Method

As mentioned above, the Delphi method is a tool for controlled debate among anonymous experts for the purpose of rationally considering the full range of informed opinions on a complex issue. Diagrammatically, the concept behind the Delphi method can be illustrated as shown in figure 3–20.

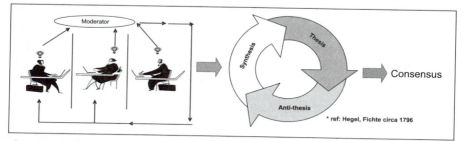

Fig. 3–20. Concept behind Delphi method

Under certain conditions, the Delphi method can be one of the most effective ways to identify and classify risks.

Enterprise risk management application

As mentioned previously, as an enterprise risk management application, this tool is most appropriate in several circumstances. Such circumstances involve its usefulness for identifying and classifying risks when key issues can be clearly articulated, they involve a high degree of uncertainty, and they require the judgment of experts because of their complexity. Ideal Delphi applications fall into the following categories:

- Answering a specific, single-dimension question where geographic distance restricts face-to-face meetings.

- Determining a point forecast for some future value or future event's date when there is significant uncertainty.

- Determining the desirability of some future state. Questions dealing with desirability ask for judgments about whether an event ought to occur and ask for the basis of the recommendation.

- Determining the means (or strategy) for achieving or avoiding some future state. Questions dealing with policy or strategy, for example, should explore the traditional reporter's questions of *who, what, when, where, how* (or *how much*), and *why* as they relate to the importance of achieving a particular goal or objective.

- Determining a range of opinions either to provide different scenarios or to provide the bounds on a numerical simulation.

- Determining the contributing factors or drivers to a particular outcome or risk.

This tool is least appropriate in the following situations:

- When immediate decisions are needed. The Delphi method is time intensive because of its requirement to screen and select experts, carefully design a questionnaire, and perform multiple rounds.

- When the answer can be obtained from some published source or can be derived with a calculation using predefined parameters.

Complex forecasts involving multiple factors are particularly problematic applications for the Delphi method because the results can become confusing and inconclusive.

Process

The process for implementing a Delphi process is diagrammed in figure 3–21.

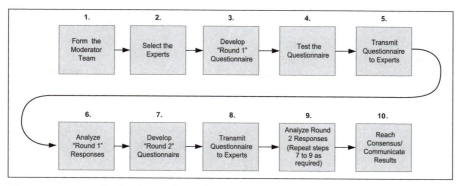

Fig. 3–21. Process for implementing Delphi

Some key considerations for application of this process to enterprise risk management are given in the following discussion.

Formation of the moderator team and selecting experts. Once the focal issue has been identified and clearly defined, there are many ways to find and select experts. However, the following issues should be considered:

- Do candidates consider themselves experts in this field?

- How many times per week do they deal with the topic at hand?

- How many years have they worked in the field relating to the topic?

- What is their educational background relative to the topic?

- Have they published or presented at professional society meetings on this topic?

A more detailed discussion can be found in the references.

Development and testing of the questionnaire. Proper application of survey techniques is a critical part of ensuring the integrity of the information feeding the enterprise risk process. Many market research projects are poorly performed because of incompetent design and development of the questionnaire.

Questionnaire development and testing is both an art and a science, requiring training and experience to be executed properly. Market research and behavioral science courses dealing with survey methods will often cover the following considerations:

- "Setting up" questions for the respondents by providing an opening paragraph or cover letter reminding them of the objectives of the study, the schedule for the response, and a way of returning the completed questionnaire

- Making the question wording crisp, single-issued, and answerable

- Phrasing of the question so as not to introduce bias

- Selecting the most appropriate form of answer relative to the question objective (i.e., yes/no, rating scale, fill in the blank, or essay)

- Testing the questionnaire for flow, understanding, and bias by administering it to a sample group of respondents

Because of its importance to the process, the topic of questionnaire design is discussed in more detail elsewhere in this toolbox. Again, a more in-depth discussion of questionnaire design can be found in the references at the end of this chapter.

Administering the questionnaire and synthesizing the results. The distinguishing characteristics of the Delphi method relative to other forecasting techniques are the physical separation of the respondents and the role of the moderator in administering successive rounds of questioning and synthesis of results.

In the past, delivery and retrieval of the Delphi questionnaires was limited to mail, fax, or some other type of secret ballot method. Today, e-mail, electronic bulletin boards, and instant messaging provide new ways to administer Delphi rounds. The paradox is that the more electronic, impersonal, and repetitive the communication becomes, the less likely the respondents are to maintain an interest in the survey. Administering the surveys through personal interviews has been suggested by one of the founders of the method, Dr. Theodore Gordon, as a way of maintaining a more interpersonal approach. However, personal interviews can be time-consuming, require experienced and knowledgeable interviewers, and do not provide as controlled a process of feedback to the respondents.

Thus the Delphi approach is best used as an information gathering technique when geographic separation, scheduling constraints, or group dynamics cause more direct methods such as face-to-face workshops to be impractical.

What if after the workshop, the risk analyst wants to dig down and discover the "root causes" of an issue? How should the analyst peel the layers off the onion of a problem and proceed to arrive at the key drivers for its resolution? The next tool could be used to answer that question. *Cause and effect diagramming* is an analytic approach used in many areas of operational risk management, from process hazard analysis to system reliability studies. It is also the basis for decision trees used for financial options valuation. Thus, this next tool is not new to the field of risk management. However, it has some interesting new applications for information integrity and enterprise risk management, which are explored in the following discussion.

Cause and Effect Diagramming

For the purposes of this book, the three tools described that illustrate the relationship between two or more elements or variables will be termed *cause and effect diagrams*. Cause and effect diagrams can be useful in linking risks, drivers, and indicators, but they are also a good way of documenting the logic behind why it is important to gather particular pieces of information. The three types of diagrams to be described here are bow-tie diagrams (sometimes called *tree diagrams*), influence diagrams, and the information integrity matrix. The three diagram types are shown in figure 3–22.

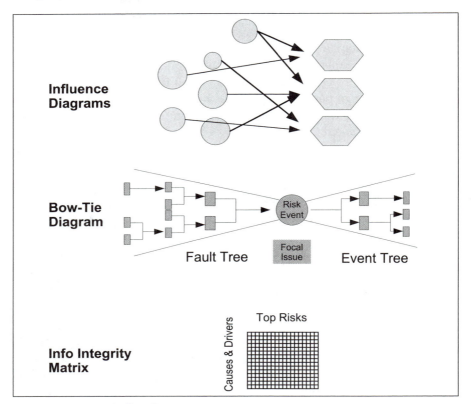

Fig. 3–22. Cause and effect diagrams

Employing these tools is an important step toward ensuring that risks are adequately described and monitored via reliable information sources. By using a combination of the three techniques, the information intensive risk drivers can be uncovered, thus providing assurance to stakeholders that adequate information due diligence has been performed.

Discovery Tool 6: Cause and Effect Diagrams

The steps involved in using these three diagrams in the discovery phase of the information integrity process are shown in figure 3–23.

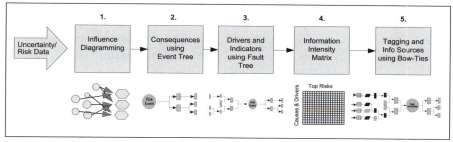

Fig. 3–23. Combination of three techniques

Step 1 in the process is to develop an influence diagram (sometimes called the *relations* or *affinity* diagram) to understand the relationship between uncertainties or risks on the one hand, and the resulting consequences and impacts on the other. When used for showing the linkage between risks, consequences, and impacts, influence diagrams rely on a graphical notation to display relationships between risk factors and their possible consequences and impacts. Even if relationships are implicitly understood, textual descriptions are often clumsy, and numerical or spreadsheet models are too tedious to be used to effectively communicate and clarify relationships. In these cases, influence diagrams can be a useful communication tool. The general steps in developing an influence diagram are as follows:

1. Assemble risks and uncertainties from the risk identification phase or from a list of uncertainties identified by the strategic planners, upper management, or risk management consultants.

2. Extract the corporate goals or metrics from the company's financial statements or from the results of the stakeholder analysis.

3. Brainstorm on the potential consequences and impacts of various risks identified. If a workshop approach is used for the brainstorming, more information on workshop facilitation tips can be found in the workshop facilitation discussion elsewhere in this chapter. (*Note:* The "consequences" can be either positive or negative.)

4. On a sheet of paper, or in a drawing application, plot the uncertainties, risks, consequences, and impacts using the notation or symbols.

5. Link the risks to consequences and to the goals, metrics, or impacts using lines or arrows.

6. Determine the uncertainties or risks that are the most critical to organizational success by examining the linkages.

For the simplest influence diagrams, circles, hexagons, and arrows can be used to display variables, outcomes, and the relationships between them. More advanced applications of influence and other cause and effect diagrams use rectangles to indicate decisions and circles versus double-lined circles to distinguish between probabilistic (i.e., "chance") and deterministic variables. The distinction between chance and deterministic variables becomes useful when modeling the system quantitatively using a Monte Carlo simulation using the influence diagram. One computer application for converting an influence diagram to a quantitative model has been promoted quite extensively by a company called Lumina Decision Systems, using their Analytica software tool.

Finally, for purposes of information integrity diagrams, two new symbols can be added: the parallelogram, to symbolize leading indicators, and the cylinder, to symbolize information sources. The range of symbols that can be used for information integrity cause and effect diagrams described in this monograph is shown in figure 3–24.

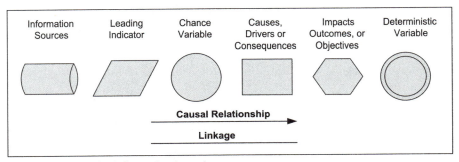

Fig. 3–24. Shapes for information integrity

As mentioned, influence diagrams can be used as a way to analyze the natural links between different aspects of a complex situation. As an example, I have extracted the following list of uncertainties from the public documents of one large oil and gas company:

- Commodity prices

- Hydrocarbon reserve estimates

- Geological success

- Competition for acreage

At this point, the term *uncertainty* will be used instead of *risk*, because risk implies that an assessment of the likelihood and the consequences has been made. Uncertainties, on the other hand, are missing one or both of these assessments. Thus, one of the purposes of the cause and effect diagrams is to convert uncertainties into risks by assessing their likelihoods and consequences.

Therefore, if the preceding steps are followed, and an influence diagram is drawn of the possible consequences and impacts related to these four uncertainties, it might look like figure 3–25.

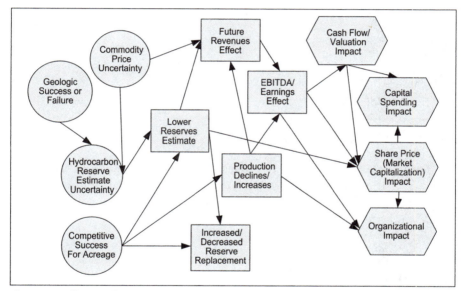

Fig. 3–25. Influence diagram

Although rather complex looking, this does allow visualization of the possible consequences (rectangles) and final impacts (hexagons) due to each uncertainty by following the causal arrows. If just one of these uncertainties (commodity prices) is isolated, it can be analyzed further using the second cause and effect technique, the *tree diagram*.

Tree diagrams are used extensively for probability calculations supporting safety analysis and financial options. Often they are one of the first steps in a quantitative analysis and include the assignment of probabilities at various decision gates. In turn, each probability is then "worked back" to arrive at a cumulative probability for a specified event. In this example they will be used strictly *qualitatively* to show the range of consequences and the link to various impacts. Effectively this is a type of *factor analysis*. Sometimes decision trees are put together to form what is called a *bow-tie diagram* (due to its characteristic shape). In the bow-tie diagram in figure 3–26, the left-hand side of the diagram is typically called the *fault tree*, while the right-hand side is called the *event tree*.

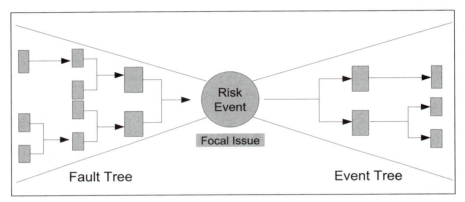

Fig. 3–26. Factor analysis bow-tie

For information integrity purposes, the fault tree/event tree technique will be further refined using the symbols previously presented as an additional notation, incorporating the following distinctions between the types of information:

- Key forces

- Driving factors

- Leading indicators

- Information sources

- Immediate consequences

- Resulting impacts

Distinguishing between the different types of information is useful because it allows information to eventually be classified as critical/noncritical and external/internal. In turn, this is useful when qualifying the accuracy and reliability of various information sources. It also provides a nomenclature that is consistent with the language used to develop *futures scenarios*, a technique profiled in the disposition chapter of this book (see the scenario analysis tool in chapter 5).

Strictly speaking, the term *bow-tie* as used in safety analysis includes *controls*, a feature that will not be dealt with in this text for purposes of information integrity. Controls are mitigating actions at various stages in the fault tree or event tree that act to minimize either the frequency or the consequence of the event. Since in this application the bow-tie diagrams are only being used as a risk identification technique, different tools will be presented in later chapters to put information integrity controls in place.

Returning to the influence diagram example of the commodity price uncertainty, the right-hand side of the bow-tie diagram could be developed (step 2 in the process) by starting with the focal issue and asking, "What if?" What would be the impacts on the financial results or on the operational goals? This questioning exercise could be performed using one-on-one interviews with experts, facilitated workshops, or even a Delphi session. (For further reference, these three techniques are described elsewhere in this chapter.) The results of this successive questioning process related to the commodity price uncertainty could be as shown in figure 3–27.

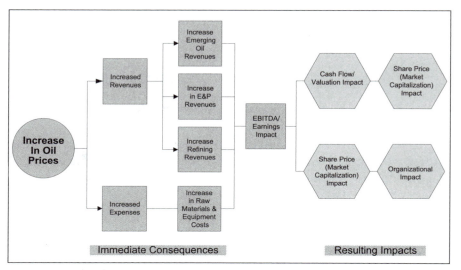

Fig. 3–27. Results of step 2, event tree analysis of commodity price uncertainty

Using oil price increase example

Applying a similar approach to the left-hand side of the bow tie diagram, two specific questions should be addressed: What are the causes of this uncertainty? What factors drive these causes?

Some of results of step 3 in the process (i.e., discovering the key forces) using this same example might look as shown in figure 3–28.

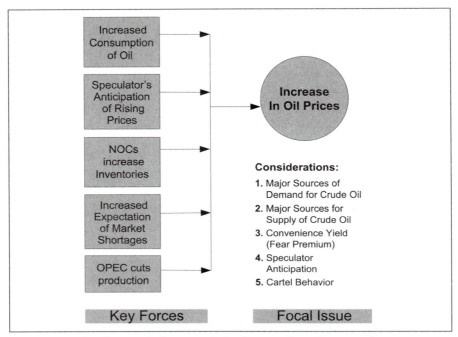

Fig. 3–28. Results of step 3, fault tree analysis of commodity price uncertainty

Expanding this analysis and fault tree out to the left, through the levels of *driving factors* and *leading indicators*, a diagram can finally be arrived at that would show information sources. An outline of the resulting information integrity bow-tie diagram is shown in figure 3–29.

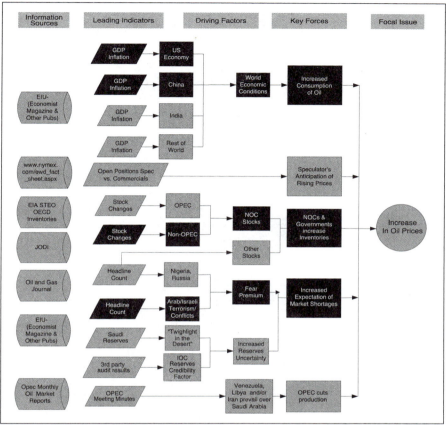

Fig. 3–29. Information integrity fault tree

The black symbols in figure 3–29 on the fault tree side of the diagram illustrate which elements in the process may have been determined to be factors that are highly *external information intensive(EII)*. This means that the key force is critical to manage the risk, and its driving factor requires accurate, reliable information *from outside the company.* But how can these driving forces be determined? At this point, the information integrity matrix technique is useful.

An information integrity matrix is nothing more than a grid of the risks on one axis versus the causes and drivers on the other. The intersection of these is where a qualitative assessment of the information intensity can be determined and recorded. For purposes of this illustration, if commodity price and reserves estimates are selected as the uncertainties and then plotted against their respective driving factors, the matrix in figure 3–30 illustrates the result.

Driving Force	Uncertainty	Commodity Price	Reserves Estimates
Escalation in Material, Equipment and Labor Costs		O	●
Production Plans		O	O
Long Term Contracts		O	O
US Economy		●	●
Chinese Economy		●	●
Indian Economy		◉	◉
Rest of World Economy		◉	◉
PSA and JV Agreements		O	O
Strategic Plans		O	O
Effect of Speculation		◉	◉
OPEC Stocks		◉	◉
Non-OPEC Stocks		●	●
License Agreements		O	O
Strategic Plans		O	O
Nigeria Fear Premium		◉	◉
Russia Fear Premium		◉	◉
Arab/Israeli Terrorism		●	●
World Reserves Uncertainty		◉	◉

Legend

● High EII

◉ Moderate EII

O Low EII

Fig. 3–30. Uncertainty vs. driving factors matrix

The black dots can then be used to code or color in the driving forces on the previous fault tree diagram to document what information is important to the organization's success.

What this information intensity matrix demonstrates is the following:

1. There are certain driving forces that are more important to monitor than others (i.e., those with the black dots = high EII).

2. These high EII driving forces require information from outside the company.

3. These high EII driving forces are common to more than one uncertainty.

The conclusion is that in order to control the uncertainties that are most important to success, reliable information sources must be found for at least five factors: escalation in costs, the U.S. economy, the Chinese economy, non-OPEC stocks of crude oil, and the latest events relating to the Arab/Israeli conflict and terrorism. These are shown as cylinders in the fault tree diagram. (*Note:* The previous example should be considered as illustrative of how to use these cause and effect tools. It may not represent the results of other data gathering on these two types of uncertainties.)

Other considerations. *Mind mapping* involves a software program called Mind Map, developed by Tony Buzan, that is used to generate ideas. It can also be used to link risks to consequences as an alternative to influence diagrams. However, the mind mapping approach makes it more difficult to see the consequences and impacts that may be common to more than one risk.

Sometimes only a limited amount of information can be obtained from brainstorming sessions, workshops, interactive discussions, and internal analysis using decision support tools. To get further, it is necessary to interview someone face to face. As with the other data gathering approaches, surveying and interviewing techniques provide a systematic process involving planning, attention to detail, and competent execution. These are critical to gathering solid, reliable information.

Surveying and Interviewing Techniques

Surveying and interviewing are forms of organized data collection using "primary" market research techniques. Primary market research deals with information that comes from someone who has experienced or witnessed the event or activities in question. In other words, the interviewer "got it directly from the horse's mouth" as opposed having read it somewhere.

Surveys generally refer to a standardized or structured data gathering activity using a questionnaire. Interviewing refers to face-to-face data gathering. Effective market research instrument design, testing, and administration are not simple undertakings, and in-depth market research should be performed by professionals with university-level training and experience in this field. Thus, the technique described in this chapter is meant to provide only an overview of the process of questionnaire design and surveying techniques. It also is meant to point out a few rules of thumb regarding information gathering during the discovery phase of the information integrity process.

Discovery Tool 7: Selected Surveying and Interviewing Techniques

As strange as it seems, some people gathering risk information in companies never bother to actually talk with the experts! In the cases where they do some data gathering, their approach is often ad hoc, disorganized, and undocumented. Thus, the purpose of this tool is to outline a structured, defensible approach to performing surveys for use in the discovery phase of the information integrity process.

As with any form of research, to ensure consistency and comparability of results, there must be a structured approach to planning and administering the interview or survey. Surveying generally refers to a standardized or structured data gathering activity using a questionnaire or similar *research instrument* sent by mail or e-mail, or administered over the telephone. Interviewing, on the other hand, refers to face-to-face data gathering using a type of questionnaire called a *discussion guide*. As mentioned previously, effective market research instrument design, testing, and administration are not simple undertakings. If the problem is very complex, in-depth market research should be performed using professionals with university-level training and experience in this field. Thus, this tool description is not meant as a comprehensive procedure for market research questionnaire design. Instead, it is to provide the following:

- An overview of the process of questionnaire design and surveying techniques

- A few rules of thumb regarding information gathering during the discovery phase of the information integrity process

One of the clearest and most concise descriptions of the survey process is described in Nancy Tague's outstanding book, *The Quality Toolbox*.[9] Thus, the following description of surveying and interviewing techniques draws from my experience and her book. The types of primary market research that are appropriate for the discovery phase are telephone surveys, personal interviews, and use of the Delphi method as described elsewhere in this chapter. Mail surveys (e-mail/postal) and focus groups are two types of market research techniques that should be left to professional market researchers. This is because it is easy to poorly perform both of these techniques, thus wasting time and money without achieving meaningful results.

Table 3–2 below illustrates when (and when not) to use three different types of surveys in the discovery phase of the information integrity process.

Table 3–2. Different survey applications

Survey Type	Recommended Survey Applications	Best Avoided Survey Applications (use more appropriate sources)
Telephone survey/interview	Determine specialized material/equipment availability information Validate market intelligence obtained from secondary sources	Commonly reported commodity, material, and equipment price information Macroeconomic data Controversial or sensitive stakeholder information
Personal (i.e., face-to-face) interview	Uncover and probe on specific stakeholder requirements Discover competitor capabilities, technologies, and work processes Uncover data supporting political risk/market entry success factors Develop or test market new technologies or concepts	Historical data on commodity prices Overall industry and regulatory trends Background information: country risk Information available from competitors' public documents
Delphi session (see tool description elsewhere in this chapter)	Focused, single-issue problems or decisions Those requiring highly expert opinion Geographic separation Group dynamics interfere with freedom of expression	Complex or multiple issue problems Where quick turnaround answers are required

Primary sources, as mentioned before, involve interviewing experts. But a fair amount of care should be taken when interpreting the results of so-called experts. The possible effects of the expert's lack of accurate recall, bias, or careless data collection techniques should also be considered.

Process

The overall survey design process is shown in figure 3–31.

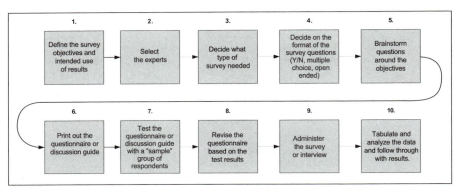

Fig. 3–31. The survey and interviewing process

Steps 1–5. A few key points to consider when planning the survey and designing the questions. The most important part of this process is to establish a clear, concise purpose and set of objectives for the survey or interview. The key issue here is focus. The following questions should be asked:

1. What problem am I trying to solve?

2. What is the essence of what I need to know and how will I use the results?

3. Are my objectives limited to the issues that can best be answered via a survey?

4. Do I need to do a survey or could I gather some of this information reliably via another means (i.e., public/private market studies, journals, technical publications, Web sites, or newswires)?

Designing the questions. Expert design of the questions involves significant practice as well as a good understanding of the psychology of the potential respondents. Thus, only an overview of some of the considerations behind questionnaire design will be provided here. A more detailed step-by-step approach can be found in college market research textbooks or in some of the references at the end of this chapter.

One good practice before beginning to develop questions is to first write the purpose and objectives down. Focus on only a few key objectives where surveys are the best (or perhaps only) method to obtain the information. Then revise and refine the objectives to make them succinct, mutually exclusive, and collectively comprehensive with respect to the purpose.

Brainstorming questions in a group is a good practice when the participants are all experienced market researchers. However, if there is a mix of people with varying degrees of market research experience, brainstorming will probably not be too fruitful. This is because the nonresearchers will lack solid criteria for the types of questions that work when administering the survey. Before analysts begin to design the questions, they should try to anticipate the types of answers expected from the respondents, as well as the number of expected respondents and how they plan to analyze the results. For example, if the analysts are looking for decisions, testing for knowledge, or trying to narrow down mutually exclusive choices, yes/no questions are effective. Examples of enterprise risk issues that could be addressed using a yes/no question are as follows:

- "Do you plan to award the concession before the end of this year?" (A question for the bidding official)

- "Are you familiar with our company's efforts over the past six months for increasing our overall liquidity through the repurchase of long-term debt?" (A question for the bond rating analyst)

Yes/no questions are often good ways to begin discovering more in-depth information. These could be followed by qualifying questions in an open-ended or multiple choice format. Numerical rating and numerical ranking questions are often useful when trade-offs or shades of a difference must be determined. Open-ended questions are useful when it is important to not only get the answer to a question, but also the feelings of the respondent relative to the issue. Open-ended and probing questions are good when talking with an expert and exploring the *key forces*, *driving factors*, and *leading indicators* behind certain risks in the preparation of a cause and effect diagram. These questions are also useful when researching background information to develop futures scenarios. (*Note:* Cause and effect diagrams and futures scenarios are two tools described elsewhere in this book.) However, open-ended questions will take more time to analyze if there are many respondents.

Steps 6–9. Some important points about testing the questionnaire and gathering the information. Testing the questionnaire is important because poorly designed questionnaires will be frustrating to administer and will probably yield unsatisfactory results. There is nothing worse than beginning the survey with a qualified respondent only to discover that the questionnaire wording is confusing, the questions are redundant or rambling, or the survey takes too long to administer. The worst situation is when the respondent becomes successively bored, impatient, then irritated. Testing and refining the questionnaire on a small group before launching the actual survey is one way to reduce the chance of this occurring. A few things Nancy Tague mentions in her book to look for when testing the survey are as follows:[10]

- Which questions are confusing?

- Which questions seem to be leading the respondent to a particular response or are biased?

- Were any questions redundant?

- Were the answer choices clear?

- Were they interpreted as you intended?

- On the average, how long did it take for a respondent to complete the survey?

- For a questionnaire to be sent to the respondents, were there any typographic or other printing errors?

- After gathering the trial responses, was it difficult or awkward to tabulate and analyze the data?

(*Note:* Concerning the length of the survey, from my experience, the ideal length of a survey is 20 minutes. If it takes more than 30 minutes to get through the questions in the trial run, you should reduce the number of questions.) The risk analyst should use feedback from the preceding list to distill the questionnaire or discussion guide down to a workable document.

When administering the survey, the objective is to avoid acting or sounding like a telemarketer. The best surveys are those that seem like a free flow conversation among peers. This is accomplished by knowing as much as possible about the respondent's business and the topic being researched prior to starting the survey. Knowing the respondent personally always helps as well.

Step 10. Some important points about analyzing and using the results. Given the availability and ease of use of simple databases, using the right information technology applications is an important part of efficiently and effectively managing the survey results. Thus, tabulating the information in MS Word, Excel, or in a hard copy format is inefficient and unacceptable from a traceability/adequacy of documentation standpoint. Instead, a simple database program such as MS Access or Filemaker Pro should be used to input, tabulate, analyze, and report on the survey results. Prior to administering the survey, the database should be preformatted with the question fields, sorts, and reports that will be used. In that way, the results can be input once each survey is completed, allowing the results to begin to be analyzed immediately to develop preliminary findings.

Final considerations on surveys and interviewing. It is evident that primary market research can quickly become a complicated undertaking, but this should not be a cause for discouragement. In most cases, the purpose of the survey is not to perform a statistically valid, peer-reviewed market research study to support a doctoral thesis. Instead, it is to document and analyze expert opinion in a logical, organized manner. In this way, the risk identification process can be a source of competitive advantage, rather than using educated guesses and ad hoc data gathering.

Discovery Vignette

San Felipe Resources takes up the enterprise risk challenge

The following is the story of an integrated multinational oil company that decides to take on the challenge of implementing enterprise risk management. The plot revolves around San Felipe Resources, a fictional company with activities, characters, and situations that will seem familiar to anyone working in the oil and gas industry. The story is divided into vignettes whose conclusions go beyond a mere application of tools and offer a series of lessons learned that could be applied at any energy company. The vignettes illustrate the five fundamentals of information integrity in the context of enterprise risk management in the oil and gas industry. The story begins with some corporate background as would typically be found in the "Item 1" section of the Form 10-K of any publicly traded company.

San Felipe Resources (SFR) is a 45-year-old integrated oil and gas company with major business activities carried out via three operating segments:

1. *Exploration and production (E&P).* Explores for and produces crude oil and natural gas on a worldwide basis.

2. *Refining, marketing, and logistics (RM&L)*. Refines, markets, and transports crude oil and petroleum products, primarily throughout the Northeast, the upper Great Plains, and the south central United States.

3. *Emerging oil (EO)*. Where the company hopes to develop, upgrade, market, and transport oil products derived from heavy crude oil extracted in Venezuela's Orinoco Belt.

San Felipe Resources is an investor-owned integrated oil company, with shares traded on the NYSE under the ticker symbol SFR. Last year revenues for SFR were $46.5 billion, split fairly evenly between the RM&L and the E&P segments.

The company is a significant international exploration company and operator. By the end of the last fiscal year, SFR had conducted exploration, development, and production activities in seven countries. Principal exploration activities are in the United States, Denmark, Nigeria, the Ivory Coast, the United Kingdom, and Canada. Principal development and production activities are in the United States, the United Kingdom, Canada, Venezuela, the Ivory Coast, Gabon, and Russia.

San Felipe Resources and enterprise risk—the genesis

Dave Andersen, SFR president and CEO, has decided to embark this year upon the company's first enterprise risk initiative. This is in the wake of the Enron collapse, the mandate for Sarbanes-Oxley compliance, and pressure from a company's board and other stakeholders. The impetus for this activity is clearly compliance, but Dave's vision is that in three years, SFR will have a system in place to clearly identify, assess, and begin to manage all the company's major risks. Dave feels that if he and the board have a solid understanding of the company's major risks and his staff is managing these "big hitters" on a real-time basis, he can not only satisfy the rumblings of the board, but it would also play well with the investor community.

Who knows? Dave reasoned to himself, *Enterprise risk management might even provide us a source of competitive advantage*. A demonstrated competitive advantage was just what SFR needed. Its price-to-earnings ratio had languished for years in the 8–10 range, and enterprise risk management could be just the thing to get it to break through the symbolic level of 15. In turn, at 15, the stock would yield the strike price necessary for Dave to exercise 25% of his 225,000 stock options granted him at the end of last year! Needless to say, Dave expected his senior managers to accept his enterprise risk management (ERM) vision and kick off this initiative. He selected long-standing SFR employee and seasoned internal audit manager, Barry Craddock, to lead the project.

Barry's job was not only to develop and lead the ERM effort, but to implement and institutionalize the tools, techniques, and methodologies necessary to ensure that the external information feeding this system was indeed reliable. What Barry did not anticipate is how this ERM journey would eventually lead the executive management team to the conclusion that *the lack of reliable external information* would be the main barrier to an effective enterprise risk management system at SFR.

Criticality—Barry finds out what's important

One day, Jack Montgomery, SFR's strategic planning director, dropped by Barry's office to chat.

Barry asked, "Jack, I'm wondering if you could figure this one out. You know Dave put me on this enterprise risk initiative, and Bart and others on the financial team look at risks. How did they come up with the top risks mentioned in the 'risks' section of our 10-K?"

Jack didn't know, but he conjectured that Dave Anderson, Bart Jensen, the CFO, and some of the others on the operating committee had sat around during one of their executive retreats at the corporate lodge a few years previously and had a round-robin discussion over a few drinks after dinner.

"You know," said Jack, "they probably came up with stuff like the price of oil, whether their wells would test out, the whims of the environmental lobby, tin-horn dictators in Africa, and contingent liabilities from the last acquisition—standard oil business stuff. Then they just report on those same risks year after year with a few minor adjustments. But again, to tell you the truth, I really don't know."

Barry thought it was strange that even Jack, the strategic planning guru, was not really clued into how the company's major risks were determined, or the priorities of each risk relative to the others. Then Jack said something that let Barry know that this was not the first time Jack had thought about all this.

"If it were my money, I'd probably step back and try to look at the whole show. You know, ask myself, What really makes this place tick? I've got to run, though—I'm late for a scenarios meeting with my team. Listen, if you want to grab lunch on Thursday, we could hash this over a little more. I've got a few ideas. Why don't we try a burger at the regular place at around 11:30?" asked Jack.

"I'm all over it," Barry said. "See you there on Thursday."

Barry and Jack had discussed SFR challenges over lunch many times over the years, and this time Barry knew by the tone of his voice that Jack was onto something. Jack was a "big picture" guy in more ways than one. First, he had an ability to see things from a much broader perspective than Barry, and second, he often could tie very disparate ideas and thoughts together in diagrams that communicated information quickly to upper management. Jack was an inductive thinker with an ability to take something and project it forward. That's why he was so good at developing scenarios. Intuitively, Jack also had a knack for presenting information that was not only credible, but easy to digest. This was no doubt one of the reasons he was such a respected member of the SFR staff. He often carried around a sketch pad and used it to explain some of his ideas. He sometimes used it to make rather unflattering caricatures of the executive staff as well, something that everyone knew about and that had, by this point, become a tolerated part of the corporate culture at SFR.

Barry, on the other hand, was a deductive thinker with the ability to "drill down" to figure out the cause and effect linkages between events. He had done well as an internal auditor because he understood how to pull together findings and summarize results in a way that other "detail men" just could not. He had taken extra courses in finance, accounting, and marketing that gave him the ability to comfortably understand SFR's competitive position in the industry, and its strengths and weakness. Finally, he got along well with others and enjoyed the role of a facilitator. Even so, his experience over the years told him that the other half of the strategic equation—the opportunities and threats—was more dependent on the ability to look outward rather than inward. Together, Barry and Jack were good complements.

Over lunch next Thursday, Barry and Jack discussed how they might get a handle on what the company's major risks really were.

"The whole thing is about having a value proposition, communicating it, then delivering on it," said Jack. "This means you've got to actually identify your value chain, map it out, and create a diagram so everyone can start working off the same page."

"You're right, Jack, but it can't be some pie-in-the-sky thing, or none of the board members will believe it. We really need to back this up with the numbers," said Barry.

Barry then pulled out results of his own analysis of SFR's income statement, balance sheet, and statement of cash flows over the past six years. Jack sketched out what he thought the company's three major businesses activities were, and how he saw them fitting together, including his insights into the capital spending plan for the next four years. Together they discussed how to put something meaningful down on paper.

SFR's main revenue generators were undoubtedly refining and pipelines in the United States and offshore exploration and production in the Gulf of Mexico and off the northern coast of Africa. The company's up-and-coming business was emerging oil (EO), which involved extracting the crude and blending it at newly built upgraders in Venezuela and then shipping it to refineries in Europe and the United States. Ten years ago, Dave Anderson, then president of the refining group, had a vision to take a chance on the vast, untapped reserves of heavy crude in places like Canada, Venezuela, and Russia. Back then, SFR was one of the few U.S. independent oil and gas companies that was betting on the technology improvements, economies of scale, and tremendous demand growth from China and India that could make heavy oil development profitable. What they had not seen coming was the terrorism premium that drove up the worldwide price of crude that promised to make heavy oil development *extremely* profitable. Still, SFR could pretty much be characterized as an integrated oil company with revenues and profits split about evenly between refining, marketing, and logistics (RM&L) and offshore exploration and production. They also had below-average margins, and the new EO division had not begun to make any significant money yet, since they just finished the plan and were still paying off the construction loans. Dave knew that operating income, or the earnings before interest, taxes, depreciation, and amortization (EBITDA), was a key metric for the division heads. Their bonuses were based on this, and it played a key role in that all-important *free cash flow* and *terminal value multiple* that the valuation guys were always talking about. It did not dawn on Barry and Jack until later that in this overheated oil and gas market, these financial characteristics were the very things that made SFR a very tempting takeover target.

Together, Barry and Jack used the numbers and the sketch pad to develop a one-page value chain diagram (see fig. 3–32).

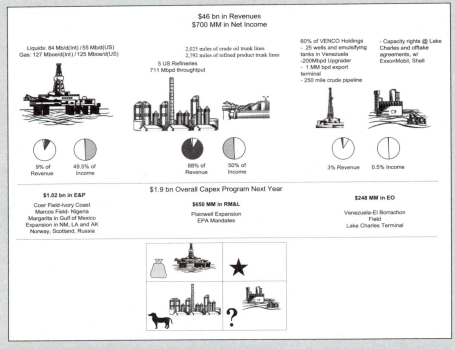

$46 bn in Revenues
$700 MM in Net Income

Liquids: 84 Mb/d(Int) /55 Mb/d(US)
Gas: 127 Mboe/d(Int) / 125 Mboe/d(US)

2,025 miles of crude oil trunk lines
2,792 miles of refined product trunk lines

5 US Refineries
711 Mbpd throughput

60% of VENCO Holdings
- 25 wells and emulsifying tanks in Venezuela
-200Mbpd Upgrader
- 1 MM bpd export terminal
- 250 mile crude pipeline

- Capacity rights @ Lake Charles and offtake agreements, w/ ExxonMobil, Shell

9% of Revenue — 49.5% of Income

88% of Revenue — 50% of Income

3% Revenue — 0.5% Income

$1.9 bn Overall Capex Program Next Year

$1.02 bn in E&P

Coer Field-Ivory Coast
Marcos Field- Nigeria
Margarita in Gulf of Mexico
Expansion in NM, LA and AK
Norway, Scotland, Russia

$650 MM in RM&L

Plainwell Expansion
EPA Mandates

$248 MM in EO

Venezuela-El Borrachon Field
Lake Charles Terminal

Fig. 3–32. San Felipe Resources value chain

"That pretty much captures it—not too much detail, but solid backup with the facts," said Barry. "Now we should also characterize these businesses—you know, cash cow, question mark, rising star, dog, and attach a few growth projections—all that strategic stuff you're good at, Jack."

Jack plotted the businesses in each quadrant in short order. Now they had a basis to begin the risk analysis. What they both agreed upon was that their perception of what was the *cash cow* and what was the *rising star* was quite different from what they had heard from the executive suite at SFR.

"We haven't done any risk analysis, and of course we don't have any probabilities, but this is at least a solid basis for figuring out what *could* be risky," said Barry. "This effectively is the basis for our corporate *risk profile*." Barry was starting to get excited at this point. "And we need our own risk metric, something like value at risk used by the trading desk, but more tied to quarter-to-quarter operational risk. What if we were to develop our own 'earnings-at-risk' metric based on some type of Monte Carlo simulation using the last few years' operating income? Granted, some of the purists in finance might have some reservations about using it, but at least it would be a starting point."

Barry could see this starting to come together: steps, activities, tools, and metrics. By this point, he thought they were really on a roll.

"Now Barry, you can do what you want, but if I were you, I wouldn't work on this any more until you at least run it by Bart Jensen or maybe even Dave," said Jack.

As they drove back to the office, Barry thought, *Jack's right, better to get some buy-in before we get too far out on a limb.* But something else kept bugging him. The more he thought about it, the more he realized that if someone like Jack were to do a SWOT analysis of SFR, the strengths and weaknesses were fairly straightforward, but the opportunities and threats (or the *O* and *T* of the SWOT) had very little substantiation. *There are so many uncertainties,* thought Barry. *We really don't have a good, solid handle on what our key risks are. We can't see out ahead of our headlamps because we don't have them turned on. We've got to have better information before we are in any position to manage our major risks. Could it be that poor external information behind the risk analysis turns out to be our biggest threat of all? On the other hand, could reliable external information lead us discover the best opportunities and really provide a competitive advantage?* Barry's head was swimming.

As soon as he got back, Barry called Nancy, Dave Anderson's executive assistant, to set up a 10-minute briefing on the value chain approach.

"Well, he's booked up all day tomorrow, but he'll be in for about 40 minutes before his 8:00 meeting in the morning. I'll pencil you in for 15 minutes at 7:30," said Nancy.

Barry thanked Nancy. He knew that if he did not get Dave's approval now, it would be an uphill battle on this whole initiative, especially with ERM naysayers like Carlos del Sordo, the company's business development manager. Also, the last thing Barry wanted was to confuse the issue at this point. It would be best to stick with a simple strategy: no PowerPoint slides, no briefing booklet, just the value chain diagram and Dave's blessing on the plan forward.

It turned out to be exactly the right approach.

"Great plan, Barry, and I like the cartoons. Now listen, we're really counting on this thing to be watertight. I know you'll do a good job at this. Keep up the good work and keep me posted on your progress," Dave said.

Barry knew that with these simple diagrams, he had captured the essence of the complex interaction of assets, processes, and plans that characterized SFR. Of course, he also recognized that the company's employees and suppliers were a critical, but missing, part of the picture. At least through the diagrams he had a graphical summary of the company's financial statements. It was just this type of graphical guide that Barry needed to take this analysis of criticality of the various risks and drivers of the company to the next level. The next step had to be some type of risk identification activity.

The usual way of identifying risks at SFR took one of two formats: a round-robin discussion among internal "experts" (which usually meant the company's executive staff at a management retreat) or a facilitated workshop consisting of a multidisciplinary team of management staff and discipline leads.

This consisted of an anonymous brainstorming by qualified experts from inside and outside the organization using a moderated electronic bulletin board. In this case, Barry would distribute the value chain diagram electronically to each of the qualified participants and ask them the following questions:

1. In each of the three segments of the San Felipe Resources value chain, what do you consider are the main risks at each stage?

2. What is the rank order of these risks in terms of probability of occurrence and consequence on the company's financial operations over the next three years?

Following the questions, respondents could record their ideas about risks in a text block on the diagram. As the moderator, Barry would take these ideas, consolidate them, and send them back to the respondents, whereupon they would have an opportunity to reconsider their responses in light of what the other anonymous respondents said. This would continue until all respondents came to a consensus on the key risks and their relative level of importance.

When Barry was able to actually execute this exercise, the results were quite telling. He found that overwhelmingly, the areas of concern for SFR were the price of oil, geopolitical concerns, regulatory risks, and the cost of equipment and materials, in order of criticality to the company's operating income, or EBITDA. What Barry also knew was that upper management told the investment community that it had little or no control over these factors. The truth was, they had little or no knowledge of these factors' drivers, their leading indicators, or how swings could affect operating income. Thus they were in no position to face the risks of the future.

To put the pieces together, Barry decided to begin with just one of the identified risk events and analyze the key forces, drivers, and leading indicators, in this case, the uncertainty behind their hydrocarbon reserves estimates. He would do this by using a factor analysis and a series of decision trees put together to form a bow-tie diagram.

The left-hand side of the diagram is typically called the *fault tree*, and the right-hand side, the *event tree*. An illustration of what he developed is shown in figure 3–33.

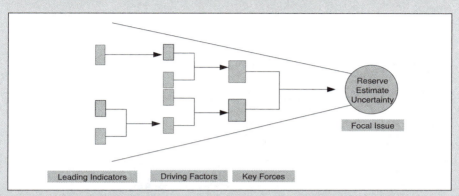

Fig. 3–33. Bow-tie diagram (A)

Adapting this bow-tie diagram to his focal issue (the uncertainty around SFR's estimate of proved reserves), Barry considered the key forces, drivers, leading indicators, immediate consequences, and resulting impacts as successive "stages" or levels of the fault or event trees, as shown in figure 3–34.

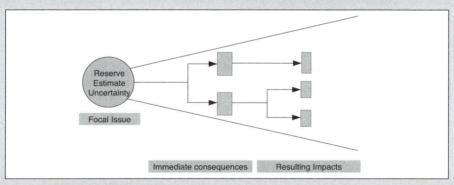

Fig. 3–34. Bow-tie diagram (B)

Developing the right-hand side of the bow-tie diagram is an inductive process. Barry started with the event and (in this case) described first the financial consequence (or result) and the impacts of a write-off of proven crude oil reserves on SFR's income statement and goals as shown in figure 3–35.

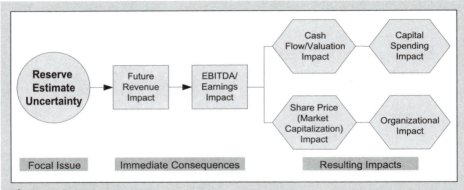

Fig. 3–35. Event tree

Conversely, developing the left-hand side of the bow-tie diagram is a deductive process of determining one by one what could contribute to the next layer of "faults." Starting again with the focal issue, the uncertainty behind their proven reserves estimates, Barry interviewed some of his reserve engineers to diagram some of the key factors behind their reserves estimates. These key factors were: the current and future operating, expense, and revenue (OER) interest holders for each asset, SFR's current and future costs of operation and development, future product prices, and agreements and plans for operations and sales of production. He was able to graphically illustrate these as shown in figure 3–36.

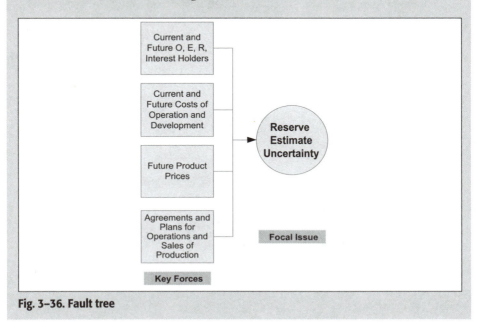

Fig. 3–36. Fault tree

Together, the fault tree and event tree formed the basic bow-tie diagram that graphically profiled the uncertainties behind SFR's reserves estimates (fig. 3–37).

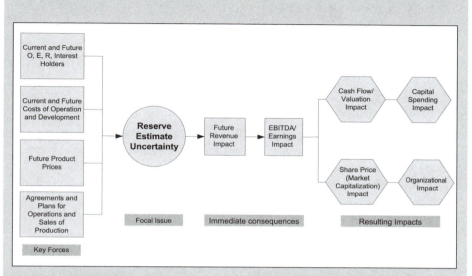

Fig. 3–37. Complete bow-tie

Of course, this was just the beginning. To better understand the picture, Barry needed to know what was driving these key forces and what the indicators of change were behind the drivers. Thus, he developed the next two layers of the fault tree, the driving factors and leading indicators, until he had a full bow-tie diagram for this key uncertainty.

Finally, with respect to one of SFR's major risk factors, Barry had an understanding of how it worked, and he could easily explain it to others. If reserve estimates really kept everyone in the executive suite "awake at night," SFR finally would have a common framework and a series of indicators to gauge when things might be getting out of control. It also dawned on him that to find the information about these indicators, he would need to have reliable information sources. Identifying the information sources was what Barry needed to turn on the headlamps, to begin to *see ahead* to changes in the company's risk profile with respect to reserves as well as the other risks and uncertainties facing SFR. Barry did not have the answer to the big questions of life yet, but at least with respect to reserves, he had a good idea of what was important. This was an important first step toward managing SFR's enterprise risks.

Competence

Barry was musing about how mundane the analyst's comments from last week's earnings call had been. Most of them just wanted to know more about third-quarter guidance and SFR's refining outlook for the upcoming driving season. However, Bruce Wonderlein, representing a large Canadian teachers' pension fund with significant SFR holdings, asked about political instability in Venezuela.

More specifically, Bruce questioned, "How would this affect SFR's capital expansion decisions next year in emerging oil?"

Very confidently and convincingly, Dave stated that there was currently less instability in Venezuela than in previous years, given the latest national election results and the new joint venture framework established by presidential decree the previous week. Granted, some would say that there have been unplanned regulatory changes in the current year in the royalty and income tax regimes. But since this new joint venture framework was consistent with the country's constitution, the possibility of new changes was more than compensated for by SFR's early mover position and its partnership with the state-run oil company. Wonderlein seemed to be satisfied for now, but later that day a powerful board member, Karen James, called Dave to ask some more pointed questions.

"Dave, I've been concerned for some time about this venture in Venezuela. We are fine with the idea of growth in new markets and Venezuela being part of your EO strategy, but I need to know that you have good people and the right information on this one," Karen told Dave.

Dave knew that when Karen brought something up like this, it was not just a passing comment. If she was talking with him about it, she was probably talking with the other board members, and maybe even doing some background research herself. He had better have a good answer soon.

The next morning Dave fired off an e-mail to Barry, saying he wanted some better backup for the political risk in all their international markets by the end of the month, starting with Venezuela. On top of this, SFR's commercial director, Carlos del Sordo, had somehow heard about the flap, and like a fly to honey, was beginning to make wild, off-handed comments in the staff meetings.

Carlos commented, "They are a bunch of crooks in Venezuela. I insist on this. We should not trust anyone there—certainly not these military colonels in charge of the oil company. They don't know anything about our business of petroleum production."

Although he was loud and abrasive at times, Carlos had the ear of Bart Jensen, the CFO, and because he was Latin American, people gave him the benefit of the doubt when it came to activities in South America. Suddenly, Barry was faced with a complicated situation both internally and externally involving Latin American political risk, a topic on which everyone who had ever been to Mexico on vacation was an instant expert. It was time for Barry to address this one by applying some bona fide expertise. He needed a trained market researcher, someone who had experience with both primary and secondary data gathering techniques. In addition, they should have a working knowledge of the culture and language of the region. A tall order, but he knew of just the person: Elena Alvarez, a newly hired analyst currently working in the finance group.

Elena reported to Bart Jensen and had been recently hired after spending four years with a world-renowned leader in consumer market research. Barry knew that she had also specialized in industrial market research at one of the more prestigious Midwestern universities. In addition, Elena had an understanding of finance and econometrics and spoke Spanish—exactly what this analysis needed. Barry happened to know that Bart Jensen was looking to put Elena on something new to test her mettle, so that afternoon Barry convinced Bart to agree to put her on this short-term assignment.

Later that afternoon, Barry and Elena began to chart the rough game plan for the political risk assessment that was to follow. Barry knew that Elena had done this sort of analysis in the past. What he did not expect was that she had a disciplined approach that involved scrupulous attention to the quality of the data behind the analysis.

"Much of the raw data can be obtained through market intelligence sources," said Elena, "which will confirm the historical perspective, a current situation analysis, and a trending assessment on each risk element." She went on to say, "The main difference between this assignment and what we did at my previous employment is that the framework we will use for this analysis—the Independent Petroleum Association of America (IPAA) political risk framework—is oil industry specific. This really allows us to hone in on relevant issues."

They had to order in pizza to finish that night, but they were finally able to link the IPAA's political risk elements to the EO segment's critical success factors for heavy oil development. Furthermore, they developed weightings for each risk element that were specific to SFR's investment in the country and the project.

Some would consider Venezuela to be politically unstable and a risky place for a foreign oil company to do business. Based on popular media reports, the country was on the verge of civil war, and nationalization of foreign assets could occur at any moment. However, rather than relying on media reports, Elena and Barry knew that they would need to perform a structured country or political risk analysis that was both industry and country specific. But if regime change were to occur in Venezuela, what could the new government look like, and would this be better or worse for foreign oil companies? Where would SFR get reliable data to support such an analysis?

There were many possible sources of information about Venezuela—the U.S. Department of Commerce and Department of State, articles in popular news magazines such as *Time* and *Newsweek*, or specialized Latin American newsletters. These *secondary* sources of information were thus termed because the raw data was not gathered directly by Barry and Elena from first-hand interviews or observation, which would be *primary* data sources. Based on Elena's experience and training, she knew they would need to use both secondary and primary data sources in order to get an accurate assessment of the political situation. Before they started, Barry and Elena began to consider the reliability of secondary data sources using a framework for the information integrity criteria involving the following questions:

- What process did these publications use to gather their information?

- How much of their data or conclusions was "repackaged" from other secondary sources?

- How disciplined and objective was their method of analyzing and citing the evidence before they came to a conclusion?

- Did they use a structured logic that included explanatory theory, empirical evidence, and the rejection of competing explanations?

- Before publication, how much external review and approval by content experts or intelligent skepticism did they apply to the data?

The information integrity criteria were essential to providing assurance that the data gathering process was sensible and honest and the information was reliable.

Of course, it was difficult to gauge or investigate the extent to which publications had a robust process. But Barry knew some surrogate "red flag" indicators for sloppy data gathering and analysis included extensive use of the passive voice, a shallow depth of information content in charts and graphs, distorted aspect ratios, and axes without labels. These were dead giveaways of careless research methods, and he and Elena found many examples of these red flags in the popular news magazines they surveyed. Because of political tensions between the U.S. and Venezuelan governments, they knew that the objectivity (and thus reliability) of the Department of State and Department of Commerce publications was questionable. Again, the popular news magazines contained more glossy photos and discussion of headline-grabbing events than useful business risk information. Finally, they included cartoonlike illustrations instead of information-rich charts and graphs. In short, there was no lack of data sources, but sifting through them to find defensible, credible sources was not easy.

After carefully examining various publications, Barry and Elena settled on the Economist Intelligence Unit (EIU), the British market intelligence research and publishing conglomerate. They considered it to be a well-substantiated source for beginning to establish historical trends and building the "current situation" for San Felipe's economic and political analysis in Venezuela.

Barry then assigned Elena her first political risk task, which was to prepare a Venezuelan political risk "backgrounder" and submit the results to him in an intracompany memorandum in one week. It would be a challenge to finish in a week, but Elena was anxious to start.

As promised, the following week, Elena delivered the Venezuelan political risk backgrounder that was the first step toward getting this political risk analysis off the ground. Figure 3–38 is an excerpt from the first page of Elena's memorandum.

Based on her preliminary analysis using the EIU data, the overall picture was not pretty.

For example, trends in two areas were disturbing: the sanctity of contracts and property rights, and kidnapping and terrorism against company employees. Even so, when compared with other foreign oil investment opportunities such as Nigeria, Libya, and Iran, Venezuela's local business culture, tradition, history, and even religion made it worth considering. It would be interesting to see if Dave Andersen's statement to the investment community earlier this week was defensible.

Barry and Elena realized that many of the issues they were to research required primary data gathering (i.e., going down and actually talking to people). Whether they gathered the data personally, or publications or consultants gathered the data, the information would have to be validated by qualified primary sources. At that point, Barry and Elena realized they would have to go on a mission to the tropics.

San Felipe Resources
Memorandum

Date: 10 June 2004

To: Barry Craddock, Enterprise Risk Manager

From: Maria Elena Alvarez, Corporate Risk Analyst *MEA*

Subject: Venezuela political risk
           Backgrounder

As requested last Thursday, I have prepared the following Backgrounder from (secondary sources only) on the Venezuelan Political Situation.

This political risk assessment considers twenty specific risk factors drawing from the Independent Petroleum Association of America's International Primer on assessing political risk.[1] The sources of data are primarily from the Economist Intelligence Unit's Risk Wire service[2], and from Transparency International's 2003 Annual Report.[3] Results are organized into three categories: Unfavorable Risk Factors with a Worsening Trend, Unfavorable Risk Factors with a Stable Trend, and Currently Acceptable or Favorable Risk Factors.

Unfavorable Risk Factors with a Worsening Trend

Track Record of Orderly Change of Government Control

There has been considerable political change, often violent in nature, over the past 15 years in Venezuela. Since 1998, when Hugo Chavez came to power, there have been periods of civil unrest, coup attempts, rewriting of the constitution, recurring street demonstrations, and significant labor unrest. The following timeline illustrates significant events that have occurred in the country over the past 5 years.

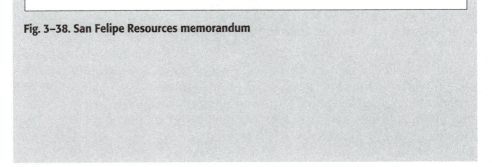

---

[1] IPAA International Primer, Chapter III, Section 2, Assess Political Risk, presented at the 2002 North American Prospect Expo(NAPE).

[2] Economist Intelligence Unit (EIU) Risk Wire, November, December 2003, January 2004.

[3] Transparency International, Global Corruption Report, 2003, Berlin, Germany.

Fig. 3–38. San Felipe Resources memorandum

The idea was to go into the country "under the wire," so to speak, as observers and data gatherers—no formal dinners or polite "let's get to know each other" sessions with locals on this trip. Their purpose from the outset was to be strictly reconnaissance. Barry could still speak Spanish, having done a four-year tour of duty in the Peace Corps in Bolivia upon finishing his undergraduate work. At the time, Barry's dad thought that this was a bit of a delay in starting to pay off the student loans, but over the years, there were various situations in which those Spanish language skills paid off. This was one of them. Barry and Elena would be able to read the local papers, talk with local trade agency officials, and carry out interviews in Spanish—a big advantage.

But like a true market research professional, Elena was polite, but direct. "Based on what I've done before, we can't just go down and try to wing it. Otherwise we'll end up with an unsubstantiated mess." She went on to explain, "The best primary research starts with a well-designed instrument, a discussion guide in this case. This discussion guide requires a clear, objective, careful design of the questions, and a certain discipline in asking the questions, so as to make the responses comparable." She emphasized, "Just because we don't get a statistically representative sample, we can still end up with substantiated inferential data. Finally, in order to keep everything straight by the end of the trip, it is essential to capture everything into a simple MS Access database."

Elena added, voicing one more concern, "Now, no one can predict the future, so I was wondering, does San Felipe ever develop alternative futures, like futures scenarios?"

"Absolutely," said Barry. "Jack Montgomery does this all the time, but usually for overall corporate strategy, not to support something like this. That's a very interesting point, though. Maybe we need to get Jack involved to develop scenarios as well," he replied. *Whoa*, thought Barry, *this is going to be a lot of work. In the end, how am I ever going to make sense of all this*?

Together Elena and Barry sketched out a plan for the next month that involved a step-by-step approach for identifying, analyzing, and managing SFR's sovereign risks in Venezuela.

With this background in hand, a research plan, and about 50% of their in-country appointments prearranged, the next Monday, Barry and Elena took Continental's night flight to Caracas.

Night flight

Caracas is the archetypal South American capital, literally a tropical paradise. From the flock of parrots that flew by Barry's hotel room window every morning at 6:15 AM to the Afro/Cuban music, the strong black coffee, and the typical dress of the women, everything here seemed to Barry to be represented in crisp, vivid colors. There were expensive cars on the road, and construction cranes dotted the skyline of this Caribbean city of 5 million. However, on closer inspection of how business is done in Venezuela, the exotic veneer gave way to a persistent lack of transparency in nearly every facet of business and social activity. Something as simple as a plan, or an implied promise to perform, was never exactly as it seemed. Like the hangover from drinking one too many Cuba Libres the night before, this lack of transparency was a nagging source of discomfort in the back of Barry's mind.

Elena and Barry's first interview was a visit to SFR's local legal council, Saenz, Lopez y Asociados, Ltda, where they met with Dora Lopez, the partner in charge of SFR's account. She gave them a briefing on the uncertainty around possible regulatory changes affecting royalty and income tax treatment. Her conclusion was surprising. Strange as it seemed, the company actually faced less regulatory uncertainty today than in the past six months because the royalty and tax regimes had just been altered by presidential decree and would soon be ratified by the country's congress. Although the treatment of foreign investors was not too favorable, it was more consistent and sustainable now than in the past, when oil companies had been given preferential treatment by the state. Barry and Elena breathed a sigh of relief. This was a confirmation of Dave Anderson's statements during the earnings call last month.

That weekend, Dora invited Barry and Elena to dinner with her and her husband, a leading Venezuelan sociologist and professor at the University of Caracas. After dinner, Elena commented that she had noted that there was a certain reserved nature to most Venezuelans in their business dealings that seemed to go beyond the norms of formality. She wondered whether this formality had a sociological root. If so, what were its effects in Venezuelan society on business and personal relationships?

The professor explained that every society is based upon trust in its institutions, and unfortunately, nearly every institution, from government to the military, labor unions, and even the church and the family, had lost its legitimacy in Venezuela.

Mmm, thought Elena, *this is a much harsher critique of Venezuelan society than I had expected. The breakdown of these institutions could be significant to our analysis.*

The professor went on to explain that the effect of this breakdown was that in Venezuela today no one operated outside their own sphere of influence, or circle of trusted acquaintances. In general, this was the basis for the general lack of transparency in business and personal dealings. He reasoned that until the society's institutions were somehow rebuilt (perhaps through a grassroots spiritual revolution), it was difficult to see how Venezuelan society could become more transparent and its social ills could be resolved.

At this point, this explanation resonated with something Barry remembered reading in *The Mystery of Capital*, a book written by Peruvian economist Hernando de Soto. The economist wrote that the existence of trust, or the ability of institutions within a particular society to guarantee property rights, was the key difference between economies that worked and those that did not.

This definitely was something to consider in their scenario development. Barry and Elena ended up a very busy week having visited the Petroleum Chamber of Commerce offices and talking with partners, suppliers, and even competitors in the local market. They used a discussion guide of 10 questions designed to confirm some of the country risk data from the secondary sources.

Their final discussions were with Colonel Montesinos, a key figure in organizational hierarchy of the national oil company. Cool, controlled, and calculating, he had been part of the country's early revolutionary movement in the 1990s and was now the national oil company's key representative in the partnership with SFR. They spoke at length in the colonel's office about the possibility of royalty increases. They also spoke about the national oil company's growing insistence on use of local suppliers for fabrication of process components such as tanks, separators, and pipe spools. Contrary to the opinions of SFR's commercial director, Carlos, Barry and Elena came away from the meeting convinced that this military man had done his homework. He was quite capable of understanding and running a petroleum business.

In the end, they had the results of interviews with more than 40 knowledgeable professionals in Venezuela and had captured the comments and observations in their desktop database in MS Access for analysis. They were ready to go home and start building scenarios.

Discovery: Parting Shots

There are a few observations that could be considered at this point concerning the vignette and the application of the tools, as follows:

1. Why did it seem that SFR's upper management was caught off guard by the political risk questions of board member Karen James? Could it be that SFR's president, Dave Anderson, had underestimated Karen's sensitivity to this issue? If SFR had performed a structured stakeholder analysis, could they have been more prepared and not have been forced into the subsequent efforts?

2. The competence displayed by Barry's coworker, Elena Alvarez, proved invaluable to structuring an approach and gathering the data for the trip to Venezuela. What would SFR have done had they not recognized the strengths of this new employee with experience from another industry (i.e., consumer products)? Would they have relied on the supposed in-house "expertise" of their sales manager, Carlos del Sordo? Would Barry have tried to muddle through a trip to Latin America without adequate preparation? Often companies are not aware of and do not leverage the capabilities that new employees have attained at a previous company. As our workforce becomes increasingly more transient, we cannot afford to waste these "hidden" talents of our new employees. This is particularly true with those coming from another industry. Tried and proven methods in one industry (such as consumer products) may be new and revolutionary enough in the energy business to give an oil and gas or electric power company a competitive advantage!

3. The use of facilitated workshops seems to be the predominant risk identification method at many companies. How could electronic communications be used to more efficiently identify risks using previously time-consuming and/or costly research methods such as focus groups and the Delphi method? Could it be that we are trapped in a 1970s mindset regarding use of technology for risk identification?

4. Do you think any of the stakeholders who have an auditing or management systems background have developed their own informal checklists of things they look for in a company's presentation of earnings projections? How valuable would it be for the energy industry's reputation with investors and the media if the industry developed and promoted its own standard checklist or governance guidelines?

References

1. Porter, M.E., and V. E. Millar. 1985. How information gives you competitive advantage. *Harvard Business Review*. (July/August).

2. Committee of Sponsoring Organizations of the Treadway Commission. 2004. *Enterprise Risk Management—Integrated Framework and Application Techniques*. (September). New Jersey: COSO.

3. Johnston, D. 2005. *Introduction to Oil Company Financial Analysis*. Tulsa: PennWell.

4. U.S. Securities Exchange Commission. EDGAR electronic forms and filing system. http://www.sec.gov/edgar/searchedgar/companysearch.html

5. Johnston, D. 1992. *Oil Company Financial Analysis in Nontechnical Language*. Tulsa: PennWell.

6. Cobb, C. G. 2005. *Enterprise Process Mapping: Integrating Systems for Compliance and Business Excellence*. Milwaukee: ASQ, Quality Press.

7. Toastmasters International. 1979. The discussion leader. Advanced Communication and Leadership Program. Santa Ana, CA: Toastmasters International, Inc. pp. 20–22.

8. Thomson, N. 2007. Facilitation. Microsoft PowerPoint presentation. UK: Det Norske Veritas.

9. Tague, N. R. 2004. *The Quality Toolbox*. 2nd ed. Milwaukee: ASQ, Quality Press.

10. Ibid.

Assessment 4

Assessment is the second phase in the external information integrity (EII) process, and as shown in figure 4–1, it corresponds closely to the "risk assessment" COSO activity.

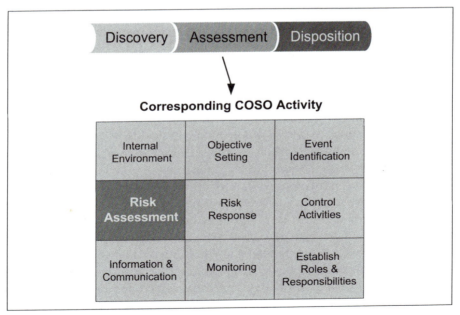

Discovery	Assessment	Disposition

Corresponding COSO Activity

Internal Environment	Objective Setting	Event Identification
Risk Assessment	Risk Response	Control Activities
Information & Communication	Monitoring	Establish Roles & Responsibilities

Fig. 4–1. EII process and assessment

One of the similarities between the EII definition of assessment and that of the COSO framework is that both involve analysis and measurement of some parameter. The COSO enterprise risk framework uses risk assessment techniques to analyze and measure *risks* once they have been identified during event identification. It uses both quantitative and qualitative methods to assess these risks based on their likelihood and impact. In a similar way, assessment for purposes of EII is analysis and measurement of important parameters surrounding *externally gathered information*. It also uses qualitative and quantitative methods (or tools) to measure and classify information. Some of the tools are even the same for both COSO and EII. Thus, there are similarities in how to perform the assessments, even though the area of application is different. Where COSO risk assessment and the EII assessment differ is in what is being analyzed and measured (risks vs. external information) and the parameters (likelihood/impact vs. criticality, consistency, and accuracy).

As mentioned in the description of the discovery phase in chapter 3, the EII assessment is often the missing strategy ingredient in the enterprise risk management (ERM) process. This is because the EII assessment actually drives the results of ERM beyond a defensive, threat mitigation posture and into the offensive arena of sustainable competitive advantage. As such, assessment tools relating to information integrity to be used during ERM implementation are described in this chapter. As previously mentioned, this is by no means an exhaustive treatment of ERM tools. However, those I have profiled provide a good starting point for anyone to analyze and measure external information for criticality, consistency, and accuracy. A general road map of the assessment phase illustrating the tools to be profiled is shown in figure 4–2.

Upon inspection of these tools, it can be seen that they all involve some level of either characterization or quantification of information. The first tool, information testing and validation, provides an information validation road map or stage-gate process upon which all the other assessment tools expand. The second tool, governance guidelines for information integrity, is probably the most useful high-level tool for those in positions of corporate oversight, such as board members, bond rating agencies, stock analysts, and regulators. These guidelines serve as a type of litmus test of information integrity. A failing score on the questions in the governance guidelines means stakeholders should expect managers to demonstrate evidence of how they have *reasonable assurance* behind the reliability of their information. The other tools are familiar to anyone who has done quantitative risk modeling. What is new is that they are detailed here step-by-step, and again, they are for validation of information with the goal of providing competitive advantage through stakeholder assurance.

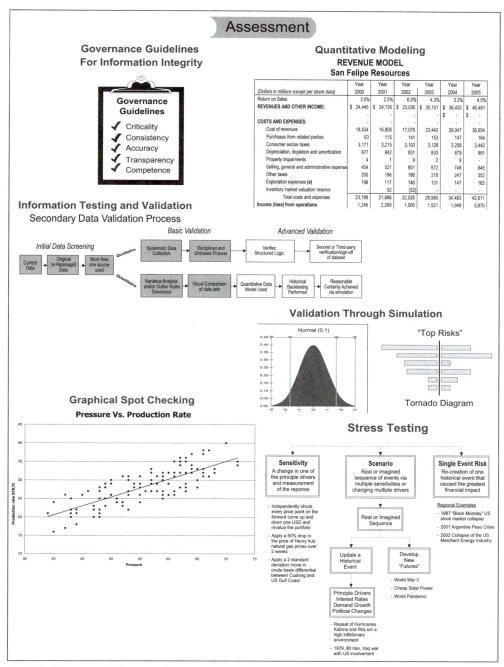

Fig. 4–2. Assessment phase road map

Assessment Toolbox

As with the discovery phase toolbox, the following detailed description of the assessment tools is meant to be a step-by-step "cookbook" approach toward their use. They should be in enough detail to aid any board member, shareholder, analyst, or manager who is interested in ensuring that due diligence has been performed in the pursuit of *adequate assurance* in the gathering of external information. The format for the presentation of the tools is the same as with the discovery phase: presentation of the tool summary, followed by a more detailed guide to implementation.

The first of these tools serves the top of the organizational pyramid of stakeholders: those concerned with corporate oversight and governance. It provides a convenient checklist for board members, rating agencies, and analysts. It also provides overall guidance to every layer of the organization, from analyst to chief executive, concerning the maturity of their organization regarding reliable information.

Starting at the Top: Corporate Governance Guideline for Information Integrity

Good corporate governance means having reasonable assurance that the assets of the corporation are safeguarded and that stakeholder value is created. Those responsible for corporate oversight have a responsibility to ensure good governance by ensuring the reliability (or integrity) of information. In turn, the integrity of the information is assured through the proper gathering, validating, and processing of information. As surprising as it may seem, there is no internationally recognized standard or set of guidelines for how to test for reliable information.

Governance Guideline: Criticality, Consistency, Accuracy, Transparency, and Competence

The corporate governance guideline for information integrity presented in this book provides a proposed standard in the form of a checklist for board members, analysts, auditors, and regulators. Its purpose is to assess the reliability of externally gathered information feeding any management decision-making process. Organized along the lines of five information integrity fundamentals of criticality, consistency, accuracy, transparency, and competence, the guideline sets the standard for anyone in a corporate oversight position. It is, in effect, a reasonable assurance litmus test for the integrity of externally gathered information.

Assessment Tool 1: Corporate Governance Guideline for Information Integrity—A Checklist for Directors, Officers, and External Analysts

Criticality | Yes | No

Criticality of external information is a measure of its materiality, or the information's sensitivity to the outcome of the analysis. Establishing critical information needs provides management focus so that it can control critical external information and not become distracted with information that has a relatively minor bearing on the organization's risk profile.

1. Has the organization analyzed its current and historical commercial, financial, and operational information to determine what constitutes the main activities in its value chain? ☐ y ☐ n

2. Has the organization identified and mapped value drivers and threats to the key activities in its value chain? ☐ y ☐ n

3. Has the organization compared the relative importance of one value driver to another? ☐ y ☐ n

4. Has the organization identified the external information needed to understand and monitor each value driver? ☐ y ☐ n

Competent Application | Yes | No

Information collection and analysis must be performed by people who are competent in the data gathering and interpretation techniques relevant to the type of information being gathered.

5. Do the individuals gathering external data have some training in market research or data gathering from an accredited university? ☐ y ☐ n

6. Are the individuals gathering and analyzing market data experienced in using primary and secondary market research techniques? ☐ y ☐ n

7. Do the individuals gathering and analyzing market data and other external information used for forecasting, projections, and strategy have a basic understanding of macroeconomics and econometrics? ☐ y ☐ n

8. Do the individuals performing the market research have a working knowledge of the industry, geography, language, and/or culture relating to the topic being researched? ☐ y ☐ n

Consistency

	Yes	No

Consistency implies that the information falls within some preestablished boundaries or limits that are comparable with historical trends or other known reliable information. It is a measure of precision of the data. Lack of consistency should raise questions about whether the data is representative and/or reliable.

9. For raw data and analysis drawn from published sources, have the following questions been answered satisfactorily? ☐ y ☐ n

    • Were the data and/or conclusions original to the publication (versus "repackaged" from some other secondary source)? ☐ y ☐ n

    • Was the process used by the publication to gather the data systematic and repeatable? ☐ y ☐ n

    • Was the method used by the publication to analyze and cite evidence before coming to a conclusion disciplined and objective (vs. careless or possibly biased)? ☐ y ☐ n

    • Did the publication analyst use a structured logic that included explanatory theory, empirical evidence, and the rejection of competing explanations before coming to conclusions? ☐ y ☐ n

10. Is the external data drawn from a larger historical data set (vs. one piece of point data)? Has the data been compared with other data sets either through plotting (for quantitative data) or through comparison with previous period data? ☐ y ☐ n

11. Have any corroborating parameters been established that would indicate that the data is reasonable? Have any information integrity rules for variance been established that could automatically identify suspicious outliers? ☐ y ☐ n

12. Is there any verification and sign-off on the critical assumptions and data by a second- or third-party specialist? ☐ y ☐ n

Accuracy

	Yes	No

Accuracy is a measure of how directionally and/or absolutely close we are to an objective truth. This includes the timeliness of the information. A standard to strive for is attainment of reasonable certainty of the accuracy of the information.

13. Was the most current data available used? ☐ y ☐ n

	Yes	No
14. Was more than one source of data used to develop the final data set?	☐ y	☐ n
15. Was some type of documented qualitative or quantitative model used to generate the data? Where appropriate, has a probabalistic simulation been performed to establish, within a specified degree of confidence (say 90%), reasonable certainty regarding accuracy of the data?	☐ y	☐ n
16. Has validated historical information been used as a basis for assumptions, projections, or estimates? Has any qualitative or quantitative backtesting of the data been performed to measure performance of historical projections vs. actuals?	☐ y	☐ n

Transparency

	Yes	No

Transparency is traceability of critical information sources and substantiation of critical assumptions. For purposes of this information integrity standard, the lack of transparency is a result of ignorance or negligence rather than willful manipulation or malfeasance.

	Yes	No
17. Are the assumptions logical, well founded, and clearly documented?	☐ y	☐ n
18. Is there documentation of an information trail that leads back to some information source?	☐ y	☐ n
19. Can the information be traced back to a reputable third-party standard or source?	☐ y	☐ n
20. Is the information captured in a well-structured, secure, searchable electronic database?	☐ y	☐ n

The second tool in this toolbox is oriented toward the internal team in an organization: the internal business analysts, technicians, supervisors, managers, and executives who are responsible for ensuring that their information is reliable. It provides a framework for the "nuts and bolts" of actually checking secondary information. This framework deals with the most basic question regarding information validation: How can the reliability of information be tested?

A Framework: The Information Testing and Validation Process

Application of information testing and validation techniques provides assurance of both the consistency and the accuracy of secondary data used for modeling and decision making by means of a structured, repeatable validation process.

These validation techniques deal principally with information from secondary sources, i.e., information drawn from something other than first-hand observation. Secondary information is often the only source available to the analyst, and thus these tool descriptions serve as a quality control guide to the use of secondary information. Examples of the information for which this approach would be applicable are market trends, political risk information, macroeconomic data, historical and projected costs, future revenues, and equipment reliability data.

Appropriate application of these tools assures compliance with the consistency and *accuracy* fundamentals of the information integrity process. Figure 4–3 describes the general process behind the validation of secondary sources of data and information. The process can be divided into three segments: the initial screening, the basic validation, and the advanced validation of two types of information—qualitative and quantitative data. The secondary data validation process is summarized in figure 4–3.

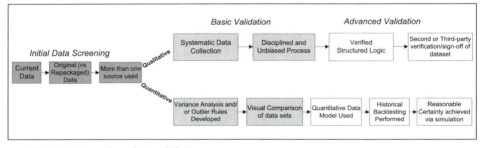

Fig. 4–3. Secondary data validation process

The most appropriate enterprise risk management application for these tools is in risk assessment when critical data is being gathered to qualify and quantify risks. The approach can also be used for data inputs to any type of business model that relies upon external information.

Assessment Tool 2: Information Testing and Validation

The objective of this monograph is to describe an approach and various techniques for validating information from secondary sources. Application of these techniques provides assurance of both the consistency and the accuracy of secondary data used for modeling and decision making by means of a structured, repeatable validation process.

First it is useful to describe the difference between primary and secondary sources. Some good definitions have been given by university schools of journalism. Thus, the following descriptions are drawn from online writing guides published by Purdue University and the University of Southern California-Santa Cruz.[1,2]

Primary sources are contemporary accounts "written by someone who experienced or witnessed the event in question" (i.e., got it directly from the "horse's mouth").[3] Primary sources can include data that has been directly gathered by the author through observation or measurement. These sources "may also include published pieces such as newspaper or magazine articles (as long as they are written soon after the fact and not as historical accounts)" by eyewitnesses.[4] Expert opinion can be considered a primary source, but the possible effects of the expert's lack of accurate recall, bias, or careless data collection techniques should be considered when using the data. If the expert opinion is suspect, it should be validated by another expert or a secondary source.

Secondary sources interpret primary sources. Secondary sources "can be described as at least one step removed from the event or phenomenon under review."[5] Secondary source materials "interpret, assign values to, conjecture upon, and draw conclusions about the events reported in primary sources."[6] Secondary source accounts "are usually in the form of published works such as journal articles or books, but may include radio or television documentaries, or conference proceedings."[7]

As mentioned above, this monograph deals primarily with information from secondary sources, i.e., information drawn from something other than first-hand observation. Secondary information sources are often the only resources available to the analyst, and thus this monograph serves as a quality control guide to their use.

Enterprise risk management application

The technique's most appropriate enterprise risk application is in risk assessment when critical data is bei qualify and quantify risks. The approach can also be used fo any type of business model that relies upon external informa of the information for which this approach would be applica trends, political risk information, macroeconomic data, projected costs, future revenues, and equipment reliability da application of this tool assures compliance with the cc accuracy fundamentals of the information integrity process. ' less useful for gathering primary information where more sta control and primary market research techniques might be m

Initial data screening

Initial data screening is the minimum level of quality control to be applied to input data, and three questions should be answered in the screening process:

- Is the data current?

- Is it repackaged?

- Is it sufficient and precise enough for use?

One of the most important screening questions is one of timeliness, i.e., determining whether the most up-to-date information is used. To determine whether the data is current, the analyst should perform the following steps:

1. Track down the source of the data and look for its documented publication or copyright date, ISBN number (if a book), and author(s).

2. Perform an Internet search on the source to get the publisher's contact information and an indication of the latest publication date.

3. Contact the publisher and/or author and ask if the publication represents the most current data available.

If only old data is available, the analyst should be prepared to defend why it is still relevant for use.

Another important question about the data is whether it was original to the publication or was "repackaged" from some other secondary source. Repackaging or drawing heavily from some other source makes the data suspect because the further removed it is from a primary source, the more susceptible the work is to misinterpretation and/or manipulation. In the words of Edward Tufte, a noted expert in the field of statistics and information sciences, "Repackaging adds its own special interpretive filter to the critical process of learning from evidence.... Consumers of evidence should stay reasonably close to primary sources and to evidence-interpreters who provide honest unbiased readings. There's almost always something to learn from a first-rate primary source."[8] On the other hand, concerning what are called "repackagers" in this text, Tufte notes that "secondary bureaucracies of presentation may lack the technical skills and substantive knowledge to detect mistakes."[9]

There is a disturbing trend among many popular periodicals and newspapers: they unabashedly pull from the *Washington Post*, the *New York Times*, the Associated Press, Reuters, or the BBC news wires. To comply with their news source license agreements and avoid plagiarizing, the repackagers may give credit to the original sources, but rarely will they perform sufficient quality control on the content. According to journalism expert Sarah Harrison Smith, news publications such as *Time* once employed dedicated fact checkers, but no longer do so.[10] Thus, if original sources are not as rigorous as they once were about quality control, the reliability of information from repackagers is even more suspect. Any publication that regularly reprints and publishes from others is a repackager and should be considered untrustworthy. An analyst who finds that data in one report or publication is drawn from another should find the original and examine it carefully rather than relying on the repackaged source.

Finally, an important initial data screening determination is that of sufficiency and precision. The key questions to ask are: How much data is enough? Was more than one source of data used to develop the final dataset?

Other than the direct marketing of refined products to consumers, most oil and gas companies are in the wholesale (or business-to-business) marketing of their products. The practice of business-to-business market research differs from consumer market research in that the sample size is often small. It is thus difficult to statistically prove that it is representative of the population. This makes the determination of sufficiency of data for business-to-business market research more of an art than a science. Even so, there are a few best practices in business-to-business data gathering that should be followed to give some assurance of reliability. The first is not to rely on only one source of data. At the very least, a "second opinion" should be gathered and the data points compared to determine their degree of consistency.

Again, reliance on a single data source does not allow more than an intuitive "gut check" of the data. Use of only a single source of data should raise concerns about whether the data set used in any model is representative or reliable.

The first three screening checks for data (timeliness, avoidance of repackagers, and use of more than one source) are the minimum data quality control checks that an analyst should employ to "scrub down" data collected from secondary sources.

Basic validation techniques

The initial screening of the data described above is necessary, but it is not sufficient to provide any reasonable level of assurance for critical data. To provide validation beyond simply screening, a few qualitative and quantitative tests should also be applied to the data. The first of these tests deals with checking for consistency, again using more than one data source.

One method for checking for consistency is through plotting, graphing, and other structured visual comparison techniques. Plotting more than one set of data allows trends and outliers to be quickly identified and compared. In this sense, consistency is an indicator of the precision of the data. Consistency also implies that the information falls within some preestablished boundaries or limits that are comparable with historical trends or other known reliable information. This is similar to a variance analysis that an accountant would do to find mistakes or outliers. Have these limits or rules been established? A more detailed description of applying various visual comparison methods is provided in a later section of this chapter, "Graphical Spot-Checking."

Another best practice for ensuring consistency is to determine whether the data was collected using a preestablished *taxonomy*, or industry standard nomenclature and set of definitions. Having a taxonomy ensures that the basis of the data is the same or comparable for all input data sets used. For example, for equipment reliability data, taxonomies have been developed by the American Institute of Chemical Engineers, Center for Chemical Process Safety (CCPS).[11] The CCPS taxonomies are used to gather data from across the process industry for its plant and equipment reliability database (PERD). Among other advantages, the PERD methodology standardizes plant, unit, and specific equipment failure modes and definitions so that comparable reliability data can be gathered and combined from different companies and plants. In this way, regardless of the source, users of the data can be assured that at least the basis of data collection is the same.

Other basic validation questions include the following: Was a systematic and repeatable process used by the publication to gather the data? Does the publication reveal anything about its process of data gathering? Is the report methodology perfectly clear? If the answer is *no* to any of the above questions, the data is suspect. To address these issues, a good practice is the dissemination of a standard methodology for data gathering by the publication source. For example, the Economist Intelligence Unit (EIU) and the PIRA Energy Group both publish their methodologies. PIRA offers courses in its commodity supply and demand forecasting methodology, and the EIU publishes its general approach to economic analysis on its Internet site.[12] Both of these organizations pride themselves on having more than a "black box" approach to development of economic data. Some multilateral organizations have also begun to tighten up their process and have published their methodologies. For example, the Joint Oil Industry Data Initiative (JODI), coordinated by the Organization of Petroleum Exporting Countries (OPEC), is an oil industry database sponsored by seven international agencies interested in "quantifying and qualifying the availability and timeliness of basic monthly oil data."[13] As with the CCPS, the JODI secretariat has established a standard taxonomy and methodology for the collection of oil production data worldwide. This provides information consumers with a much better degree of assurance about the validity of the data.

Another possible concern with the data collection methodology has to do with the possible bias of the author or the editor reaching conclusions. Important questions to explore in this regard are: Is there any reason to believe the publication may be biased? Who paid for the study? Was the method used by the publication or report to analyze and cite evidence before coming to a conclusion disciplined and objective (vs. careless or possibly biased)? In this regard, government-sponsored information is always suspect, as is information used to promote a product or service, such as research by stock brokerage analysts and pharmaceutical manufacturers.

Advanced validation of the process and data

For many applications, initial screening and basic validation is sufficient to gain assurance that the data gathering was not spurious. However, in order to meet the increasingly stringent requirements of regulators, credit rating analysts, institutional investors, and auditors, *best of class* validation may be required. The advanced validation techniques (particularly the quantitative methods) that will now be described have been developed and used in financial services and energy trading companies and represent best practice in validation. With increased pressure from stakeholders, I expect these will become standard practice at publicly traded energy companies as well.

To truly test the soundness of the researcher's analytical process, the analyst should take a more in-depth look at whether the conclusions of a research report could stand up under the scrutiny of scientific peer review. An important deductive question was developed by Edward Tufte in his book, *Beautiful Evidence*, to test the process of arriving at a conclusion.[14] Tufte's questions is, Did the publication analyst use a structured logic that included explanatory theory, empirical evidence, and the rejection of competing explanations before coming to conclusions? Notice the influence of Tufte's mathematical and scientific training in asking this question without resorting to confusing statistical jargon. This is a succinct logic sequence that anyone could follow.

Another quality control hold point is dedicated checking. As mentioned in Sarah Harrison Smith's book, *The Fact Checker's Bible, A Guide to Getting It Right*, best practice among the world's most respected publications is to at times employ a team of "fact checkers" to carefully pore over the manuscript and catch mistakes before publication.[15] Scientific journals and academic publications require extensive peer review. Best practice in nuclear power plant engineering design requires "dedicated checkers" on calculations. Third-party design reviews are frequently required in oil and gas industry offshore production systems. If a second set of eyes for checking is recognized as best practice in these areas, why should it not be applied universally to critical business data? Work that goes either unchecked or is not peer reviewed is not very credible. Therefore, for reports providing data that is critical to financial and strategic modeling and decision making, the following question should be asked: Was there any verification and sign-off on the critical assumptions and data by a second- or third-party specialist?

Along the same lines as checking is the establishment of some preestablished standards to check against. Questions that might be asked include: "Have any corroborating parameters been established that would indicate that the data is reasonable?" and "Have any information integrity rules for variance been established that could automatically identify suspicious outliers?" Without any preestablished criteria, a variance analysis or third-party checking can become quite subjective.

Modeling and simulations

In the absence of hard data about the future, modeling provides another level of assurance that there is some logic behind input data. Modeling is used extensively in risk management and forecasting, but sometimes models are used to actually generate the input data. For example, in the field of petroleum reserves estimating, the Society of Petroleum Engineers states that petroleum reserves and "future production performance can be estimated through a combination of detailed geologic and reservoir engineering studies and mathematical or computer simulation models."[16]

Whether models are used to generate reserves information, equipment reliability data, or revenue forecasts, a few quality assurance questions related to modeling should be considered. First, was validated historical information used as the basis for assumptions, projections, or estimates? Second, if a model was used, has any qualitative or quantitative backtesting of the data been performed to measure historical vs. actual projections? Drawing from the field of banking and finance, the Basel Committee on Banking Supervision, an international banking regulatory body, states that "backtesting is a technique for evaluating the quality of a firm's risk measurement model."[17] The Basel Committee also stated that "the essence of all backtesting efforts is the comparison of actual trading results with model-generated risk measures....In some cases, however, the comparison uncovers sufficient differences that problems almost certainly must exist."[18] Again, the Society of Petroleum Engineers states in its 2001 standard on reserves estimating that "the validity of the mathematical simulation models is enhanced by the degree to which the calculated history matches the performance history. Where performance history is unavailable, special consideration should be given to determining the sensitivity of the calculated ultimate recoveries to the data that is the most uncertain."[19] (Notice the inference here to determining the criticality of the data by running a sensitivity analysis!} For an oil and gas company, reserves information is the most important input to cash flow forecasting and valuation models— it is *critical*. The same could be said about the risk due to exchange rate, interest rate, and commodity price fluctuations for a financial institution or trading company. Thus, backtesting as a validation technique is a standard validation procedure in these industries.

Backtesting techniques can range from simple visual observation and comparison to calculating a "t" value to test the null hypothesis using a representative sample. It is up to the analyst to determine the degree of rigor applied to a backtest, as there are few universal standards. Where backtesting has been most widely used is in the field of financial risk management and in statistical and econometric modeling. As an example of a fairly simple form of backtesting for bank portfolios, the Basel Committee has determined that the backtesting of a bank's controls can be done by simply checking to see if the bank's *value at risk* (VaR) limit is exceeded more than 1% of the time. If the regulator assumes that the banks have designed their portfolios in accordance with their risk appetite using an in-house VaR model, by counting the actual number of breaches, the regulator would be backtesting the bank's VaR model.

For risk applications other than financial trading risks (i.e., operational, strategic, and compliance), the assumptions inherent to the VaR methodology make its strict application difficult. However, the simple logic of developing a predictive model and then backtesting it using actual historical data is applicable in many different fields. Where appropriate, a probabilistic simulation can even be performed to establish, within a specified degree of confidence (say 90%), "reasonable certainty" regarding the accuracy of the data. In summary, where the information is critical to achieving a company's goals, these advanced validation steps of quantitative data modeling, historical backtesting, and reasonable assurance through simulations should be applied.

Other considerations

More detailed descriptions of the validation approaches are given in the discussion of the following two tools: graphical spot-checking and validation through simulation.

Graphical Spot-Checking

Graphical spot-checking is a generalized approach to data validation by plotting numerical data and then visually inspecting the results. It is a technique for applying a skeptical eye to data that is not known to be reliable and is the second step in the larger process of secondary data validation described earlier in this chapter.

Sometimes graphical spot-checking is called *intuitive statistics* because underlying information such as correlations, patterns, and trends can be determined "intuitively" (i.e., via visual inspection) *without* using any statistical computations. The scatter plot, which is shown in figure 4–4, illustrates one type of graph that is used for graphical spot checks.

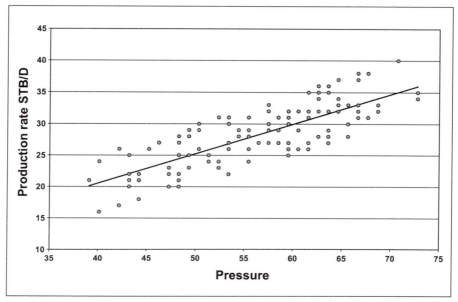

Fig. 4–4. Scatter plot example

Spot-checking for data validation often requires comparisons of one data set to another "reference" set. For example, a graph can be plotted of projected time series forecast(s) of crude oil, natural gas, electric power, or other projections vs. actual realized prices to perform a simple backtesting of the data. The graphical spot-checking process involves a five-step process for determining the relevancy and type of data, establishing the relationships and possible control limits, selecting and plotting the data on a graph, and then inspecting the results.

This tool's most appropriate application for enterprise risk management is in the data assessment phase to ensure consistency and accuracy of primary or secondary quantitative data received from others. It could also be used for quality control on internally generated data.

Assessment Tool 3: Graphical Spot-Checking

The purpose of this monograph is to describe graphical spot-checking as a generalized approach to data validation by plotting numerical data and then visually inspecting the results. Graphical spot-checking is a preliminary or basic form of numerical data validation and is best used when the data set consists of 20 or more data points. As mentioned, it is a technique for applying a skeptical eye to data that is not known to be reliable. Finally, graphical spot-checking is the second step in the larger process of secondary data validation described previously in this chapter.

How data can be most effectively communicated via visual displays and appropriate graphical approaches for data analysis is a fascinating topic, but it is beyond the scope of this discussion. For interested readers, this topic is very nicely covered in three excellent books: *The Visual Display of Quantitative Information* by Edward Tufte, Nancy Tague's *The Quality Toolbox*, and *Applied Data Analysis in Process Improvement*, by James Lamprecht.[20-22] Thus, some of the information described here draws on the works of Tufte, Tague, and Lamprecht; however, with a difference in focus. Instead of seeing how data can be analyzed or communicated *to others* through visual displays, the focus presented here is to see how visual displays can be used to scrutinize the accuracy of data *from others*.

Graphical spot-checking is a form of "intuitive statistics," a term used by Lamprecht to describe how analysts can effectively "see the data" by plotting and then inspecting the results. It is called *intuitive statistics* because underlying information such as correlations, patterns, and trends can be determined intuitively (i.e., via visual inspection) *without* using any statistical computations. In a similar way, Tufte describes visual display of quantitative information as a way of "revealing" the data. When applied to spot-checking of numerical data, the idea is to use visual displays to protect against possible sloppy data gathering, careless analysis, or the unsupported assumptions of others.

Selecting the proper graphing technique to reveal the data in this way depends upon the structure of the data and exactly how it will be used. For example, supposing a crude oil forecast is needed for a revenue model, and the analyst wants to validate a strip of forward oil prices provided by someone else. A graphical spot-checking approach may be to first plot the strip as a time vs. price scatter plot and then look for any suspicious outliers, peaks, humps, or dips in the series. Certain patterns or shapes automatically raise suspicions. For example, the infamous "hockey stick" pattern for the cash flow time series of a startup company or acquisition candidate is a commonly cited example of potentially unrealistic growth projections. However, in order to recognize the hockey stick, it may be necessary to actually plot the cash flows rather than simply look at them in tabular form.

Spot checking as a way of data validation often requires comparisons of one data set to another data set, called a *reference data set*. Visual comparisons using graphs are particularly useful for this purpose. For example, when plotting prices against time, a type of visual check or backtest can be performed of a time series forecast (or forecasts) vs. actual historical data. To illustrate how much easier it is to see differences in data when it is plotted as opposed to tabular form, consider six data series representing five-year projections of world crude oil prices made by the U.S. Energy Information Agency (EIA) between 1994 and 1999. The control or reference data set is the series showing actual historical prices. The tabular year-by-year percentage difference between the projected series and the actual prices as taken from the EIA Web site is shown in figure 4–5.

		Projected Year									
		1995	1996	1997	1998	1999	2000	2001	2002	2003	2004
	AEO 1994	6.4	-5.9	11.4	83.7	37.7	-7.9	25.0	25.1	15.0	-5.6
	AEO 1995	0.8	-11.7	4.0	69.4	25.1	-17.1	10.6	8.8	-1.6	-19.9
Series Label	AEO 1996	0.1	-14.0	0.3	63.8	21.5	-19.3	8.2	6.5	-3.6	-21.6
	AEO 1997		-3.1	4.8	62.4	16.3	-25.7	-1.5	-4.2	-14.3	-31.2
	AEO 1998			0.0	56.1	15.1	-24.4	-1.0	-5.0	-15.3	-32.4
	AEO 1999				3.8	-21.0	-47.0	-25.7	-24.6	-29.1	-41.3

Year-by-year percentage difference in prices per barrel including the effects of inflation
US Energy Information Administration- Annual Energy Outlook

Fig. 4–5. World oil prices, actual vs. reference case projections

Notice how difficult it is to make sense of the data in the tabular form provided by the EIA. Even by adding a few annotations and labels to this table to make it more comprehensible, it is difficult to comprehend because of the way that the data is presented. Based on visual inspection of the table, all that can be said is that it looks like the projections varied widely from the "actuals" over many years. A plot of the data shown in figure 4–6 illustrates much more clearly where the differences are and is an example of the power of a graph to perform a spot check on data.

What the plot of forecast vs. actual prices demonstrates is that for any year between 1994 and 1999, the government forecast inaccurately predicted the direction *and* the level of crude oil prices in the front year. Furthermore, since each *Annual Energy Outlook* (AEO) forecast is released with at least a one-year time delay from the current year, there was the added problem of timeliness. Thus the AEO for 1994 used 1993 actuals but reported an estimate for 1994. Effectively, the AEO forecasts for the front year (in this case 1995) were out-of-date as soon as they were released!

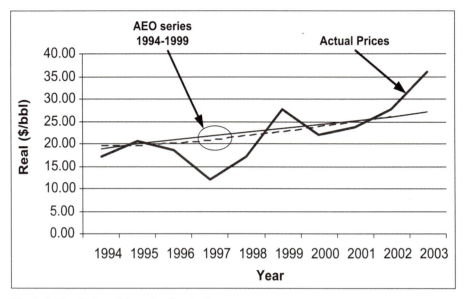

Fig. 4–6. Five EIA world crude oil price forecasts

Scatter plots can be used as a simple spot check of any type of data. A scatter plot is a visual display of two variables that have been measured or estimated (for example, measurements of equipment failure versus time). To create a scatter plot, pairs of variable data are selected, and one variable is plotted on each axis. Then the analyst looks for a relationship between them by inspecting the graph. To use the scatter plot, there should be discrete (i.e., individually collected data points) as opposed to continuous data. Finally, as previously mentioned, the analysis is most productive if there are more than 20 data points to analyze. Scatter charts can be used for spot-checking by looking for a pattern or a trend between different observations, measurements, or estimates. If there is a discernable pattern, the graph can help identify possible causes of change or suggest correlations. If the variables are correlated, the points will fall along a line or curve, i.e., the better the correlation, the tighter the points will hug the line.

One example of where the use of a scatter plot proved invaluable in spotting a problem comes from the discipline of petroleum reserves auditing. The company in question is a publicly traded exploration and production company that had not delivered on its internally generated forecast of gas production over several quarters. On top of this, the company's stock price had plunged in the preceding 18 months, despite an aggressive infield drilling program designed to boost production. In spite of their inaccurate projections, the company's geologists continued to support new drilling locations with large associated reserves that they had "proven" using their internally generated analysis. In the face of these problems, the new CEO of this company asked its independent reserves auditor, Ryder Scott Company, to provide a third-party production forecast and reserves report.

The auditor's analysis began with a review of all producing wells, past and present, and a determination of the estimated ultimate recovery (EUR) for each well. Rather than immediately diving into the geology, the auditors plotted a time series of historical performance of wells drilled at one of the company's fields slated for continued development drilling. They then plotted the company geologists' projected performance of new wells being promoted at the field. A comparison of the historical vs. the new projections is graphically illustrated in Ryder Scott's scatter plot shown in figure 4–7.

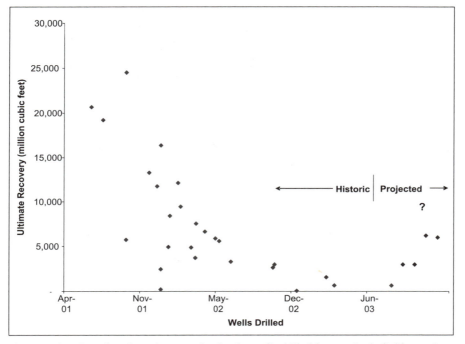

Fig. 4–7. Historic and projected gas production by wells drilled from a single field over time

The trend of dots (volumes actually produced) prior to June 2003 on the plot clearly shows diminishing returns over time for the wells that had been drilled. Yet the company geologists were unable to explain why the declining trend prior to June 2003 would be reversed with the new drilling program (shown by the dots in the future). Ryder Scott performed a similar graphical analysis on another field with more than 20 years of data, and the same (seemingly) overly optimistic projections were discovered.

It turned out that at this company, managers had been under pressure by Wall Street to drill wells, maximize production, and increase the reserve base. Consequently, their drilling program was aggressive, leaving little time for reflection upon past results. Had the managers taken a bit more time to graphically look at the trends, they might have been able to reign in the geologists' optimism and the expectations of their upper management and investors.

The so-called vintage plot utilized by Ryder Scott was just a spot check on the data. In and of itself, it did not prove very much. It ignored geology, it ignored production problems, and it could tempt someone to predict the future without regard to most of the pertinent technical data. However, from the auditor's perspective, it provided a simple and clear indication that there might be something wrong with the geologic view being presented to the company's upper management and to investors. Upon closer inspection of the actual geologic conditions, it turned out that the auditor's suspicions were correct.

Enterprise risk management application

Graphical spot-checking's most appropriate application is in the data assessment phase to ensure consistency and accuracy of primary or secondary quantitative data received from others. It can also be used for quality control on internally generated data. The following is a step-by-step description of the overall graphical spot-checking approach, beginning with figure 4–8, which outlines the process.

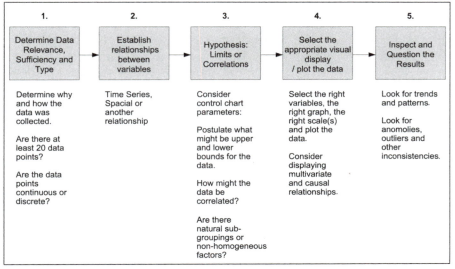

Fig. 4–8. Graphical spot-checking approach

Step 1. Determine data relevance, sufficiency, and type. Performance of this step is a way of "prequalifying" the data for use. Sometimes data is collected for one purpose but used for another. In the extreme case, data is taken completely out of the context for which it was gathered and then plugged into a model because it is the only data available. Ready access to the Internet has increased the tendency for people to cite and use inappropriate data. This is very tempting to the analyst because an Internet search is quick, simple, and inexpensive to perform. However, using Internet data encourages the analyst to lower the minimum standards for intellectual skepticism and to overlook the Internet's lack of documentation and (qualified) peer review. In addition to knowledge of how and why the data was gathered, there should be enough data to actually plot and make some inferences. As mentioned previously, Tufte states that 20 pieces of data are the minimum needed to display data that visually makes sense. Finally, to properly prequalify the data, it is important to know whether the data represents a discrete measurement, a count of something (i.e., integer data), or a constantly changing phenomenon. Knowing this helps considerably when setting up the appropriate visual display in step 4 of this process.

Step 2. Establish relationships between the variables. Relationships can be spatial (lending themselves to data maps), time series (displaying changes over time), or multivariate (comparing one variable to another). Knowing how the data was gathered or which relationships are being tested can again help the analyst plan for plotting the data to yield a meaningful analysis. Understanding the differences between data points (i.e., the range) also helps in planning, so it may be useful to calculate the range of the data immediately. In cases such as loss frequencies for safety incidents resulting from human and natural causes, these ranges could span more than one order of magnitude. Here it might be useful to consider logarithmic scales on one or both of the axes.

Step 3. Hypothesize limits or correlations. The idea in this step is to think about establishing a *control chart*, which according to Tague is a graph with a central line for the average, an upper line for the upper control limit, and a lower line for the lower control limit. More than a control chart, however, the analyst should consider how the variables are expected to relate to each other. Should they demonstrate a positive correlation? Should they demonstrate a negative correlation? Should the values increase or decrease over time? It may be helpful to consider if there are some natural groupings that the data should fall into. Once these hypotheses are established, the analyst has the basis for setting up a chart to test these presumptions.

Step 4. Select and plot the appropriate visual display. Tufte describes the topic of his research and intellectual pursuits as the "visual display [of] measured quantities by means of the combined use of points, lines, a coordinate system, numbers, symbols, words, shading, and color."[23] This is quite a broad description. It encompasses his three major categories of graphics: data maps, time series, and narrative graphics of time and space. A step-by-step account of how to actually create these graphics is beyond the scope of this description but is covered by Tague in her book.[24] Even so, the point here is not to write a prescription for which graphic to use in every situation. Instead, the decision of which graphic technique to use should depend on the data set at hand and the analyst's creativity. The checking of data has been illustrated here using a line graph and a scatter plot time series. In most cases, as long as the analyst follows the first three steps of the graphical spot-checking process, one or the other of these two types of graphics should be adequate to provide a "smell test" of the data.

Step 5. Inspect and question the results. Simple inspection of the resulting plots can reveal patterns and trends for the data that help to check for consistency. In the previous example of the gas field production, the declining recovery pattern from historical data was in stark contrast to the geologists' projected figures. Looking for other anomalies, data outliers, and seemingly contradictory trends can point out areas where there may be concerns about the reliability of the data.

Other considerations. As mentioned previously, graphical spot-checking is more of an intuitive rather than a prescriptive approach to data quality control. The preceding description provides some guidelines for its use, but the best approach is to develop a methodology based upon the types of data and nature of analysis that will be performed.

Validation through Simulation

Use of simulations is a type of scenario analysis involving a computerized technique to generate thousands of possible outcomes from a model and then drawing conclusions about the credibility of the assumptions behind the model based on the results. In this way, input variables such as a crude oil price forecasts, population and demand growth estimates, or other model inputs can be tested for their criticality. In addition, they can be validated for reliability within a specified confidence interval. Validation using simulations draws from the technique of generating random scenarios (sometimes called a *Monte Carlo simulation*) along with the various theories behind statistical inference. As mentioned previously, validation using simulation is a relatively quick method when commonly available spreadsheet simulation software such as @Risk or Crystal Ball is used.

Enterprise risk management application

One of simulation's most appropriate enterprise risk management applications is determining what is critical in a financial or other model. Criticality is nothing more than the degree of correlation of a particular input variable to a particular output.

Assessment Tool 4: Validation through Simulation

Simulations are a form of scenario development involving a computerized technique to generate thousands of possible outcomes from a model. The results from the simulation can then be used to draw conclusions about the credibility of the assumptions behind the model. In this way, input variables such as a crude oil price forecasts, population and demand growth estimates, or other model inputs can be tested for their criticality. It is also possible to validate these inputs for reliability within a specified confidence interval. Validation using simulations draws from the technique of generating random scenarios (sometimes called Monte Carlo simulations) along with the various theories behind statistical inference. Although seemingly time-consuming and complicated, today validation using simulation is a relatively quick method when commonly available spreadsheet simulation software such as @Risk or Crystal Ball is used. The mechanics of using this software are beyond the scope of this discussion. However, the following description explains how this technique can be applied to enterprise risk management to test the criticality or accuracy of input information.

Enterprise risk management application

As stated previously, one of simulation's most appropriate enterprise risk management applications is determining what is critical in a financial model. Criticality is nothing more than the degree of correlation of a particular input variable to a particular output. In a simple financial model, correlation in a qualitative sense may be easy to determine by inspection. However, if the model becomes large or complex, or if it is important to determine correlation quantitatively, computer simulation applications such as @Risk help tremendously. These computer applications are able to perform the model calculations hundreds of times before applying statistical tests to the variables. The degree of correlation or criticality is then typically displayed through a *tornado diagram* report that is a feature of most simulation software. The tornado diagram displays correlations as a series of horizontal bars labeled with the correlation coefficients, resembling a tornado. The way these steps might flow together to determine criticality is shown in figure 4–9.

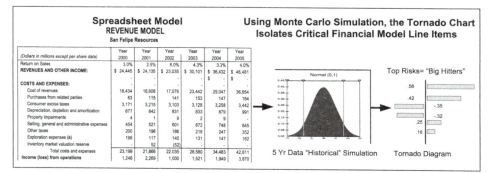

Fig. 4–9. Spreadsheet models and Monte Carlo simulation

The simulation process, its inputs and outputs

Examples of desired outputs from a financial model could be revenues, net income, cash flow from operations, return on investment, and return on capital employed. Examples of input variables for oil and gas companies would be the price of crude oil and gas, drilling costs, rig rates, contractor labor rates, and production volumes. Inputs and outputs are linked together through a series of calculations in a spreadsheet to form a model. This model represents the "base case" upon which scenarios or simulations can be performed.

Simulations require the preselection of a desired data distribution for each stochastic or chance variable in the model. This is not a simple task. Accurately and precisely determining the distribution of the data through research and massive data collection can easily become a complicated and academic study in itself. In the absence of sufficient time to collect data and/or historical data sets to support the "correct" distribution, often analysts determine that there is very little value in spending time researching the exact distribution for each input variable. If there is a sense that extreme values are much less likely than the median, but the possible outcomes are still of a continuous (as opposed to discrete) nature, then often a distribution with a type of "hump" in the middle should be used. Many practitioners select either a triangular or a PERT distribution employing minimum, maximum, and most likely estimates as the bounds. In the absence of a detailed study on what to use for a particular category of data, I would recommend using a simple triangular distribution. More can be gained by spending time ensuring that the minimum, maximum, and most likely values are reasonable than by performing extensive research on the proper distribution to use.

Once the distributions and estimates are assigned, the way to determine which financial risks might be critical to an output variable is to run thousands of scenarios using the simulation software and then look at the tornado diagram of the inputs. In practice, an analyst might first take the forecast year financial model and apply the minimum and maximum variance from the five-year historical average (in percentage terms) to each line item. The analyst would then run the simulations and analyze the tornado diagram to determine the most critical input variables. Determining the top risks (or the "big hitters") in this way provides a systematic, risk-based approach for determining and prioritizing what is critical to the business. In this way, simulation is a tool supporting the criticality fundamental of information integrity.

Similarly, simulation can be used to help validate the forecasts of others. For example, credibility criteria in the form of statistical confidence intervals could be established to test whether a third-party forecast is credible under certain assumptions. For some types of input data (for example, daily spot crude oil prices and weather data), there is a vast historical data set that is useful to get a feeling for the type of distribution to use in the simulation. Still, the analysis of the precise distribution to use could be a tedious task. In this case, the distribution fitting function often found with simulation software can be very helpful. Often a distribution fitting function is part of the software and can be used to take the historical data series and statistically "best fit" the data to a variety of possible distribution types. Creating a model, running a simulation, and comparing it with a forecast may not be a conclusive validation of a forecast or an estimate, but it at least provides a "reality check" on suspect data. In this way, simulation is a tool supporting the accuracy fundamental of information integrity.

Summary and other considerations

Monte Carlo simulation modeling has become a standard quantitative technique in many areas of risk management, from geological to project cost/scheduled risk and operational performance forecasting. Using standard simulation tools such as @Risk, simulation can now play a significant role in the integrity of the enterprise risk management process by incorporating its use into the validation of input data to support the criticality, consistency, and accuracy requirements of the information integrity process.

As mentioned above, quantitative methods such as Monte Carlo simulation require some type of quantitative model upon which to act. Thus it is useful to look at the process of quantitative modeling itself and discuss some best practices for building models in the next tool in the toolbox, *quantitative modeling.*

Quantitative Modeling

Quantitative modeling forms the backbone of business decision making. This modeling is often developed in Microsoft Excel or other data management applications. Many managers think of quantitative models in utilitarian terms: calculations developed by an analyst to quickly arrive at an answer to support a management decision.

However, in today's environment, the "quick and dirty calculation" approach to modeling is out of touch with the demands of corporate stakeholders. Compliance as well as competitive advantage can by achieved by providing assurance by adhering to three guiding principles of model design:

- Design the model with communication in mind.

- Follow a consistent process and document the model.

- Perform "internal validation" through peer review.

A recommended five-step model design process is shown in the flow chart in figure 4–10.

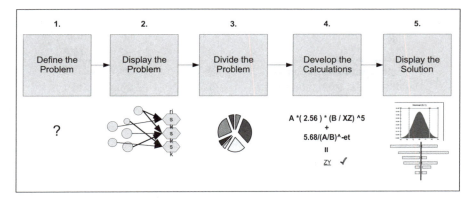

Fig. 4–10. Five-step flow chart

Assessment Tool 5: Quantitative Modeling

As mentioned previously, quantitative modeling forms the backbone of business decision making. Outputs from these types of models often take the form of reports with lines of numbers and figures. The excerpt shown in figure 4–11 from a financial statement illustrates a typical revenue model output.

(Dollars in millions except per share data)	Year 2000	Year 2001	Year 2002
Return on Sales	3.0%	2.5%	6.0%
REVENUES AND OTHER INCOME:	$ 24,445	$ 24,135	$ 23,035
	-	-	-
COSTS AND EXPENSES:	-	-	-
Cost of revenues	18,434	16,808	17,076
Purchases from related parties	63	115	141
Consumer excise taxes	3,171	3,215	3,103
Depreciation, depletion and amortization	(a) 677	842	831
Property Impairments	4	1	9
Selling, general and administrative expense	454	521	601
Other taxes	200	196	186
Exploration expenses (a)	196	117	140
	-	52	(52)
Total costs and expenses	23,199	21,866	22,035
Income (loss) from operations	1,246	2,269	1,000

Fig. 4–11. Revenue model output

Again, in today's environment, analysts and managers must think beyond mere calculations and consider financial auditor and regulator requirements for consistent and transparent models. If the model behind the report is confusing or poorly documented, then assurance is lost. To paraphrase John Ioannidis, a noted Greek medical researcher, a report's integrity depends on the process of collecting the evidence, and alert *stakeholders* "must seek some kind of assurance that the *process* was sensible and honest" (emphasis added).[25] But beyond mere compliance, the important question is, how can using best practice in model design lead to a competitive advantage?

The answer is by providing assurance to all stakeholders by adhering to the previously mentioned three guiding principles of model design:

- Design the model with communication of the methodology and the results in mind. This often means liberal use of graphics instead of just numbers or text.

- Ensure that analysts follow a consistent process and document the model as if they had to prove their case to an auditor.

- Pay attention to the accuracy of the calculations by having "internal validation" measures and have a peer check the work.

With the increased turnover of people in the energy industry, many companies have lost control of the modeling process at the very time when consistency, transparency, and accuracy are most needed to maintain or rebuild their reputation. Given this "assurance" mandate, adopting a modeling approach that restores confidence can differentiate a company from the pack in the eyes of the stakeholders.

Models designed for communication (not just computation)

Granted, designing models with communication in mind is not the most expedient way to arrive at an answer, but unless a back-of-the-envelope calculation is all that is required, then a risk analyst cannot get by with a poorly organized spreadsheet. The new era of assurance requires that the analyst design the model so it can be explained and the results communicated with more than just numbers. According to Max Henrion, a recognized expert in decision modeling and uncertainty, computer models "are, too often, an obstacle rather to than a vehicle for clear communication" because they are often neither graphical nor transparent.[26] He argues that the model building process should begin with block diagrams, influence diagrams, or other graphical forms of display that are then supported by the calculations. In fact Henrion and his company, Lumina Decision Systems Inc., promote a new software tool, Analytica, that electronically ties together influence diagrams, decision trees, and other graphics to the calculations and a simulation engine. For most model building, abandoning Excel for another software application may not be practical. Nevertheless, the *idea* of embedding graphics from the start of the modeling process and carrying them through to the display of results is a good one. Flow charts, block diagrams, and influence diagrams are effective ways to not only map out the structure of a model, but to explain the model to others once it is complete. Microsoft Visio diagrams pasted into the first few sheets of the model in an Excel workbook provide a great graphical overview of how the process works. Thus, best practice in quantitative model development (which is a left-brain activity) may actually start with a very qualitative (right-brain) visualization of the problem in the form of a drawing. As promoted by Edward Tufte, the expert in display of quantitative information, the most visually engaging information displays are data graphics that are multivariate (as opposed to single dimension), optimize the use of ink relative to white space, and incorporate textual annotations and visual contrasts.

One way that an analyst could consider how to structure the model for communication during its design is to pretend to be explaining it to an inquisitive elementary school student. If it cannot be explained to a fourth grader, then the model will probably frustrate an adult.

Consistency of the process—the auditor's viewpoint

Quality goes hand in glove with consistency. ISO 9001 is the recognized world standard for quality management systems. The two things an ISO 9001 auditor looks for in a company are an established process and consistency in its application. Much of the "best practice" that once existed within companies has been lost, buried, or forgotten due to staff turnover. Yet, best practice for most fields is available to companies through professional organizations such as the Society of Petroleum Engineers, the Project Management Institute, and the International Standards Organization. In the area of risk modeling, British author Alistair Day has developed an excellent handbook called *Mastering Risk Modelling, A Practical Guide to Modelling uncertainty with Excel.*[27]

I have developed the following flow chart (mentioned in the introduction to this tool) of a process for modeling that is supported by many of the best practices for modeling discussed by Alistair Day and others. Again, figure 4–12 acts as a guide to the ensuing discussion of modeling best practice.

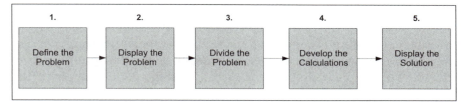

Fig. 4–12. Flow chart from Alistair Day's modeling

Guidance Questions for Robust Model Development

The following comments and questions relate to each step in the process.

Define and display the problem: steps 1 and 2

- What is the key question to be answered?

- What is the overall objective of the model?

- What should be the overall structure of the model?

- What are the inputs to and outputs from the model?

- What reports or outputs are needed?

- Who will use it?

- How can the structure, inputs, and outputs of the model be illustrated using multivariate, annotated graphics?

Divide the problem and develop the calculations: steps 3 and 4

- How can a clear layout be created with easily identified inputs, calculations, and outputs?

- What are the components of the problem, and how can they be subdivided into smaller sections?

- How can these sections be "modularized" and organized visually in the workbook for easy understanding, modification, and checking by others?

- Is there a management summary (with the final answer) physically close to the inputs area? Display of various sections of the model should be arranged such that differing consumers of information (managers, analysts, and peers) do not have to explore the full structure of the model if they want to use the model.

- In the development of the calculations, are the formulas simple, attempting to use predeveloped Excel functions and separate data tables as much as possible?

- Has internal validation been designed into the calculations to provide some quality control over inadvertent errors in the inputs?

- Will there be peer review of the calculations and formulas?

Display (and document) the solution

- Is there a version number or author name to show the exact version being used?

- Are the assumptions and background to the model well documented in one of the initial worksheets? (See the discussions on the information testing tool and the validation and documentation best practices tool elsewhere in this book for more information.)

- Is the model logic displayed graphically in the same workbook as the calculations?

- Is the model "stand-alone," or does it have troublesome links back to a centralized server, which could cause logic problems when the model is moved?

- How can the results be most effectively communicated using data-rich, multivariate graphics?

Enterprise risk management application

As mentioned, this tool's most appropriate application for enterprise risk management is in the assessment phase of the information integrity process. Appropriate application of this tool supports the consistency, accuracy, and transparency fundamentals.

Other considerations

Other tools in this book that complement quantitative model development are discussed in the following sections: "Discovery Tool 2: Enterprise Value Chain Mapping," "Discovery Tool 6: Cause and Effect Diagrams," "Assessment Tool 2: Information Testing and Validation," and "Assessment Tool 3: Graphical Spot Checking." Communication, transparency, consistency, and accuracy in models will lead to compliance, as well as stakeholder assurance of the integrity of the results. This builds a reputation and a brand, which in turn is a source of differentiation and competitive advantage.

The next discussion deals with an advanced, but increasingly more important, topic in the field of risk management: stress testing.

Stress Testing

Stress testing is a way of converting "what should happen" into "what could happen." "What should happen" is our projection, forecast, budget (or even our hopes). Almost always, before a stress test can be designed or applied, a model must be developed to represent the base case. This is sometimes called the *projected, forecasted,* or *budgeted case.* Stress testing applies a "shock" to this base case that systematically changes one or more of the variables and then compares the outcome to the original. Some of the reasons for performing stress tests are as follows:

- To identify exposures with disproportionate risk

- To identify market conditions that could lead to severe losses

- To develop and apply stress-based risk limits

- To allocate capital based on quantified exposures or opportunities

Although the concept of quantifying or at least bounding uncertainty is universal to all risk management, the term *stress testing* comes specifically from the field of financial risk. Creating and running stress tests is now expected by regulators and other stakeholders for monitoring and managing exposures at the world's banks, insurance companies, hedge funds, brokerages, and trading houses. There are three basic types of stress testing: sensitivities, scenarios, and single event risk.

Assessment Tool 6: Stress Testing—A Framework for Assessing and Quantifying Financial and Operational Risks

As mentioned previously, stress testing is a way of converting "what should happen" into "what could happen." "What should happen" is our projection, forecast, budget, or even our hopes. However, uncertainty obviously surrounds anything in the future. Thus, our projections, forecasts, budgets, and hopes are inherently uncertain. What is in question, then, is the degree of uncertainty. Stress testing provides a means of addressing this concern. It does so by designing and applying a "test" that systematically changes one or more of the variables in a situation and then compares the new test outcome to the original. Before a stress test can be designed or applied, some type of model must be developed to represent the base (or deterministic) case, which might also be called the *projected, forecasted*, or *budgeted case*. (For more information on modeling best practice, see the previous discussion dealing with quantitative modeling.)

After a base case model is developed, a simple form of stress testing might be to adjust some of the variables in the base model to calculate a high and low alternative to the base case. At its most complex, stress testing could be as involved as the creation of three or four alternate world views, each reflecting the outcome of a change in multiple variables over time. These are a type of stress test called *futures scenarios* and are described in detail in the next chapter. For boards of directors, requiring that at least some stress tests are performed is good governance. This is because it forces executives and operations managers to explicitly manage uncertainty by considering and quantifying what could plausibly happen, in addition to what they hope will happen.

Although the concept of quantifying or at least bounding uncertainty is universal to all risk management, the term *stress testing* comes specifically from the field of financial risk management. Creating and running stress tests is now expected practice for monitoring and managing risk exposures at the world's banks, insurance companies, hedge funds, brokerages, and trading houses. For example, stress testing is often a first step in establishing risk controls or limits for commodities traders. Even the most common trading metric, value at risk (VaR), could be considered the result of a stress test. This is because the definition of VaR is the maximum projected loss, over a given time horizon, within a specific confidence interval. As this definition includes the term "confidence interval," it implicitly means that there is some type of measurement of uncertainty included in every VaR calculation. Even so, it is well accepted that stress tests must go beyond measuring and monitoring VaR. This is because a VaR calculation is not able to capture the effects of "non-Gaussian" or so-called fat tail events.

One of the world's leading financial institution advisory groups, the Basel Committee on Banking Supervision, has emphatically called for banks around the world to apply market risk stress testing because they recognize that VaR monitoring does not provide enough assurance. This monograph takes from the Basel Committee recommendations for banks, along with other financial risk background papers, and considers how stress testing can be applied in other enterprise risk situations. It considers best practices, policies, and procedures for stress testing and scenario analysis from documents from the Committee of Chief Risk Officers (CCRO) and the Committee on Sponsoring Organizations of the Treadway Commission (COSO).

Since much of the literature and conceptual work around stress tests has been done in the financial risk arena, the examples and terminology described below will mention financial risk terms such as *exposures, profit and loss (P/L)*, and *portfolios*. However, the stress testing concept can easily be applied to other risk management applications. To do so, it is useful to try to "translate" some of the financial terminology into analogous asset, project, and health, safety, and environmental risk terminology. Table 4–1, although not comprehensive, illustrates such a comparison.

Table 4–1. Risk terminology comparison across different risk management disciplines

Financial Risk	Asset and Project Risk	Health, Safety, Environmental, and Insurance Risk
Exposure	Potential failure, downtime	Hazard, peril
Profit/loss (P/L)	Savings, loss, impact, failure, slippage	Consequence, emission fatality
Portfolio	Asset, plant, equipment group	People, consequence area
Limit	Risk control	Risk control, barrier
Risk decomposition	Event (or risk) identification	HAZID
Deal capture system, financial model, valuation model	Reliability model, project schedule	Consequence model, fault tree/event tree
Stress test/scenario analysis	Cases, simulations, scenarios, alternatives	Scenarios, cases

A similar but expanded comparison can be found in the International Standards Organization (ISO) Guide 73, "Risk Management—Vocabulary—Guidelines for Use in Standards." Additional guidance can be found in the ISO Standard 17776, which deals with hazard identification and risk assessment for the offshore oil and gas industry and has a section on risk management definitions.

For the purposes of enterprise risk and information integrity, the definitions will be generalized so they can be applied in any (or all) of these risk fields. For example, instead of *portfolio* or *asset, plant, or equipment group*, the term *system* will be used to encompass any of these terms based upon the types of risks being assessed.

Definitions and requirements

There are numerous definitions in the financial risk literature for stress tests, many of them confusing, contradictory, and not readily applicable to other fields of risk management. Therefore, after sorting through many sources, I have compiled the following definitions for stress tests, sensitivities, scenarios, and single event risks.

- A *stress test* is a simulationthat evaluates a system's performance under defined exceptional circumstances and quantifies the resulting impact.

- There are three basic types of stress tests:

  1. Sensitivities

  2. Scenarios

  3. Single event risks

- A *sensitivity* is a type of stress test that changes one of the principle drivers, such as the underlying price or volatility, and measures the response or impact on the system that results from the change.

- A *scenario* is a type of stress test that simulates real or imagined events by using *multiple sensitivities*, or changing multiple drivers, and evaluates their effect on a system.

- The *single event risk (SER)* is a type of stress test that uses the single past event that when applied to the current portfolio has the greatest financial impact. The value can be determined by revaluing the portfolio using historically based price, volume, correlation, or volatility scenarios and selecting the worst outcome from the resulting data set of valuations.

These definitions, including their interrelationships and examples, are illustrated in figure 4–13.

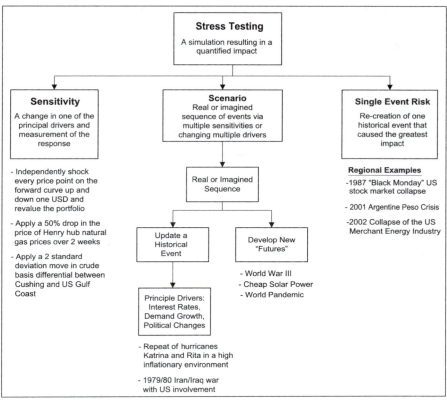

Fig. 4–13. Stress testing in energy risk management

Reasons for stress tests and recommendations for their use. Some of the reasons for performing stress tests are given in the following:

1. *To identify exposures with disproportionate risk.* As previously mentioned, there may be risk concentrations that have acceptable VaR exposures but could still suffer high losses during abnormal market conditions. This could be due to nonrepresentative behavior in the VaR calculation or a completely different phenomenon in the infrequent tail event risks as compared to those under "normal market conditions."

2. *To identify market conditions that could lead to severe losses.* This is a forensic exercise in which the risk analyst uses stress testing to simulate conditions under which the company would suffer severe financial loss. Then, acting as a risk detective, the risk analyst would piece together the *whys* behind the losses, using cause-and-effect diagrams or quantitative simulation tools that provide a tornado diagram analysis to discover drivers.

3. *To develop and apply stress-based risk limits.* As previously mentioned, because it quantifies extreme exposures, stress testing can be the first step in the development of limits or barriers.

4. *To allocate capital, based on quantified exposures or opportunities.* Applying stress tests can help the risk analyst choose between competing alternatives for investment. From a strategic standpoint, by bounding the uncertainty around events, stress tests can be an important tool for recognizing and quantifying upside opportunities. In turn, the ability to do this better than competitors can form the basis of competitive advantage.

As previously mentioned, the Committee of Chief Risk Officers (CCRO) has compiled information on best practice in governance and risk management for commodity trading companies. This includes best practice in the areas of valuation and risk metrics. Paraphrasing the CCRO valuation and risk metrics white paper, the following are attributes for good stress testing:[28]

1. *The stress tests are appropriate for the system and its risks.* This includes making sure key assumptions, drivers, and vulnerabilities are appropriate to the system being analyzed. In contrast to the Basel II approach of attempting to standardize stress testing across the organization, stress testing should be a customized activity. Thus it is very important for the risk analyst to be keenly aware of both the market conditions and the potentially unique risk profile of each portfolio (or system).

2. *The stress tests should be stressful enough to yield a discernable shift in profit and loss (P/L).* It does no good to marginally stress the system and then conclude that exposures are minimal. Again, the risk analyst must be creative enough to know that he or she cannot perform these stress tests by rote and still expect to effectively discover the exposures.

3. *The stress tests must be plausible.* The "aliens invade the Earth" scenario will do nothing but destroy the credibility of the analyst's risk group within the organization. If seemingly wild scenarios are appropriate, they should be grounded in a "story" or in some historical occurrences. For more information on extreme scenarios, see the *futures scenario*s discussion in the next chapter.

4. *The stress tests should be designed so that risks (and results) are transparent and documented.* An example of a good documentation format for stress tests is given at the end of this discussion.

5. *The stress tests should not be compartmentalized (i.e., must be universal).* This allows for linkages among identified markets.

Another authoritative source for risk management, the COSO II framework, states the following concerning stress testing (which they term "risk assessment"):

- *The events should be evaluated from the viewpoint of both likelihood and impact.* This evaluation "normally uses a combination of qualitative and quantitative methods. The positive and negative impacts of potential events should be examined, individually or by category, across the entity. Potentially negative events are assessed on both an inherent and a residual basis."[29] *Residual* is that risk that is created or remains after some type of risk management strategy is applied to mitigate the exposures.

- "In risk assessment, management considers the mix of potential future events relevant to the entity and its activities. This entails examining factors—including entity size, complexity of operations and degree of regulation over its activities—that shape the entity's risk profile and influence the methodology it uses to assess risks."[30]

Given the recommendations from the CRO and COSO documents, I have developed a conceptual approach to developing stress tests, called *exposure assessment*, as described in the following.

A process for exposure assessment via stress testing. Exposure assessment via stress testing can help quantify the exposures resulting from specific types of risk. Stress testing in financial risk management relies on the results of a risk decomposition to identify risks types and drivers that are potentially material. As mentioned previously, this is simply another word for *event identification* in project risk management or a *HAZID* in the health and safety risk world.

An overview of the major elements of exposure assessment is shown in figure 4–14. Again, the word *system* can be substituted for portfolio, and *potential losses* or *impacts* for exposures, in order to generalize the approach for nonfinancial risk applications.

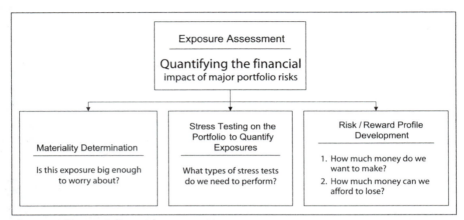

Fig. 4–14. Elements of exposure assessment

The focus of this monograph is to provide guidance for the middle block of the diagram, "stress testing on the portfolio to quantify exposures," dividing the process into fours steps as shown in figure 4–15.

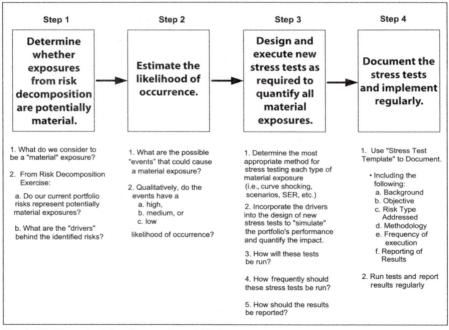

Fig. 4–15. Stress test development, a multistep process

Stress test development steps

Step 1. As mentioned above, step 1 starts with examination of the event identification or HAZID process here described as *risk decomposition*. Event identification and materiality were dealt with extensively in the "discovery" chapter of this book, so the focus in this discussion will be on steps 2, 3, and 4.

Step 2. Likelihood of occurrence. In markets with little or no forward pricing data, and frequent economic and regulatory structural changes such as those in developing countries, a quantitative assessment of the likelihood of occurrence is often not possible. However, it is important to get an indication of the likelihood of occurrence to be able to prioritize which exposures are more dangerous than others. The high likelihood, potentially high materiality exposures would then require more frequent stress testing and reporting of results. Therefore, identified events leading to a "potentially material" exposure should at least be qualitatively categorized as "high," "medium," or "low" likelihood of occurrence.

Step 3. Determining the most appropriate stress testing methods. According to three noted risk management practitioners, Aragonés, Blanco, and Dowd, stress test types fall into four main types, which differ in how they are constructed.[31]

1. The first type of stress test uses either actual scenarios from recent history, such as the 1987 equity crash, the bond market crash of 1994, the 1994 Mexican peso crisis, and the 1997 East Asian crisis and its aftermath. In these scenarios, the effect on profit or loss of repeats of past historical events is simulated.

2. The second type of stress test uses *imagined futures scenarios*, either by updating historical events with current conditions or by developing alternative "futures" through a strategic planning approach involving group brainstorming. This is a process that was pioneered by Royal Dutch Shell in the late 1970s and is currently employed by some corporations for corporate planning purposes.

3. The third type of stress test uses predefined scenarios that have somehow proven to be useful in practice. For example, a risk analyst could simulate the impact on the P/L of a fall in the stock index of x standard deviations, or of a change in an exchange rate of $y\%$, or of a yield-curve shift of x number of basis points.

4. The fourth type of stress test is a mechanical search stress test. A mechanical search stress test uses automated routines to simulate changes in risk factors, evaluate P/L under each set of risk factor changes, and report the worst-case results. For example, a very common stress testing procedure is to "shock" certain prices or returns to particular values, assume that other prices take their usual values, and derive the firm's risk exposure accordingly. This approach is conceptually straightforward and easy to carry out, but it is questionable because it ignores correlations between the stressed prices and other prices. In addition, recent empirical evidence suggests that the failure to allow for these correlations can misrepresent the true maximum exposures.

Given the varied nature of assets and transactions within a company's portfolio (or the "system"), the selection of the appropriate stress test for each identified exposure type will need to be analyzed on a case-by-case basis.

Step 4. Documentation. In order to ensure that stress testing is more than simply an ad hoc activity and that it is performed consistently, stress tests must be documented. Overall, an undocumented process is, at best, weak; at worst, it is nonexistent. In any case, lack of documentation is poor management. Aside from the quality assurance advantages, documentation provides auditors and analysts with proof that a reasonable effort is being made to assess financial risks within the organization. To assist with stress test documentation, we have developed a suggested template that includes all of the essential elements of a well-documented procedure: background, objective, methodology, frequency of execution, and reporting. This template is presented in appendix A.

Other considerations

For sensitivity analyses, risk analysts should take care not to extrapolate or generalize the results unless they are certain that the system reacts to change in a linear fashion. In real situations, this is seldom the case, so if risk analysts must generalize results, they should perform adequate sampling to determine the "shape" of the behavior across the entire system. As previously mentioned, this monograph draws extensively from the financial risk management literature. Risk analysts should be creative in application of this approach to other areas of enterprise risk management!

Recommended Template for Stress Test Documentation

Stress Test Name

Background

This should describe the following:

1. What the geographic scope and functional scope are (i.e., market risk, safety risk, project risk of the major project, trading book, etc.)
2. How we decided to use this stress test
3. Why we think this test is adequate

Objective

This should describe why we are doing the scenario or stress test (i.e., what it is meant to accomplish).

Risk Type Addressed

This is a description of the following:

1. Which risk type or types this test is meant to address
2. The possible materiality of the exposure (i.e., under which circumstances an exposure would be large, and how this compares with our risk tolerance)

Methodology

This should describe the following:

1. Who will perform the test
2. How it is performed (which models or tools are used, which curves are stressed, which assumptions are changed, etc.)

Frequency of Execution

This should describe the following:

1. How often we plan to run this test
2. Why we have selected this frequency of execution

Reporting

This will answer the following questions:

1. To whom will the results of this test be reported?
2. What is the format of the report?
3. What is the medium by which this will be reported (daily position report, risk management committee report, special weekly report, risk engine report, etc.)?

Assessment Vignette

The San Felipe Resources vignette continues, as Barry and Elena confront more challenges to their implementation of enterprise risk management. A plot is brewing among powerful corporate stakeholders to create havoc in the boardroom.

Blessed assurance

Karen James was sitting at home when her mobile phone rang, and she saw the country code "7" and a string of numbers pop up on the screen—a Russian telephone number. She knew that it probably was the one person in Russia she preferred not to talk to: Victor Komarovsky.

Komarovsky was a minority shareholder in SFR who had an impressive history as a Russian entrepreneur and industry investor. Originally a commodities trader, he had built a fortune in the post-Yeltsin era as a leading investor in Russian industries ranging from automotive parts to insurance, construction, and the secretive diamond industry. By 2001, he was firmly entrenched as one of Russia's "oligarchs" and had family ties by marriage to former president Gorbachev. Over the past few years, Komarovsky had begun to branch out of Russia, focusing on European steel and other commodity companies, and now owned part of a small private Canadian oil and gas producer, along with his shares in SFR.

Komarovsky had very clear ideas regarding how a business should be organized. He believed in the "stick to your knitting" school of business management and had a reputation for being a critic of both industrial conglomerates and vertically integrated companies. To him, "stick to your knitting" meant that even companies like SFR, with its upstream, midstream, and downstream businesses, should probably be broken up. Throughout Europe, Komarovsky used his understanding of the growing power of shareholder rights to force companies to spin off some of their profitable divisions and change out management to increase share prices. Over the past two years, Komarovsky had increased his interest (financially and otherwise) in SFR.

"Hello," said Karen, taking the call with some hesitation.

"Hello, Karen, this is Victor Komarovsky. How are you?"

"Very well, Victor, thank you. It's so good to hear from you. I haven't seen you since the World Economic Forum in Davos. How have you been?"

"Quite well, thank you. Yes, it has been about a year, hasn't it? I was wondering if you had seen some recent news describing the new corporate governance metric developed by this group, PRA?" said Komarovsky, in slightly broken English.

PRA, or Proxy Rights Advocates, was a stock research and investor advocacy group that focused on corporate governance issues and gave advice to institutional investors on shareholder-led proposals. Increasingly, PRA was becoming a force for change in the industry, and oil company boards and upper management had begun to take notice of their reports and recommendations. Karen was curious as to where Komarovsky was heading with his call.

"I know of them, yes. What have you seen, Victor?" Karen asked.

"Oh, just a benchmarking study they recently performed—one of those joint industry projects. I didn't think much of it at first, but I was talking with Bruce Wonderlein the other day, and he seems to think that it might warrant a few questions at the next board meeting. I'm afraid the report did not mention San Felipe in a very flattering light."

Karen's heart began to pound. She knew that unfavorable publicity mentioned by a powerful investor was never a good thing.

"In particular," Komarovsky continued, "Bruce and I were wondering about one of the PRA criteria that was...let me read it now—yes, here it is—'evidence of a process in place to verify the accuracy of external information used for material assumptions, data inputs to economic models, forecasts, and guidance to stakeholders concerning risks.' Do you think San Felipe has something in place to cover this?"

Karen was stumped. She had not dug down into this level of detail on how SFR's management actually verified the accuracy of external data and assumptions. She was beginning to see, however, that Komarovsky would try to use this as his vehicle to question whether the management of SFR had things under control. Furthermore, the fact that Komarovsky had talked this over with Bruce Wonderlein, one of SFR's major institutional investors, meant he was already gathering his allies and maybe even preparing for a proxy fight.

"You know, Karen, I thought this might be kind of interesting to you from the standpoint of, how you say, fiduciary responsibility," Komarovsky continued.

Karen recognized this last comment for what it was: a veiled threat to her position on the board. If a group of outside investors like Komarovsky and

Wonderlein were beginning to lose confidence in the upper management, they could be pushing for a board shakeup as well!

"I wanted to give you an advance on this. You know, because we are old friends," said Komarovsky menacingly.

"I appreciate that, Victor, and I'll take a closer look at this. Thanks for your concern. You take care now, and let's not wait until the next meeting in Europe to get together. I know you must be coming over here more often, and I would enjoy catching up over dinner the next time you come to town. Please do drop me a line before your next visit," Karen said nervously before she hung up.

She immediately placed a call to schedule a sit-down talk with SFR's top two executives, Dave Anderson and Bart Jensen.

Back at SFR headquarters, Barry and Elena were considering the fault tree diagram for crude oil price risk, which most of SFR's management realized by now was their key risk factor.

"Unless we have data, this diagram is nothing more than a nice little conceptual framework for how oil prices behave," said Elena. "And unless that data is validated somehow, all the assumptions behind our market strategy and this company's risk profile are nothing more than hot air."

Barry knew she was right. They needed to gather data, and they needed to prove to themselves that the data was credible and reliable before they began any analysis. Now the big question arose in both of their minds: What could they use for a systematic process to ensure reliable data?

Barry wondered aloud if anyone in science or industry had developed an overall standard or set of guidelines for what he would consider "information integrity." Out of professional pride, Barry really wanted to do things properly, and he wished that there was such a standard. He thought it was highly unlikely that anyone cared or would check up on whether SFR actually had a system for validating their market data, or whether he was following that system. To most of the men and women at SFR, validating information seemed like a long way from finding and producing oil. Barry did have to admit, validating market information seemed like a purely back office function. Even so, he could imagine bond rating agencies such as Standard & Poor's or Moody's had developed their own checklists or guidelines to apply to energy companies such as SFR. What would this set of information integrity guidelines look like?

Never in a million years would Barry have suspected that at that moment, a storm was brewing in the boardroom over this very issue.

After a few fruitless Internet searches, some serious inquiries of academics at nearby Baylor University, and a few calls to a well-respected technical standards and classification consultancy, Barry and Elena both came up empty-handed. Frustrated and tired, they broke for lunch.

Over brisket and beans at his favorite barbeque shack by the old stockyards near downtown, Barry had a long talk about their information integrity dilemma with his retired friend, Ralph Johnson. For many years, Ralph had been the president of a well-respected petroleum reserves estimating and auditing consultancy and had always been one of Barry's professional mentors. Ralph was about to give Barry a tremendously valuable clue as to how to solve this problem.

"What you might do, since you can't find anything *directly* testing the reliability or accuracy of market data sources and assumptions," stated Ralph hesitantly, "is take an approach from another context, some other field, where they also need to test for accuracy of information and apply it to testing market information. One of these areas is financial statement auditing to the requirements of Sarbanes-Oxley Section 404. Now I know this is a bit of a stretch, but the accounting auditors have a concept called 'reasonable assurance' that the SEC has specified as a standard for reliable financial statements. Reasonable assurance testing is not very well defined, but even so, maybe you could look at the methods that the accountants use and adapt them somehow to your situation."

"That is very interesting, Ralph," said Barry with a bit more animation. "What about from your own field of petroleum reserves auditing. Is there anything similar to reasonable assurance that you've used?"

"Yes, there is a concept that the Society of Petroleum Engineers and the World Petroleum Council have jointly defined as 'reasonable certainty' of recoverable reserves. As petroleum reserves auditors, we use four specific methods to determine whether reserves can be classified as proven or not. Reasonable certainty plays a part in that determination. If a deterministic method is used, the definition of 'reasonable' is pretty subjective and is defined as simply 'a high level' of certainty. If a probabilistic method such as simulations is used, the reasonable certainty criterion is that there is at least a 90% probability that the recovered reserves will meet or exceed the estimate. Finally, there is one more thing I'd like to stress, Barry. Petroleum reserves information is inherently imprecise, and no matter what we do, we cannot assure absolute accuracy. We can only ensure that through a systematic approach, we reduce the variability in the process. We can then say that we are implicitly improving the accuracy of the estimate."

"Again, this is very interesting, Ralph. I'd like to ask you a favor. Could you come over to the office this afternoon to explain this reasonable certainty concept and the four methods to my colleagues and me in more detail?" asked Barry.

Ralph went home to put on a coat and tie, and later that afternoon, showed up at the SFR headquarters building.

Ralph enjoyed the role of seasoned advisor and sage to large oil and gas companies. After all, he had spent his entire career in the business, and he continued to talk about prospects and developments with his old oilfield buddies at the monthly lunch meetings of the Pioneer Oil Producers Society. Keeping up with Barry and going over to the SFR headquarters building from time to time made him feel like he was still a contributor and influencer to a great American industry. (In fact, others recognized Ralph's achievements, and unbeknownst to him, he was being considered as one of the International Petroleum Association of America nominees for their annual Chief Roughneck Award.)

Ralph had an easygoing way of presenting technical information that was succinct, yet complete. He did this by getting straight to the point and then drawing on analogies for illustration. What made him so useful for this assignment was that Ralph was able to draw from his experience and then extend it by analogy from reliability tests for reserves information to reliability tests to ensure information integrity.

Ralph started by referring to the definitive standard for reserves estimating and auditing, the Society of Petroleum Engineers *Standards Pertaining to the Estimating and Auditing of Reserve Information*.

"If we look at the standard, we can see that there are four acceptable methods described for developing a reserve estimate. Now back when I was a reserves auditor, I wanted to see the extent to which one or more of these methods were used. Similarly, if I were a financial auditor, (or even an investor in SFR), I would want to make sure that someone in your strategic planning or risk management department was doing something similar. Let's see how these methods could be extended to check any type of information," continued Ralph.

Ralph then went on to explain each of the four methods, along with ideas about how each could be applied to information integrity. The first method he discussed was the volumetric method.

Method 1. The volumetric (i.e., direct calculation or observation) method. This method requires the engineer to use owners maps, geologic maps (perhaps from third parties), and reports. The engineer also uses results from physical tests with instruments and tools, such as well logs, core samples, well completion, and well performance history, as well as an estimated recovery efficiency factor to calculate the probable volumes in a reservoir.

The information integrity counterpart to this could be a series of calculations that leads (logically) to the data that would be used in the analysis. The calculation might rely on reports made by other internal staff members, third-party consultant reports, direct observation, or primary data gathering, data that was gathered using some data collection techniques, and a scaling factor or rule-of-thumb ratios.

Elena said, "That sounds straightforward enough if you trust how the data itself was gathered, i.e., if you trust the tools, instruments, and competence of the people gathering the data. I'm afraid this is a big 'if' when it comes to some of our market information."

"You are right, Elena," said Ralph. "Even though much of the data we use from well logs, for example, is gathered using instruments and tools, and the process is fairly standardized, human error does occur. This in turn would affect our reserves estimates. Over time, I would say that an experienced reserves auditor will get to know who is careful and who is not."

Ralph then presented the second method, the historical method.

Method 2. The historical method. This method looks at history, determines if it is sufficient, and "extends the trend." The historical method evaluates the performance history and could include an analysis and projection of producing ranges, reservoir pressures, oil/water ratios, gas/oil ratios, and gas/liquid ratios.

The information integrity counterpart to this might be that if analysts have enough historical data, they can plot it (or extend it forward) to "project out" what the estimate might be. It does require some assumptions about history being a good indicator of the future.

A second interpretation of how analysts would apply the historical method would be to simply check how the forecast compares with the actuals using an error metric, such as standard deviation, for example. Then the analysts could use this as an indicator of the reliability of the current data.

"Mmm," said Barry, "this sounds a bit like what some people in the financial risk management department of a commodities trading company would do. The so-called middle office group of a trading shop would develop tests for pricing information. To ensure some level of accuracy, they would perform what they call "backtesting" on the market data that feeds their forecasting models. I wonder if we could backtest the crude forecasts we use to develop our earnings guidance?"

Ralph then explained the third method, or the model method.

Method 3. The model method. This method involves the development of a mathematical model through consideration of material balance and computer simulation techniques.

The information integrity counterpart here could be a Monte Carlo simulation that attempts to describe "how things should be" under given conditions by assigning a distribution to the data using a three-point estimate. The simulation method runs thousands of possible scenarios in a short period of time. The result of the simulation allows the analyst to determine probabilities of whether a certain estimate will be exceeded or not.

"One area outside of geology and reservoir engineering where I've seen simulations applied to check for accuracy is in the area of project schedules," said Ralph. "For example, say a contractor comes to you with a pretty aggressive construction schedule for your project, and you have a concern about his ability to meet that schedule. To get a feeling for the reliability of his completion date, you could ask him to supply a project plan (which is a type of model) in some software like MS Project or Primavera. Then you could run a simulator on that plan to determine the 'level of confidence' you would expect for the completion date."

"I've also seen this used in financial risk management circles," said Barry, "where banks and oil traders make a decision about continuing to trade based on the existing degree of risk of their portfolio. To make those decisions, sometimes they perform Monte Carlo simulations on their portfolio model to calculate a metric called 'value at risk.' The value at risk, or VaR, tells them how 'at-risk' they are to losing lots of money should the market move against them. On the compliance side, an additional advantage of this approach is that because it is probabilistic, it would satisfy the SEC's 'risk-based' approach requirement for reasonable assurance."

"Sort of like killing two birds with one stone," added Elena.

"I like it," concluded Barry.

Ralph then explained the fourth method, or the analogy or comparison method.

Method 4. The analogy (or comparison) method. This method makes an analogy of one reservoir to another if geographic location, information characteristics, or similar factors render such an analogy appropriate.

The information integrity counterpart in this case might be for the analyst to take some data for another country, or situation known to be accurate, and compare it to the country or situation under study.

It might also involve the use of multiple data sources for the same piece of information, thus providing an internal "checks and balances" for the data.

Sort of like not getting all your eggs from one information basket, thought Barry.

Thus Ralph's simple information briefing had turned into a sort of brainstorming session on Barry and Elena's information integrity problem. They had many ideas for testing the reliability of their data using the concepts of *reasonable certainty* from the field of petroleum reserves auditing and *reasonable assurance* from the field of financial statement auditing. To organize their thoughts, they created the following chart (table 4–2) to compare and contrast the two concepts.

With these methods and approaches in mind, Barry and Elena returned to their problem at hand: the integrity of market information feeding SFR's forecast of crude oil prices for the next five years. The fault tree diagram they developed provided their conceptual model of oil price behavior. Now what they needed was to look at various information sources that would feed this conceptual model. Thus they began to examine the next level of the fault tree: the information sources. Figure 4–16 illustrates the entire fault tree, the driving factors, leading indicators, and information sources that they would use to determine crude oil price behavior.

Table 4–2. Reliability of information: reasonable assurance and reasonable certainty

	Reasonable Assurance of Reliable Financial Statements	Reasonable Certainty of Recoverable Reserves
Specific Tests	"Such a level and degree of assurance as would satisfy prudent officials in the conduct of their own affairs"	Using deterministic methods: Provide a high degree of confidence Using probabilistic methods: Achieve a 90% probability that quantities will meet or exceed estimates
Approach and Techniques	Top-down, risk-based approach, focusing on first establishing materiality	Four methods: • Volumetric (direct calculation) • Historical performance • Modeling/simulation • Analogy (comparison)
Caveats	Reasonable assurance does not mean absolute assurance. "Reasonableness" does not imply a single conclusion or methodology but encompass the full range of potential conduct, conclusions, or methodologies upon which an issuer may reasonably base its decisions.	Reserve information is imprecise due to the inherent uncertainties in, and the limited nature of, the database upon which the estimating and auditing of reserve information is predicated. The methods and data used in estimating reserve information are often necessarily indirect or analogical in character rather than direct or deductive. The extent and significance of the judgments to be made are, in themselves, sufficient to render reserve information inherently imprecise.
Reference	*Management's Report on Internal Control over Financial Reporting. Staff Statement. U.S. Securities Exchange Commission.*	*Standards Pertaining to the Estimating and Auditing of Oil and Gas Reserve Information.* 1997 SPE/World Petroleum Council Resolution.

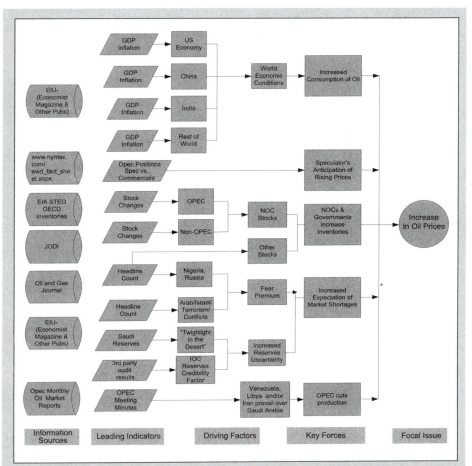

Fig. 4–16. San Felipe Resources conceptual model for crude oil price behavior

They then gathered SFR's crude oil "price deck," or the series of oil prices for the next 10 years that the finance group was using to develop its earnings forecast. Basically, the corporate assumption was that oil prices would increase over the next eight years at the same rate of projected U.S. economic growth (assumed to be at 3%/year), thereafter leveling out to $50/bbl as shown in figure 4–17.

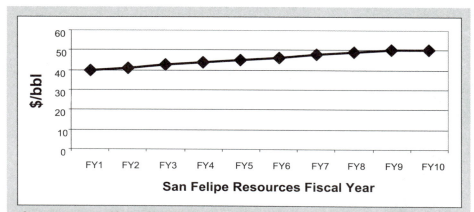

Fig. 4–17. Imported low sulfur light crude oil price forecast (San Felipe Resources)

The problem was that there seemed to be no logic behind these assumptions. Most oil economists agree that energy consumption and GDP are positively correlated, but this does not mean that prices, consumption, and GDP are correlated on a one-to-one basis. Barry and Elena realized that there were serious problems with the assumptions inherent in their company's price forecast. So they turned to their conceptual model for help. In this way, they were effectively applying Ralph's third method, the model method, to find a more substantiated oil price forecast.

One of the data sources that was frequently cited was the Energy Information Administration (EIA) *Annual Energy Outlook* (AEO) forecast. The data was readily available in electronic form off the Internet, so they used the current EIA five-year forecast (fig. 4–18).

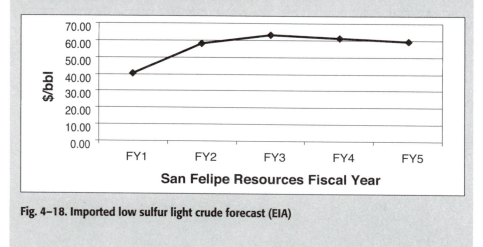

Fig. 4–18. Imported low sulfur light crude forecast (EIA)

Even though they knew that the EIA had petroleum economists and sophisticated forecasting models, they still wondered how reliable this forecast was. So they decided to try to apply Ralph's second method, the historical method, and compare EIA historical forecasts to actual prices. They did this by performing a simple backtest using a technique called *graphical spot-checking* of the EIA forecasts. They selected five historical EIA forecasts termed *AEO series* and compared them to the actual prices for the years 1999–2004. Unfortunately, the results (as shown in fig. 4–19) were not very reassuring.

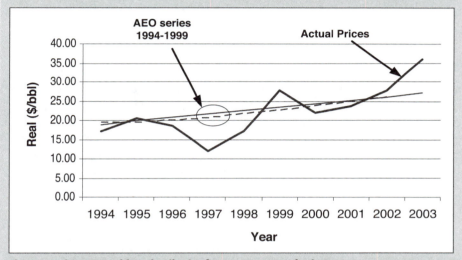

Fig. 4–19. Five EIA world crude oil price forecasts vs. actual prices

What the plot of forecasts vs. actuals demonstrated in figure 4–19 was that for any year between 1994 and 1999, the government forecast either inaccurately predicted the direction or the level of crude prices in the front year and also over a five-year horizon. Furthermore, there was a problem with timeliness. Each *Annual Energy Outlook* (AEO) forecast was released with at least a one-year time delay from the current year. Thus the AEO for 1994 effectively had 1993 actuals and a 1994 estimate. Since their 1994 estimate did not match the 1994 actual prices at the time of release, the AEO forecasts for the front year (in this case 1995) were out-of-date as soon as they were released. Barry and Elena determined that they needed an estimate that was more timely and consistent than that provided by the EIA.

The road to reliability: timeliness and consistency

Barry and Elena then broadened their search, reconsidering each of the possible information sources from their oil pricing model. They looked at one multilateral source, the International Energy Agency (IEA), and a British source, the Economist Intelligence Unit. They considered *Oil & Gas Journal* data, as well as that from the futures markets off the NYMEX. What they found was that with the exception of the NYMEX real-time pricing information, most of the data sources offered data from a historical perspective. Those sources provided good lagging indicators, but Barry and Elena needed more immediate and forward-looking information than was available from many of these sources. After much searching, they finally came upon the Organization of Petroleum Exporting Countries (OPEC) Web site that described what it called the Joint Oil Data Initiative (JODI) World Database. The stated goal of JODI was, according to its Web site, to "quantify and qualify the availability and timeliness of monthly oil data." Upon looking carefully at the JODI data, they saw that there were seven independent contributors to this database, including OPEC itself. Furthermore, JODI apparently performed some due diligence on the data. They had applied a rating to the information received and reported on it along three criteria, as shown in their legend (fig. 4–20). This was exactly what Barry and Elena were after!

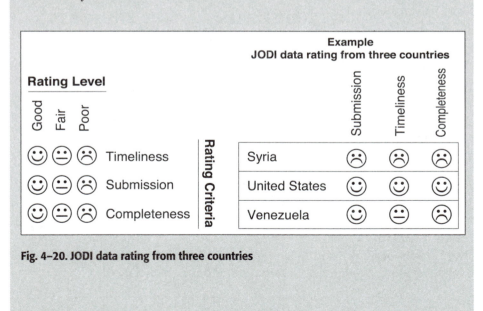

Fig. 4–20. JODI data rating from three countries

The JODI database did not provide price projections. However, for country production data and other supply/demand information required by their conceptual model, the JODI database provided the consistency they needed to make some of the SFR assumptions and future price projections more defensible. By comparing data from the seven different contributors, the JODI World Database achieved, at least to some extent, the intent of Ralph's fourth method, checks and balances by analogy and/or comparison.

There was one other technique that Barry remembered from his talks with someone from SFR's treasury department. SFR had a number of adjustable rate loans, making interest rate fluctuations potentially hazardous to SFR's liquidity. The assistant treasurer once explained to Barry that the treasury group was concerned about a liquidity crisis due to swings in interest rates that could threaten their bond ratings. To ensure that they were not in danger of possible downgrades, the treasury analysts regularly practiced simple, but effective, interest rate risk management. They not only monitored their corporate liquidity on a nominal or "budgeted" set of assumptions, but they routinely developed alternative cases that the assistant treasurer called "stress tests." These stress tests took the form of scenarios, sensitivities, or single event risks that were a variation of the budgeted or base case. Combined with the base case, these stress tests provided more than a deterministic analysis. They were the first step to a risk-based approach to financial controls.

Barry and Elena at last had everything they needed to create a systematic approach to do some spot checks on the reliability of information they used in their enterprise risk system. They were now in a position to begin to write their own information integrity policy manual for SFR.

Assessment: Parting Shots

There are a few observations a risk analyst might consider at this point concerning the vignette and the application of the assessment tools:

1. If you were on the board of directors of a large integrated oil company and were considering application of the 20-question governance guidelines for information integrity presented in this chapter, what level of compliance with the questions would you be willing to accept from your company's management? Consider how you would customize the application of these guidelines to your company by incorporating the concept of "fit for purpose" into the acceptance criteria.

2. Assuming that corporate stakeholders are a 21st-century energy company's customers. What methods and tools from the field of industrial market research could be used to segment, specify, and quantify stakeholder needs?

3. What are the growing competitive threats facing the world's existing investor-owned energy companies? Who are the emerging competitors, from what countries will they come, and how are they threatening to "change the rules of the game?"

4. How does geopolitical instability affect trust between companies and stakeholders, and what is the effect of a breakdown in trust on requiring assurance through certification processes?

References

1. Hamid, S. 2005. Research, understanding the types of resources. Purdue University Online Writing Lab. (August). http://owl.english.purdue.edu/workshops/hypertext/ResearchW/resource.html

2. Lyons, K. 2005. How to distinguish between primary and secondary sources. University Library, University of Southern California Santa Cruz. (November). http://library.ucsc.edu/ref/howto/primarysecondary.html

3. Ibid.

4. Ibid.

5. Ibid.

6. Ibid.

7. Ibid.

8. Tufte, E. 2006. *Beautiful Evidence*. Chesire, CT: Graphics Press LLC. www.edwardtufte.com

9. Ibid.

10. Harrison Smith, S. 2004. *The Fact Checker's Bible, A Guide to Getting It Right*. New York: Anchor Books.

11. Arner, D. C., and W. C. Angstadt. 2001. Where for art thou failure rate data? Presented at ISA Conference, Houston, TX, September 11. http://www.aiche.org/CCPS/Active Projects/PERD/Publications/FailureRate.aspx

12. Economist Intelligence Unit. A methodology that sets the standard. http://www.eiu.com

13. International Energy Forum Secretariat. 2006. *Joint Oil Data Initiative Manual*. Riyadh, Saudi Arabia. November. http://www.jodidata.org/FileZ/ODTmain.htm

14. Tufte, E. 2006.

15. Harrison Smith, S. 2004.

16. Society of Petroleum Engineers. 2001. *Standards Pertaining to the Estimating and Auditing of Oil and Gas Reserve Information*. (June). Society of Petroleum Engineers. p. 8.

17. Basel Committee on Banking Supervision. 2005. *Amendment to the Capital Accord to Incorporate Market Risks*. Basel Committee on Banking Supervision, Bank for International Settlements. November. Accompanying document: Basel Committee on Banking Supervision. 1996. *Supervisory Framework for the Use of "Backtesting" in Conjunction with the Internal Models Approach to Market Risk Capital Requirements*. (January). p. 2.

18. Ibid. p. 2.

19. Society of Petroleum Engineers. 2001. p. 8.

20. Tufte, E. R. 2004. *The Visual Display of Quantitative Information*. 2nd ed. Cheshire, CT: Graphics Press LLC. www.edwardtufte.com

21. Tague, N. R. 2004. *The Quality Toolbox*. 2nd edition. Milwaukee: ASQ, Quality Press.

22. Lamprecht, J. L. 2005. Intuitive statistics, the value of graphs in decision making. Chapter 1 in *Applied Data Analysis in Process Improvement*. ASQ, Quality Press.

23. Tufte, E. R. 2004.

24. Tague, N. R. 2004.

25. Ioannidis, J. P. 2005. Why most published research findings are false. *Public Library of Science Medicine*. 2 (August). e124.

26. Morgan, G. M., and M. Henrion. 1998. Analytica: a software tool for uncertainty analysis and model communication. Chapter 10 in *Uncertainty, a Guide to Dealing with Uncertainty in Quantitative Risk and Policy Analysis*. New York: Cambridge University Press. p. 258.

27. Day, A. L. 2003. *Mastering Risk Modelling: A Practical Guide to Modelling Uncertainty with Excel*. UK: Pearson Education Limited.

28. Committee of Chief Risk Officers. 2002. *Governance and Controls*. Vol. 2 of 6. Committee of Chief Risk Officers, Organizational Independence and Governance Working Group. White paper. November 19. CCRO.

29. Committee of Sponsoring Organizations of the Treadway Commission. 2004. *Enterprise Risk Management—Integrated Framework and Application Techniques*. September. New Jersey: COSO. p. 47. Draft of Executive Summary can be accessed at http://www.erm. coso.org/Coso/coserm.nsf/vwWebResources/PDF_Manuscript/$file/COSO_ Manuscript.pdf

30. Ibid. p. 47.

31. Aragonés, J. R., Blanco, C., and K. Dowd. 2001. Incorporating stress tests into market risk modeling. *Institutional Investor*. (Spring).

Further reading:

Murtha, J. 2000. *Decisions Involving Uncertainty: An @Risk Tutorial for the Petroleum Industry*. Newfield, NY: Palisade Corporation.

Disposition 5

The third phase of the external information integrity (EII) process is termed *disposition* because it involves deciding to take action based on the results of an assessment of the information. Thus, more than the other two EII phases, the disposition phase uses strategic tools to support management decisions. As such, it corresponds closely to the "risk response," "information & communication," and "monitoring" activities of the COSO enterprise risk framework, as shown in figure 5–1.

The similarity between the EII definition of disposition and that of the three activities of the COSO framework is that they both involve information processing to bring external information in-house for action. The COSO enterprise risk framework and its predecessor publication on internal control were the response of accounting and finance trade groups to the governance and accounting scandals of the late 1990s. The timing of the ERM publication in 2004 provided an example of how a holistic, risk-based approach could be taken toward compliance with the U.S. Sarbanes-Oxley Act of 2002. However, since the publication of the COSO framework, corporate governance trends have evolved, underscoring the need for the application of specific tools as described in this chapter. One such trend is the increased demand by stakeholders for transparency of information used for decision making. To deal with this, our *documentation guidelines* and *enterprise risk register* tools describe ways that information should be captured, stored, and communicated to reinforce transparency in decision making. Another trend is increased geopolitical uncertainty and how it affects foreign direct investments. Of course, political risk has always been a consideration for multinational oil companies. Today, however, there is a resurgence of resource nationalism, with its familiar cycle of nationalizations, expropriations, and unilateral abrogation of contracts by host governments. To face these challenges, two strategy tools are presented: *political risk* and *scenario analysis*. These tools will be used to consider the potential threats (and opportunities). Finally, the broad and ongoing strategic issue is addressed concerning how threats and opportunities can be identified through superior market intelligence using a procedure for *environmental scanning*.

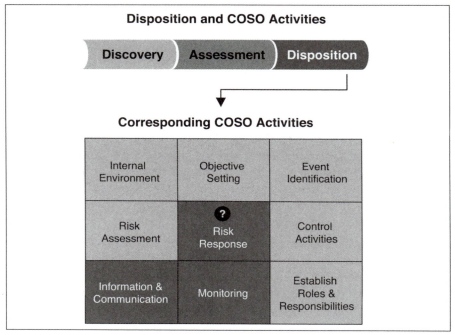

Fig. 5–1. EII process

As in previous chapters, a general road map or outline of the disposition phase illustrating the tools to be profiled is shown in figure 5–2.

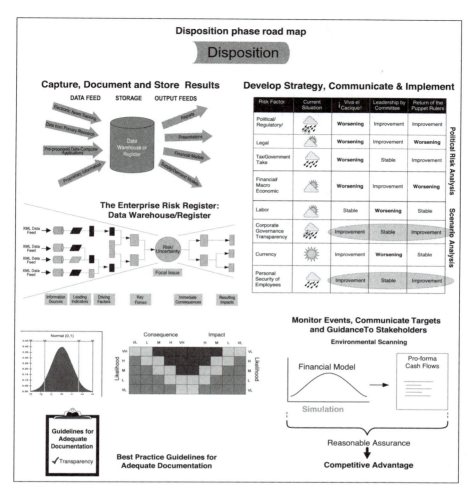

Disposition phase road map

Disposition

Capture, Document and Store Results

DATA FEED   STORAGE   OUTPUT FEEDS

Electronic News Tracking

Data from Primary Research

Pre-processed Data-Computer Applications

Proprietary Information

Data Warehouse or Register

Reports

Presentations

Financial Models

Supply-Demand Models

The Enterprise Risk Register: Data Warehouse/Register

XML Data Feed

Risk/Uncertainty

Focal Issue

| Information Sources | Leading Indicators | Driving Factors | Key Forces | Immediate Consequences | Resulting Impacts |

Normal (0,1)

Consequence   Impact

VL L M H VH   H M L VL

Likelihood

Guidelines for Adequate Documentation

✓ Transparency

Best Practice Guidelines for Adequate Documentation

Develop Strategy, Communicate & Implement

Risk Factor	Current Situation	¡Viva el Cacique!	Leadership by Committee	Return of the Puppet Rulers
Political/ Regulatory/		Worsening	Improvement	Improvement
Legal		Worsening	Improvement	Worsening
Tax/Government Take		Worsening	Stable	Improvement
Financial/ Macro Economic		Worsening	Improvement	Worsening
Labor		Stable	Worsening	Stable
Corporate Governance Transparency		Improvement	Stable	Improvement
Currency		Improvement	Worsening	Stable
Personal Security of Employees		Improvement	Stable	Improvement

Political Risk Analysis

Scenario Analysis

Monitor Events, Communicate Targets and GuidanceTo Stakeholders

Environmental Scanning

Financial Model

Pro-forma Cash Flows

Simulation

Reasonable Assurance

↓

Competitive Advantage

Fig. 5–2. Outline of disposition phase

Upon inspection of these tools, it is evident that they all involve some process for capture, documentation, and display of information. Again, some of these tools should look familiar since they have their basis in the quality management, decision analysis, strategic planning, and market research techniques that have been developed over the past 20 years. However, as with the other tools presented in this book, the disposition tools have been refined for ensuring better information leading to competitive advantage.

Disposition Toolbox

This final set of tools deals with communication, documentation, and action. As with the discovery and assessment tools, each of the following detailed tool descriptions provides a process for its implementation that is both rational and defensible. They also complete the basic information integrity toolbox, which is critical to a robust enterprise risk system.

Management decisions often rely on analysis of reams of data, but at the core, uncertainty remains as the chief challenge of decision making. Stress testing was introduced in chapter 4 as way to convert "what should happen" into "what could happen." Yet performing a stress test is only a step in the right direction. The results must still somehow be addressed. Furthermore, most stress tests require a quantitative model, yet most problems in life are qualitative by nature! To address these concerns (the need for action and a tool for uncertainty that deals with qualitative or conceptual models), the first disposition tool is presented. This tool is a stress testing technique from the field of strategic planning: *scenario planning*.

Scenario Planning

Scenario planning is a strategic risk management technique for considering what could happen in the future and its possible impact on a company's business drivers. The goal of scenario planning is not to obtain an accurate picture of tomorrow, but to establish the basis for good decision making. Its origins come from two unlikely sources: the theater and warfare. Scenario building skills include storytelling and market research, combined with an understanding of finance and operations. In the words of Peter Schwartz, one of the world's leading practitioners of the art of business scenario planning, "Scenarios are stories about the way the world might turn out tomorrow."[1]

Disposition Tool 1: Scenario Planning

As mentioned, scenario planning is a strategic risk management technique for considering what could happen in the future and its possible impact on a company's business drivers. As such, scenarios can be used as the basis for a new business strategy or they can be a way of testing the robustness of an existing plan. In either case, they fall into the category of stress testing the company's assumptions about the future. In financial risk management, the concept of creating a scenario falls somewhere between performing a sensitivity analysis and applying the concept of single event risk to a portfolio. The diagram in figure 5–3 illustrates how sensitivities, scenarios, and single event risks fit together under the umbrella of stress testing for energy risk management.

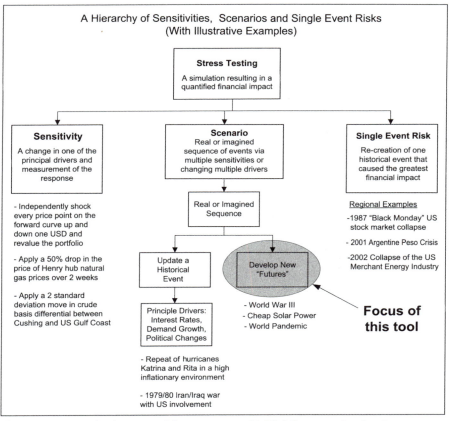

Fig. 5–3. Stress testing in energy risk management highlighting scenario planning

As shown in figure 5–3, sensitivities measure the effect of modifying one driver at a time. Single event risk varies one or more drivers based on a major (or extreme) event. In contrast, scenarios incorporate changes in many different events and drivers at once to create new "futures." The focus of this tool is to describe how to develop "futures scenarios" for energy risk management in order to know what external information is critical to monitor to have assurance that risks are being managed. In this way, scenario planning is a key tool supporting the criticality fundamental of assuring information integrity.

Challenges of the scenario development approach. Author and futurist Peter Schwartz states in his seminal book, *The Art of the Long View*, that scenarios are **not** predictions, but rather stories about the way the world *might* turn out tomorrow.[2] Additionally, scenarios are more than simply the high/low/base case approach common to engineering or economic analysis. This is because the high and low cases are often no more than a type of sensitivity off of the base case rather than a real scenario as has been defined in this text. Instead, the scenarios might need to be almost "way out there" in order to capture the spectrum of possible (yet plausible) outcomes. Another requirement is that they must capture the imagination of the audience in order to break through their barrier of disbelief or preconceived notions. On the other hand, in contrast to pure theater, these business stories must be believable and have a basis in fact in order to be effective. Balancing the visionary and artistic with the realistic and factual is difficult because it involves both right- and left-brained thinking. One additional challenge for scenario planning is having a systematic process for scenario development, effectively answering the question, "Where do I begin?" Thus development of futures scenarios is the process of visualizing, articulating, and communicating fantastic but plausible stories in a systematic and repeatable manner.

Elements of good scenarios. Scenarios should start with a strategic business decision to be made. The business decision is the kernel of the scenario development process, and often other tools and techniques are woven together with scenario planning to arrive at a decision. For example, a decision to enter into a new foreign market requires use of the political risk tool supported by the scenario analysis and information testing and validation techniques described elsewhere in this book. The decision to invest in a new technology might involve a Delphi session to flush out critical uncertainties that, in turn, feed into the scenario process.

After the strategic decision is identified, it is necessary to research a solid basis of background facts. As mentioned previously, factual background information provides a credible, realistic foundation for the business story. This means that as a minimum, the analyst should establish a solid foundation of external information about customers, suppliers, and competitors as well as social, political, and economic trends affecting the decision. Best practice is to have experienced market researchers gather this information using surveys, reliable secondary data sources, and information testing and validation techniques.

Visualization, articulation, and communication are the keys to developing robust scenarios. Projecting into the future (visualization) requires a certain degree of right-brained thinking, and to be effectively communicated, these projections must be molded and articulated into stories with different themes. It is tempting to develop just three stories, but the disadvantage to three scenarios is that it feels too much like the high/low/base case format often used for management decision making. Using high/low/base cases leads decision makers to select the base case as the "most likely" or "most probable," and then they forget about the high and low cases. By doing this, the analyst is encouraging forecasting rather than a risk-based approach. In contrast, the purpose of futures scenarios is to discourage forecasting by presenting the spectrum of possibilities, which is the essence of a risk-based approach. To do this requires careful formulation of mutually exclusive themes, each with its own catchy but descriptive title. It may seem trite to label each story with a clever little title for a business presentation. However, without this theatrical technique, it is difficult to communicate the essence of each theme or to capture the imagination of the audience (so they will suspend their preconceptions).

Scenario building—a road map. One of the main challenges of building scenarios is knowing where and how to start. The scenario building process as mentioned above must begin with a question, and it must be based upon solid factual information, but beyond this, what is a step-by-step process for developing scenarios? Figure 5–4 illustrates one process for scenario building that has been used by multinational oil companies. The exclamation marks indicate the information integrity "hold points" in the process, where it is important to obtain reliable factual information.

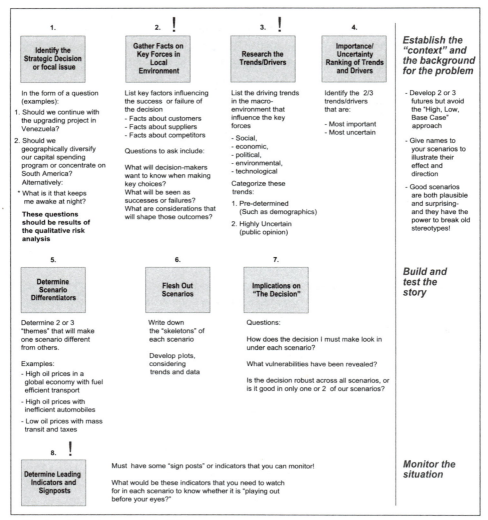

1.

| Identify the Strategic Decision or focal issue |

In the form of a question (examples):

1. Should we continue with the upgrading project in Venezuela?

2. Should we geographically diversify our capital spending program or concentrate on South America? Alternatively:

* What is it that keeps me awake at night?

These questions should be results of the qualitative risk analysis

2. !

| Gather Facts on Key Forces in Local Environment |

List key factors influencing the success or failure of the decision
- Facts about customers
- Facts about suppliers
- Facts about competitors

Questions to ask include:

What will decision-makers want to know when making key choices?
What will be seen as successes or failures?
What are considerations that will shape those outcomes?

3. !

| Research the Trends/Drivers |

List the driving trends in the macro-environment that influence the key forces

- Social,
- economic,
- political,
- environmental,
- technological

Categorize these trends:

1. Pre-determined (Such as demographics)

2. Highly Uncertain (public opinion)

4.

| Importance/ Uncertainty Ranking of Trends and Drivers |

Identify the 2/3 trends/drivers that are:

- Most important
- Most uncertain

Establish the "context" and the background for the problem

- Develop 2 or 3 futures but avoid the "High, Low, Base Case" approach

- Give names to your scenarios to illustrate their effect and direction

- Good scenarios are both plausible and surprising-and they have the power to break old stereotypes!

5.

| Determine Scenario Differentiators |

Determine 2 or 3 "themes" that will make one scenario different from others.

Examples:
- High oil prices in a global economy with fuel efficient transport

- High oil prices with inefficient automobiles

- Low oil prices with mass transit and taxes

6.

| Flesh Out Scenarios |

Write down the "skeletons" of each scenario

Develop plots, considering trends and data

7.

| Implications on "The Decision" |

Questions:

How does the decision I must make look in under each scenario?

What vulnerabilities have been revealed?

Is the decision robust across all scenarios, or is it good in only one or 2 of our scenarios?

Build and test the story

8. !

| Determine Leading Indicators and Signposts |

Must have some "sign posts" or indicators that you can monitor!

What would be these indicators that you need to watch for in each scenario to know whether it is "playing out before your eyes?"

Monitor the situation

Fig. 5–4. Steps to scenario building

Enterprise risk management application

The scenario analysis technique's most appropriate enterprise risk management application is in risk assessment of potentially large consequence, difficult-to-quantify oil and gas venture risks (or uncertainties) after they have been identified. Typically, scenarios are most valuable in assessing the following categories of risks:

- The risks of pandemics, world terrorism, and natural disasters

- Political risk

- Regulatory risk

- Risks of entry into foreign markets

- Risks of the launch of a new technology

- Strategic and market risks, such as those resulting from dramatic commodity price changes, increased competitive threats, and increased customer buying power

Scenarios are not as useful as other standard risk and quality management tools and techniques for assessing operational risks, such as supply interruptions, health, safety, and environmental risks, project risks of schedule delays, cost overruns, and financial risks.

Other considerations

Scenario planning is not an easily mastered technique. Successful scenario planning requires competence in market research, strategy development, and facilitation, as well as a global perspective on risk and considerable practice. The value of scenarios is often not appreciated by those who have not worked in strategic planning. However, many companies and nongovernmental institutions use scenarios as part of their planning process. Examples include Shell International Ltd., which produces and publishes the *Shell Global Scenarios to 2025* and the World Economic Forum, which produces the annual *Global Risks* reports.[3,4]

Our second tool, political risk analysis, builds on the ability to develop scenarios and applies the filter of regulatory, legal, labor, social, and other nontechnical factors associated with doing business to the scenario planning process. The energy industry faces specific challenges in terms of political risk that are conveniently framed by the structure of a document published by a leading oil and gas industry trade association, the Independent Petroleum Association of America, which I reference in the following tool description.

Political Risk Analysis

The goal of a political risk analysis is to provide a bounded spectrum of possible political/economic outcomes upon which business managers can make risk control decisions. This method is a systematic, qualitative approach for analyzing the political risks facing an energy company. It relies heavily on techniques used in political science, scenario development, and market research.

The most appropriate application of political risk analysis for enterprise risk management is in risk identification for a foreign energy investment project. To comply with the requirements of the information integrity competence fundamental, it is important to have analysts who are knowledgeable about (foreign) country history, language, and culture, as well as strategic planning and market research methods. A robust process is also useful, as is a checklist of questions to expose domestic political issues, international business practices, and various political issues within the country in question.

Regardless of the political risk analysis framework used, the analyst should adapt it to the specifics of the company and country under consideration. This can be done by carefully considering the characteristics of the company and the investment, and then "mapping," or matching those characteristics against the elements of the generic framework selected. For example, an oil industry service company would be much less concerned with the risk of expropriation than a drilling rig contractor or an operator with significant assets on the ground. Adapting the political risk framework and weighting each element relative to its bearing on the problem at hand is an important part of the political risk analysis process.

Disposition Tool 2: Political Risk Analysis

This method is a systematic, qualitative approach for analyzing the political risks facing an energy company. What is political risk? One of the best definitions available for energy companies is given by the Independent Petroleum Association of America (IPAA) in the *Assessing Political Risk* supplement to its *International Primer*. To quote the IPAA document, political risk analysis involves the identification and assessment of events such as "expropriation, revolution, civil disorder, creeping expropriation, unilateral imposition of new taxes and royalties, imposition of export controls or withdrawing licenses for export or import, exchange control restrictions and other factors that reduce or destroy the value of an international energy venture."[5] There are three important implications to this definition. First, political risk does not cover technical or market risks. Second, it is not concerned with political change that has little or no impact on the value of the venture. Finally, political risk analysis is not political forecasting or prediction. The goal of a political risk analysis is to provide a bounded spectrum of possible political/economic outcomes upon which business managers can make risk control decisions.

This method relies heavily on the techniques used in political science, scenario development, and market research. Thus, to perform a reliable political risk analysis, the analyst should have a certain degree of competence in each of these areas. Each field, in turn, has its own body of knowledge from which it draws. Political science depends upon the fields of sociology and history, and scenario development depends upon military strategy and theater. Finally, solid market research provides the critical "glue" that holds political science and scenario development together to yield credible, defensible analyses and recommendations.

While the IPAA document mentioned previously gives an excellent overview of the political risk process, it does not provide a step-by-step approach to its implementation. Therefore, the purpose of this monograph is to expand on the IPAA approach and provide additional guidance on implementation as well as on the quality of information required for successful political risk management. More in-depth discussion of both scenario analyses and market research techniques are given elsewhere in the text.

Enterprise risk management application

The most appropriate application of political risk analysis for enterprise risk management is in risk identification for a foreign energy investment project. It is less well suited to quantitative analysis since it relies heavily the inherently qualitative "futures scenarios" process described later in the text. To comply with the requirements of the information integrity competence fundamental, it is important to have analysts who are knowledgeable about (foreign) country history, language, and culture, as well as strategic planning and market research methods. The overall process for political risk analysis that will be explored is shown in figure 5–5.

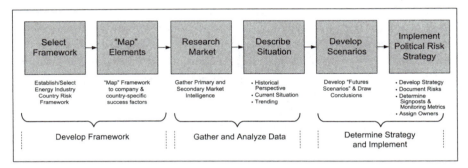

Fig. 5–5. The political risk analysis process

Detailed description of the political risk process

Developing the framework. As mentioned, the IPAA provides a robust framework specific to the oil and gas industry for political risk. However, the IPAA framework is not easy to use as a tool because it is in narrative form. Another well-developed framework is the International Project Risk Assessment checklist tool developed by the Construction Industry Institute (CII).[6] Although not specific to the energy industry and not as in-depth in the areas of creeping nationalization and the sanctity of contract law as the IPAA document, the CII approach may be easier to implement because it provides checklists. Combining the elements of the IPAA document with the checklist structure of the CII tool, a sample energy industry political risk checklist is shown in figure 5–6.

Domestic Political Issues	Favorable	Acceptable	Unfavorable
1. Ease of exit strategy	☐	☐	☐
2. Governmental delays in processing permits, applications, etc.	☐	☐	☐
3. Level of politically motivated interference due to sovereign economic dependence on oil and gas revenues	☐	☐	☐
4. Restrictions on operations due to local laws, culture, traditions, religion and history	☐	☐	☐
5. Track record of orderly change of government control	☐	☐	☐
International Business Practices	**Favorable**	**Acceptable**	**Unfavorable**
6. Level of corruption and bribery	☐	☐	☐
International Political Issues	**Favorable**	**Acceptable**	**Unfavorable**
7. Ability to use international law	☐	☐	☐
8. Boundary disputes between adjoining or adjacent countries	☐	☐	☐
9. Creeping nationalism	☐	☐	☐
10. Currency controls	☐	☐	☐
11. Expropriation of assets by the national government	☐	☐	☐
12. Unilateral U.S. government sanctions and U.S. caused business interruption and asset seizures	☐	☐	☐

Fig. 5–6. Political risk checklist

Regardless of the generic framework used, the analyst should adapt it to the specifics of the company and country under consideration. This can be done by carefully considering the characteristics of the company and the investment and then "mapping" or matching those characteristics against the elements of the generic framework selected. For example, an oil industry service company would be much less concerned with the risk of expropriation than a drilling rig contractor or an operator with significant assets on the ground. Craft labor conditions and boundary disputes with neighboring countries would be less of a concern for a British engineering company working in Norway than a Canadian independent oil and gas exploration company operating in Nigeria. Thus, adapting the framework and weighting each element relative to its bearing on the problem at hand is an important part of the *develop framework* phase of the political risk process.

Gathering and analyzing data. If developing the framework allows the analyst to know what data is needed, the *gather and analyze data* phase involves knowing how to get the information to feed the analysis. From an information integrity perspective, this is perhaps the most important step in the process. In spite of this, information gathering is often performed carelessly and in an unstructured manner by people who have little experience or training in market research. Internet searches combined with the "executive world tour" approach to gathering information (where an upper-level executive drops into the country for a day or two, talks to some people over lunch and dinner, and then flies out with his mind made up) are poor excuses for political risk data gathering. Instead, the most reliable market intelligence available using international market research techniques should be used. The appropriate depth of market research will depend upon requirements and will dictate use of secondary (public and private published sources) or both secondary and primary (interviews, surveys, and site visits) techniques.

Political risk data gathering should be carried out with the same level of care and competence as with any technical or financial analysis. This means that the sources of the data must be credible. To be credible, they should be tested by the accuracy fundamentals criteria in the information governance checklist and using the information testing and validation tool presented in chapter 4. It also means that well-established market research techniques for activities such as questionnaire design, conducting interviews, and gathering information from published sources should be used. Finally, capturing the information and documenting the sources and dates gathered in a simple market intelligence database is essential to ensure transparency of the process. The results of this phase yield a historical perspective, a current situation analysis, and a trending assessment on the risk elements for each country environment analyzed.

Determine strategy and implement. Strategy development takes into account the current situation and trends and uses expert judgment to create an overall game plan or path forward for the company. Like risk management, which often considers the full spectrum or "distribution" of possibilities, strategy development is not forecasting and should not be a deterministic exercise. Instead, strategy development should also consider a spectrum of possibilities. Thus, creating scenarios is an important political risk step between gathering the data and implementing the plan. As mentioned before, an accepted approach to developing scenarios is to combine solid market research with a strategic planning approach pioneered in the 1960s, called *futures scenario planning*, which is covered in the last tool. Based on Peter Schwartz's book and the writings of others, it can be said that the critical phases of scenario planning as applied to political risk analysis are as follows:

1. *Establish the context or the background for the problem by determining the company's goals and objectives for foreign market entry.* This phase also includes gathering the market intelligence as previously mentioned.

2. *Build and test the story.* This includes developing three or more possible stories or futures scenarios.

3. *Plan the strategy.* Instead of selecting one scenario as the base case, the futures approach requires that the risk analyst consider all of the scenarios and plan the strategy based upon the commonalities (or common conclusions) that can be drawn across all of the scenarios. By developing possible future political/economic scenarios together with the operations team in a facilitated project workshop, the risk analyst can project the potential impact of events on the critical success factors of the project and the business. Again, this is not meant to yield a forecast, but instead uses a systematic process to put reasonable parameters around the conceivable range of consequences.

Once the scenarios have been developed and commonalities analyzed, they form the solid basis for investment decisions, resource assignment, and political risk control.

Reliable data and systematic analysis are the foundations of robust decision support. Increasingly, however, decision support is not the only goal of a successful enterprise risk system. *Assurance* is emerging as the gold standard for stakeholder trust in future performance, and thus a significant strategic goal of the 21st-century company. Those "pesky" interested parties—in the form of auditors, regulators, board members, and investors—are clamoring for this assurance. External and internal stakeholders today demand assurance of a reasonable decision-making process through adequate documentation of assumptions and information. The following discussion provides guidance on how a risk analyst can know when the documentation is adequate.

Documentation Guidelines for Assumptions and Externally Gathered Information

One of the main issues regarding documentation of information is that of sufficiency. How much documentation of the process, the sources, and the assumptions is enough? The answer is not simple. Given the broad group of interested parties (i.e., stakeholders), there cannot be a "one-size-fits-all" prescriptive standard for adequate documentation. Instead, a set of *principles-based guidelines* for documentation should be used.

The following are three basic principles for documentation of external information:

1. Documentation should provide transparency of the information integrity process to all stakeholders. It is not merely the immediate users of the information who require adequate documentation, but everyone with an interest in the company's success. Thus, there should be a system for transparency and traceability that everyone can trust. This does not mean the documentation is made freely available to anyone for the asking, but it does mean that it can be quickly delivered if required to satisfy powerful stakeholders.

2. Transparency includes traceability back to reputable information sources. Important questions here include the following:

   - How much documentation is there of an information trail leading back to some reputable third-party standard or source?

   - Is the information captured in a well-structured, secure, searchable electronic database?

3. Transparency involves substantiation of critical assumptions. Are the assumptions logical, well founded, and clearly documented?

Without documentation, there is no evidence, and without evidence, there is no assurance of reliability. In general, the questions in the information integrity governance guidelines presented in chapter 3 provide a good starting point, or litmus test, to determine whether there are deficiencies in the documentation of the process.

Disposition Tool 3: Documentation Guidelines

We now return to the question previously posed concerning how much documentation of the process, the sources, and the assumptions is enough. The answer requires us first to identify how critical the information is to our objective and then to understand to what degree others may depend upon its accuracy. The more critical the information is, the more care should be taken with its documentation. A utilitarian approach would consider only the requirements of those likely to use the information for decision making. At first glance, this sounds reasonable. For example, the market analyst might gather demand growth information used by the development planners to help them select between different field development options. Following this logic, it would seem reasonable that the planners' requirements dictate the level of documentation of the market researcher's sources and data gathering process. However, this assumes that there are generally accepted standards for documentation, the planners have a quality assurance mindset, and that they are competent in a field outside their own (i.e., economics). Unfortunately, these conditions are rarely met. Furthermore, documentation is not only for the benefit of the immediate user, but for overseers and auditors as well.

In addition to the criticality of the information and the degree to which others depend upon its accuracy, a third factor, the expectations of stakeholders, is a key concern regarding documentation. Given the broad group of interested parties, there cannot be a "one-size-fits-all" prescriptive standard for adequate documentation. As suggested previously, a set of *principle-based guidelines* for documentation should be used instead. Describing these principles and providing guidance for their application is the purpose of this documentation guidelines tool.

The three basic principles behind documentation of external information will now be described in more detail. The first principle introduced was the importance of the transparency of the information integrity process to all stakeholders. As mentioned, it is not merely the immediate users of the information who require adequate documentation, but everyone with an interest in the company's success. Thus, there should be a system for transparency and traceability that everyone can trust.

The first question is whether an information integrity process exists at the company. If it does not exist, in order to provide at least a minimum level of assurance, one should be created. For example, the recommended information integrity process for secondary data presented in chapter 4 as part of the assessment phase is shown in figure 5–7.

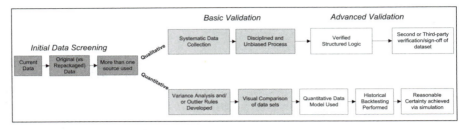

Fig. 5–7. Secondary data validation process

For primary information, written criteria to qualify sources and notes from surveys and personal interviews are probably a minimum level of documentation required.

For critical information where this or another process is adopted, is there documentation to demonstrate that the process actually was followed? Without documentation, there is no evidence, and without evidence, there is no assurance of reliability. It should be noted that the scope for adequate transparency as discussed here does not consider willful fraud and malfeasance. People can always create documentation to cover up fraudulent behavior, but fraud and malfeasance are dealt with through Sarbanes-Oxley legislation (in the United States) and its ensuing internal controls and auditing process.

The second principle requires traceability back to reputable information sources. As mentioned previously, important questions to ask include the following:

- How much documentation is there of an information trail leading back to some reputable third-party standard or source?

- Is the information captured in a well-structured, secure, searchable electronic database?

- Concerning substantiation of critical assumptions, are the assumptions logical, well founded, and clearly documented?

In general, the questions in the information integrity governance guidelines presented in chapter 4 provide a good starting point or litmus test concerning any possible deficiencies in the documentation of the process.

Other considerations

There are some established standards and best practices for documentation of models, quality management systems, and projects that are useful to consider when looking at requirements for adequate documentation of information. Although not precisely dealing with assumptions and external information, a few pertinent notes from these references are worth considering, such as the following:

- *Mastering Risk Modelling*, by Alastair Day, provides an excellent set of guidelines allowing for transparency in risk modeling.[7] Mr. Day's guidelines include how to design a risk model so that it can be easily explained to others. Although not strictly dealing with the quality of the documentation supporting inputs, his recommendations regarding layout of the model and the visual display of inputs, calculations, and outputs facilitate model transparency by simplifying the format of risk models.

- The U.S. Energy Information Administration (EIA) has its *EIA Standards Manual* for information it collects and distributes dealing with modeling, assumptions, and data sources.[8] Although not very detailed, it looks like a first draft attempt by this government agency toward guidelines for adequate documentation of information. For the risk analyst putting together a company specification for information documentation, this EIA manual might be a good starting point for an outline of what could be included.

- Technical Report ISO/TR 100013, *Guidelines for Quality Management Systems Documentation*, produced by the International Standards Organization, provides principles and a recommended structure for quality policy manuals.[9] The most relevant section of this standard for purposes of information integrity is "Records," Section 4.11. This says that "records state results achieved or provide evidence indicating that the activities indicated in the documented procedures and work instructions are performed. The records should indicate the compliance with the requirements of the quality management system and the specified requirements for the product."[10]

- From the field of offshore oil and gas production, Det Norske Veritas (DNV) is currently revising two of its recommended practices for documentation of offshore projects: *Standard Documentation Types, DNV-RP-A201* and *Documentation of Offshore Projects, DNV-RP-A202*.[11,12] These two standards are very specific to drawings and specifications. They provide a taxonomy or classification system for offshore facility documentation called a *classification information breakdown structure*. The most relevant section of these standards is Section 1.2 of the RP-A201 covering "General Requirements to All Documentation." This section covers a specification for labeling of drawings, including legends, symbols, what should be in the title block, and requirements for revision numbers.

Enterprise risk management application

Adequate documentation may seem solely like a compliance-related activity. However, when the purpose of documentation moves from merely satisfying the auditor to satisfying the stakeholders, documentation becomes a tool for assurance. In this era of investor, regulator, and auditor crisis of confidence, assurance is the ultimate strategic weapon in the battle for competitive differentiation.

Documentation of information can be facilitated with a tool for capturing and storing the raw data. The most complex of these types of tools has been developed to support commodities trading and marketing transactions. For both commercial and legal reasons, every detail of a complex transaction is often electronically documented at the end of each trading day, including how its value changes over time. Documentation in this area is so important that an entire industry has developed around creating this specialized deal capture software. In the area of operational risk management, electronic risk registers are an analogous tool to the deal capture software. As described in the next section, the requirements for modern risk registers have grown beyond the capabilities of the Excel spreadsheet.

Enterprise Risk Register

The use of a risk register (sometimes called a *risk log*) to capture and track risks is a well-established risk management practice. Use of the risk register tool has today become common practice for storing and communicating results from health, safety, environmental, project, or equipment reliability risk workshops. In its basic (or "standard") form, a risk register is the listing of an organization or project's identified risks, often using Microsoft Excel as a data capturing and reporting tool. However, this minimalist approach to risk registers is inadequate for integrating and aggregating the data from all the different workshops and risk register spreadsheets on a corporate level. A number of new tools, some of which are shown in figure 5–8, can act as modules to the standard risk database, enhancing the capabilities of the standard risk register to create the enterprise risk register.

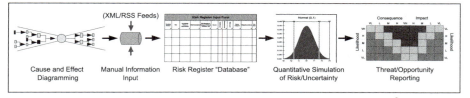

Fig. 5–8. The enterprise risk register

Disposition Tool 4: Enterprise Risk Register

As mentioned previously, in its standard form, a risk register is no more than a listing of an organization or project's identified risks, often using Microsoft Excel as a data capturing and reporting tool. However, the standard risk register cannot provide adequate levels of consistency, accuracy, and transparency to support the demands for assurance from today's corporate stakeholders. The standard risk register is equally deficient in its ability to support strategic-level management decisions because of its limitations as a communication tool. This tool description explains why the standard risk register is inadequate for enterprise risk management. It also describes the characteristics of an enhanced risk capture and communication tool called the *enterprise risk register*.

In its publication called *The Green Book*, the procurement arm of the Treasury of the United Kingdom describes a risk register as a type of log that lists all the identified risks, the results of their analysis, and the status of the risk.[13] An example of a standard risk register for capital projects illustrating typical input categories is shown in figure 5–9.

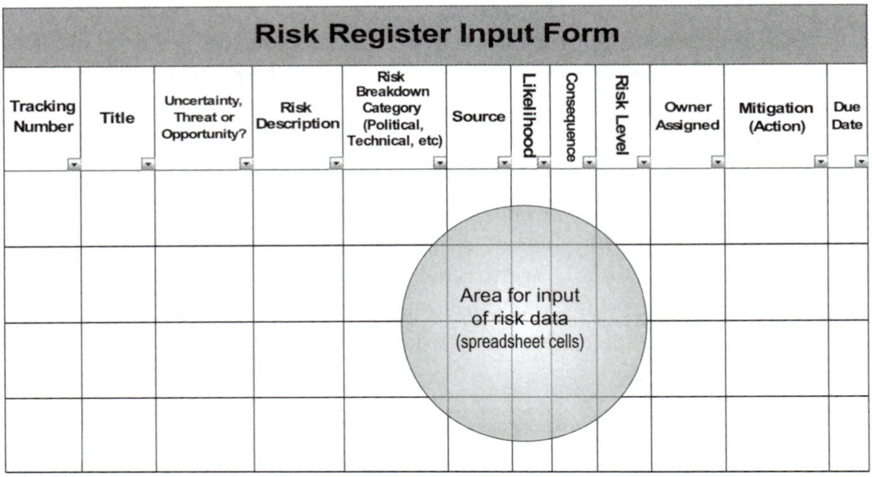

Risk Register Input Form											
Tracking Number	Title	Uncertainty, Threat or Opportunity?	Risk Description	Risk Breakdown Category (Political, Technical, etc)	Source	Likelihood	Consequence	Risk Level	Owner Assigned	Mitigation (Action)	Due Date
					Area for input of risk data (spreadsheet cells)						

Fig. 5–9. Risk register input

Quoting from *The Green Book*, the following is a "fitness for purpose checklist" of questions for a risk register:

1. "Is the Risk log part of a [broader] framework for managing risk?

2. Does the status indicate whether action has been taken or is in a contingency plan?

3. Are the risks uniquely identified (including to which project they refer if the risk relates to a programme)?

4. Has each risk been allocated an owner?

5. Is access to the risk log controlled?

6. Are activities to review the risk log in the stage plans?

7. Have costs been identified for each risk as a "risk allowance?"[14]

This checklist represents the bare minimum of what a risk register should achieve. Furthermore, in many companies today, the risk register is part of what could be called a *minimalist risk process* that includes just three activities: risk identification, qualitative risk assessment, and risk communication. Following this process, the results of the risk identification and qualitative assessment are often manually typed into a spreadsheet register serving as a flat file (as opposed to a relational) database. Finally, the severity of the threats in terms of probability and impact are communicated to management through use of a risk matrix as shown in figure 5–10.

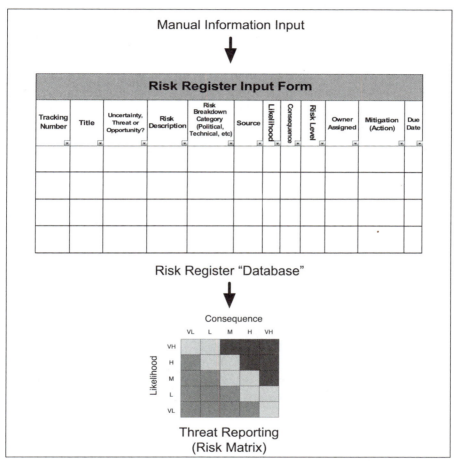

Fig. 5–10. Standard risk register process

Use of the risk register tool has today become common practice for storing and communicating results from health, safety, environmental, project, or equipment reliability risk workshops. However, when integrating and aggregating the data from all the different workshops and spreadsheets is attempted on a corporate level, the minimalist approach and its tools prove to be inadequate. This is because the standard risk register cannot provide the levels of consistency, accuracy, and transparency needed to support the demands for assurance from today's corporate stakeholders. Risk registers in Microsoft Excel do provide (at the very least) a documented way of capturing the organization's risks. However, there must be strict control on where the spreadsheet is stored, who can access it, and how information is entered. Otherwise, spreadsheet risk registers quickly become uncontrolled documents with little or no consistency across users. Given these deficiencies, how should the standard risk register be "enhanced" to create a robust enterprise risk register?

First, to deal with the problem of "multiple versions of the truth" described previously, best practice is to have a centralized database with standard, predefined fields employing various user levels of security. Conceptually, this is a big shift from a simple spreadsheet to a "data warehouse" concept, as illustrated in figure 5–11.

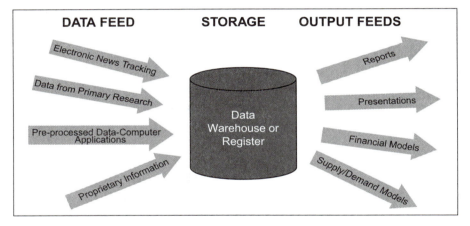

Fig. 5–11. Data warehouse or register

One of the first things a risk analyst might notice about figure 5–11 is that it includes many inputs and outputs that are supposedly not related to risk management. For an enterprise-level application, these inputs and outputs are important. Enterprise needs and drivers are more strategic than those of a project or a health and safety activity for which risk registers are traditionally used. Enterprise inputs and outputs should draw from the broad range of social, technological, environmental, economic, and political categories, instead of simply the impacts and drivers for failure of a piece of equipment or the hazards in a health and safety risk register. Conceptually, the requirements for design of this risk register should be changed from simply an aggregator of risks or a record of actions. Instead, it should be an information system for receipt, storage, and communication of all the data needed to support the risk management process *on the corporate level.* This is a significant change in scope. To illustrate this, the following bow-tie diagram in figure 5–12 compares the scope of a standard risk register to that of the expanded, or enterprise-level, risk register.

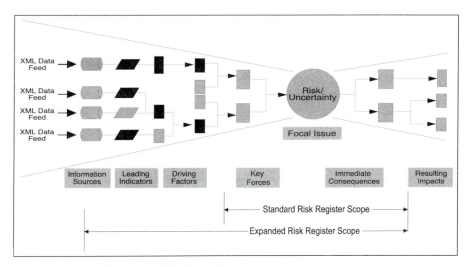

Fig. 5–12. Standard vs. expanded risk register

The darkened blocks in figure 5–12 represent strategic driving factors and leading indicators that require gathering information from outside the organization based on a *criticality analysis* to determine external information intensive elements. In turn, this external information can today be received in real-time using what is called *electronic data feeds* using RSS (Really Simple Syndication). Each of these RSS data streams is coded in XML (Extensible Markup Language), a programming language that contains electronic labels (or *metatags*) attached to different categories of data within the stream. In this way, when the data comes into the expanded risk register, the metatag directs the routing of the data to different fields in the risk register database. In terms of having current information, this is a tremendous advantage over manually typing information into the standard risk register. Furthermore, reporting for enterprise risks goes beyond warnings of threats, showing opportunities as well. Thus, various new risk tools form "modules" in the register to support the entire enterprise risk process, as illustrated in figure 5–13.

Fig. 5–13. Enterprise risk register

Notice that cause and effect diagramming is at the front end of this system. This is critical for defining what goes into the risk register from the external environment by identifying the external information intensive drivers, leading indicators, and the sources for information. Once identified, RSS/XML feeds can be set up to load the register (in real-time as required) with this external information. This information is combined with the manually input information from risk identification workshops, competitor assessments, and general environmental scanning. (See the next tool in the disposition toolbox, *environmental scanning guidelines*, for more information.) The "back end" of the register should have a quantitative module that allows for Monte Carlo simulations of uncertainty, including "mapping" of risk events to various uncertainties in the line items of a financial, market, or other numerical operations model. Finally, reporting of this enterprise risk register system would include display of both threats and opportunities in a matrix.

Enterprise risk management application

As has been shown, the enterprise risk register's application is in all three phases of the external information integrity process: identification, assessment, and disposition. However, the tool's real strength is in mobilizing the attributes of accuracy, consistency, and transparency toward effective communication of risk to internal and external stakeholders. This communication is becoming more and more critical to supporting transparency of the enterprise risk management process. Board members cannot provide adequate oversight unless information is clearly and succinctly communicated to them. Senior managers also cannot make good risk-based decisions unless information is effectively communicated to them. To effectively communicate, graphical interfaces and displays are increasingly being integrated into information systems that collect and process risk data. The enterprise risk register concept represents the next wave in risk communication and the leveraging of risk management to achieve competitive advantage through better corporate decision making.

Other considerations and further enhancements

Value chain development and influence diagramming are two graphical methods described in the "Discovery Tool 2: Enterprise Value Chain Mapping" and the "Discovery Tool 6: Cause and Effect Diagrams" sections elsewhere in this book. These two additional tools should be considered as modules of the enterprise risk register that enhance communication. Finally, display of the current situation, trends, indicators, and warnings in a type of electronic scoreboard, called a *risk dashboard*, could also be considered an enhancement to the enterprise risk register concept. More information on the basics of executive dashboards can be found in a description by a software developer called the Noetix Corporation.[15]

Awareness: the first step toward developing a market view. Until now, the importance of tools and techniques for processing market information has been discussed from the viewpoint of the information already being in place. However, one of the most fundamental questions is, how does an organization get good market information in the first place? Equally important is how the risk analyst maintains an understanding of market trends and events that are constantly changing. These two issues have been pondered by market analysts, strategic planners, and other information experts for many years. If reliable market information is at the very heart of an effective enterprise risk management system, the next tool, *environmental scanning*, becomes as important to risk managers as any simulation tool or analysis technique. In fact, the lack of systematic environmental scanning represents a significant threat to the organization due to market ignorance. Thus, from a strategic standpoint, environmental scanning is one of the most important tools for company success.

Environmental Scanning

Environmental scanning is a systematic process for maintaining an awareness of the events and trends occurring in different fields (society, politics, technology, and economics, among others) that could have an impact on the organization. Rather than a hard and fast procedure, implementing an environmental scanning process is a discipline born out of the organization's attitude, aptitude, and maturity regarding risk, uncertainty, and gathering external information. Perhaps the best characterization of the appropriate environmental scanning approach for today's energy company is the idea of "constantly searching with a purpose." Although the process is not easily standardized, a simple series of steps for environmental scanning incorporating all the major elements of an information integrity framework is shown in figure 5–14.

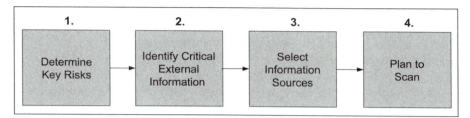

Fig. 5–14. Steps for environmental scanning

Environmental scanning yields better information. According to numerous academic studies over the past 40 years, this better information has led to greater control and improved financial performance in industries ranging from food processing to health care. In spite of the cited benefits and general awareness of environmental scanning as a business practice, there is a surprising lack of consistency or standardization of an environmental scanning process in the energy industry. This is primarily due to a dearth of market research expertise within many energy companies today.

Disposition Tool 5: Environmental Scanning

As mentioned previously, environmental scanning is a systematic process for maintaining an awareness of events and trends. There is an extensive body of knowledge published over the past 40 years dealing with environmental scanning as a business practice. A review of just one paper on environmental scanning published by Dr. Chun Wei Choo, a noted academic researcher in the area of information sciences at the University of Toronto, lists more than 35 references.[16] Furthermore, the application and benefits of environmental scanning have been well documented in the information science literature. Therefore, rather than simply repeating the work of others, the purpose of this monograph is to orient the reader toward how environmental scanning should be used in the context of information integrity and enterprise risk management.

Environmental scanning is a discipline born out of an organization's attitude, aptitude, and maturity regarding risk, uncertainty, and gathering of external information. The way that better information relates to levels of uncertainty and degrees of assurance is illustrated in figure 5–15, which is adapted from the work of Dr. Bryan Wynne, a scientist at the University of Lancaster in the UK.[17]

Fig. 5–15. Degrees of assurance

Environmental scanning leads to better information, and better information to greater control and improved performance. Dr. Choo references six different studies involving companies in industries ranging from food service to health care that show superior financial performance for companies that have a deliberate and concerted environmental scanning effort.[18] In spite of the cited benefits and general awareness of environmental scanning, there is a surprising lack of consistency or standardization of an environmental scanning process. This lack of process often results from individual managers' incompetence in market research techniques, including how to conduct surveys, gather secondary market data, and perform product or service market testing. In the energy industry, this lack of attention to market research seems to be particularly prevalent. Market research experience is not seen as a core skill set nor as a potential source of competitive advantage at most oil and gas companies. Thus, the resulting inexperience affects how energy professionals view (or choose not to view) world events and market forces. As a result, these individuals shape their organizations' behaviors toward formalized environmental scanning. To provide an assessment of how a particular company may stack up, the risk analyst could consider a method for categorizing one company's level of environmental scanning maturity that has been in use for more than 40 years.

In his seminal book, *Scanning the Business Environment*, published in 1967, F. J. Aguilar identified four modes of environmental scanning.[19] These modes of scanning are *undirected viewing, conditioned viewing, enacting,* and *searching.* Dr. Choo has taken this maturity model further, and generally characterized each level. I have prepared a synopsis of these levels in table 5–1.

Table 5–1. Environmental scanning maturity levels for organizations

Mode	Description	Pros	Cons
Undirected Viewing	Passive and unstructured receipt of information through personal contacts and ad hoc information gathering. Subjective/reactive response to external events.	Avoid the costs associated with organizing a system for market intelligence.	Always a follower. Likely to be hit "broadside" by unexpected market developments.
Conditioned Viewing	Passive receipt of "normal" industry information filtered through sources of information selected on the basis of "conditioned" perceptions of the environment built up over time and experience. Reactive and somewhat subjective response to industry events.	No change in paradigm or cultural shift within the organization needed. Minimal time and expense needed for subscriptions to trade journals. Gradual changes are recognized and companies can "jump on the bandwagon" as market shifts occur.	Market intelligence consists of "yesterday's news." Gradual and out-of-date shifts in the market are recognized, but trends and major changes are missed until it is too late to have a first or second mover advantage.
Enacting	"Trial and error" market research through test marketing of new ideas and concepts. Lobbying and product promotion to try to favorably influence the environment.	The company sometimes stumbles upon a successful idea. From time to time, the environment is influenced by the company's promotional activities.	Never able to get out ahead of the curve or to understand why something works until after the fact. Minimal organizational learning achieved.

Mode	Description	Pros	Cons
Searching	Characterized by active and ongoing market intelligence based upon targeted information needs. Organization is likely to have its own scanning unit whose staff systematically analyzes data to produce market forecasts, trend analysis, and intelligence reports.	Surprises in the market are reduced, and there is an opportunity to get out ahead of the curve, shape the environment, and create competitive advantage through differentiation.	This costs money and requires a change in attitude and a new market research skill set on the part of individual staff members.

Strategically placed individuals within an organization make it either an active or passive participant in the market for information. The level of authority, resources, and influence that these people have directly affect the organization's level of environmental scanning maturity. One chief executive I spoke with in a struggling energy company felt that because his external environment changed so slowly, the market information obtained through personal contacts and ad hoc data gathering by his salespeople was adequate. This comment clearly illustrated how little he understood about his own environment. This environment was in fact changing so rapidly that he did not see the private equity investors that entered his business environment with a vengeance, forcing a strategy direction at one of his major competitors. Given this attitude at the top of the company, it is not surprising that *undirected viewing* was the norm throughout his organization.

In contrast to this minimalist approach, a modified form of *searching* is needed to support today's energy company obligations for information integrity and enterprise risk assurance. Thus "constantly searching with a purpose" is perhaps the best characterization of the appropriate environmental scanning approach for today's energy company. To determine this purpose requires individuals and the organization to adopt a systematic environmental scanning process. Figure 5–16 illustrates such a process, incorporating the tools and techniques from this book.

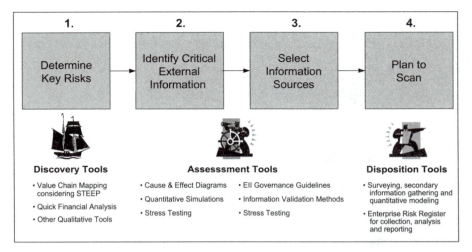

Fig. 5–16. Environmental scanning process

As shown in figure 5–16, implementing a robust environmental scanning process is akin to setting up the information integrity process. The key to effective environmental scanning is to know what to look for, determine where to find it, and separate the important from the trivial. With these considerations, the discovery, assessment, and disposition tools previously described in this book are ideal for setting up a scanning process. Discovery tools such as enterprise value chain mapping, stakeholder analysis, and the Delphi method help identify the needed information by identifying risks and uncertainties relative to specific stakeholder objectives.

A word of caution is warranted here. Risk identification can cause a risk analyst to be blindsided by unexpected events if it is too narrowly focused. Thus, instead of limiting the scanning activity to general economic news found in the local newspaper's business section or to technical information in trade publications, the risk analyst should consider a broader range of topics. This is not easy, but there is an approach that helps keep the scope broad enough: the STEEP taxonomy. During the value chain mapping process, results of the risk identification can be classified into "buckets" using a method of categorization widely used by futurists and strategic planners called *STEEP* (social, technological, economic, environmental, and political). There is nothing magical about STEEP, but it has stood the test of time as a sufficiently broad, memorable acronym for information gathering. Another advantage is that market researchers have compiled inventories of magazines, books, and other information sources that fall neatly into each STEEP bucket. This makes the "where to look" part of information gathering easier. One representative listing is given in a book on market researchers called *A Primer for New Institutional Research*, in the chapter by J. L. Morrison.[20]

Even though the sources are identified, they still must be qualified and the critical information highlighted, sifted, and assessed. It is here that assessment phase tools such as cause and effect diagramming, quick financial analysis, and stress testing become useful. An illustration of how cause and effect diagramming can be combined with identification of sources is shown in figure 5–17, with the tree diagram showing crude oil prices, the critical factors and indicators in black, and some reputable information sources to monitor.

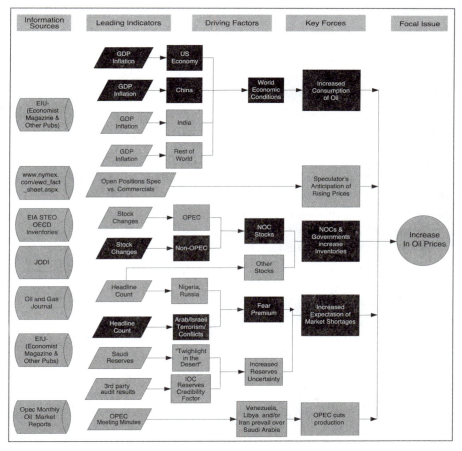

Fig. 5–17. Cause and effect diagram for crude oil prices

(A step-by-step process for cause and effect diagramming was detailed in its tool description at the end of chapter 4.)

Once the information sources have been selected, a plan to scan must be established, or real market intelligence will be nothing more than good intentions. In some cases, planning could mean commissioning a dedicated task force within the company to perform environmental scanning. However, a more effective approach is to start to change the organizational culture from an inward to an outward focus, such that everyone in the company (to varying degrees) performs environmental scanning. To be acted upon, the resulting market intelligence should be supported by an incentive-based performance management scheme, such as measurement of an individual's key performance indicator, spot bonus, or other technique. In this way, risk analysts can ensure that the information actually gets filtered back into the enterprise risk and strategic planning process. Once the basis for a system is set up (i.e., steps 1, 2, and 3 in the preceding process), individuals can set up their own plans for "continually searching with a purpose" by gathering information through personal contacts, scanning periodicals, and electronic sources.

Other considerations. Environmental scanning is by definition a less structured process than other information integrity tools that have been profiled in this book. This may cause frustration among those who want a "cookbook" approach. Unfortunately, environmental scanning is a very right-brained activity and thus does not lend itself to more of a prescriptive approach than I have outlined here. For a fascinating discourse on the philosophy behind this lack of structure, I would encourage anyone to read Peter Schwartz's seminal book on scenario analysis, *The Art of the Long View*.[21]

We now continue with our energy company vignette, as the San Felipe Resources executive management team decides what to do about Barry's findings from his structured market intelligence and analysis efforts in the pursuit of enterprise risk management. Along the way, Barry discovers just what type of high-stakes game enterprise risk management can be.

Disposition Vignette

Back at headquarters the next Monday morning, Elena and Barry were seated facing the whiteboard in Jack's office on the eighth floor, waiting for Jack to begin their crash course in scenario building.

"The first step toward scenario development is to think of this as theater. Imagine you're writing a skit, or better yet, telling a story," said Jack, beginning his lesson.

This statement would not have seemed at all out of place coming from someone in SFR's PR department, but coming from Jack Montgomery, the man in charge of guiding the executive committee in the development of a business strategy, it was quite a shock. It made Elena question whether he took the company's future very seriously.

Jack went on to say, "All our careers, we have been conditioned to thinking in linear terms: sequentially, deductively, using primarily the left side of our brains. This is not all bad. It helps us stick with a process and form well-reasoned, logical arguments. But when it comes to creating scenarios, linear thinking is not always the best. When we think sequentially and try to come up with scenarios, it often leads us instead to sensitivities. You know, change one of the variables then rerun the analysis to create the standard 'high,' 'low,' and 'base' cases. In this way, instead of scenarios, you end up with just the base case and two sensitivities. What we're striving for with scenario development is multiple base cases. We are also trying to capture the imagination of our audience by assigning names to our scenarios. Again, it is in this way that scenarios are like theater."

Jack went on to explain that although building and telling a story was a fictional exercise, in order to be effective, it needed to be substantiated with credible, factual information. If the scenarios were not plausible, people would not suspend disbelief, letting loose of their preconceived ideas about what could happen in the future. The naysayers (Barry thought immediately of SFR's commercial director, Carlos del Sordo) would immediately try to shut down the scenario builder. This is why the Venezuelan market intelligence that Barry and Elena had gathered over the past two weeks was so crucial. It not only provided both of them with assurance that their conclusions were solid, but it gave their scenarios credibility in the eyes of others.

The question in many investors' minds regarding political risk is one of political instability, or regime change. What is often missing in this type of analysis is careful consideration of the effect of a possible regime change on a particular foreign investment. In the case of Venezuela, Barry's concern was not with the small modifications or adjustments to the tax regime (which had already occurred). Instead, he was interested in the possibility of a constitutional change making nationalization of private property perfectly legal under Venezuelan law. Barry and Elena agreed that this change was an example of a "scenario logic" that was to be considered as part of their scenario analysis later. In fact, they reasoned that the goal of their Venezuela political risk exercise should be to feed a political risk scenarios process. For this they would need the help of someone who had done scenarios before—their expert in strategic planning, Jack Montgomery. Over coffee and donuts that morning, they listened to the master, who turned out to be invaluable to mapping out the scenario process.

Behind his demeanor of a likeable but frustrated artist, Jack had an analytical side that stemmed from his graduate studies in engineering and policy decisions at Stanford. There he had worked with Peter Schwartz, the noted futurologist who wrote the seminal guide to scenario planning, *The Art of the Long View*. After graduating, Jack spent time at Sandia National Laboratories in the early 1990s, where he was involved in classified work for an obscure federal government agency that reported directly to the U.S. National Security Chief. No one really knew what he did at Sandia, but one thing was clear to Barry: Jack's approach to scenario analysis was not something he had just dreamed up the day before.

On the whiteboard in Barry's office, Jack sketched out the scenario development process for Barry and Elena as it related to political risk scenarios in Venezuela. It very closely followed the Peter Schwartz methodology. The three of them then determined the points in the process that would require market intelligence and designated them with exclamation marks as shown in figure 5–18.

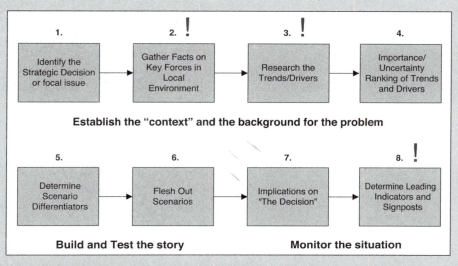

Fig. 5–18. Scenario development process

The focal issue, or in this case the decision of whether to continue investment in Venezuela or not, stemmed from the value chain analysis and the company's corporate strategy. From these two sources, it was clear that the emerging oil (EO) segment was the company's "rising star." It also implied that now was the crucial moment to make a decision on whether to continue to rely on Venezuela as the "vehicle" for success in emerging oil or to consider redirecting capital spending, possibly to the Canadian oil sands.

Scenario development and executive summary

Over the next week, Barry and Elena worked with Jack and his team to complete the eight steps of Jack's scenario development process and develop three Venezuelan political risk scenarios.

To document their work thus far, they decided to publish an executive summary memo addressed to the strategic planning group.

San Felipe Resources Memorandum

Date: 25 June
To: Strategic Planning Team
From: Barry Craddock/Elena Alvarez
Subject: Venezuelan Risk Assessment—Political/Economic
 Scenario Analysis
(SFR fiscal years 1 to 5)

Scenario Background

The enterprise risk team performed this analysis using the standard methodology normally employed by the SFR strategic planning group.

In Venezuela, every commercial risk is related to the uncertainty in the political situation. This in turn is dependent upon the price of crude oil. For purposes of this executive summary, we consider three scenarios and discuss the investment risk climate for San Felipe Resources.

Scenario I: "Return of the Puppet Rulers"

Oil prices fall back to $15/bbl, and the cutback in social programs leads to a lack of support by the masses for Hugo Chavez. The Venezuelan military decides that it must take control of the increasingly unstable political process and arranges for an "Afro/Caribbean-style democracy" by controlling the referendum outcome and forcing Chavez to resign. Behind the scenes, they offer him the option of either execution or political exile in Paraguay, and he chooses the latter. The generals step in to "stabilize the country" and set up a timetable for a transition to a civilian-led "puppet" government controlled by the military. In the interim, military leaders either pay off or begin to execute dissenters, and by fiscal year 3 after the referendum, there is tight military control of Caracas, Maracaibo, Puerto La Cruz, and all facilities of Petróleos de Venezuela S.A. (PDVSA).

However, armed guerrilla groups will have formed in the eastern parts of the country near Merida. By fiscal year 4, the puppet regime is elected via rigged elections, and it changes the constitution, tightly restricting labor rights in the oil sector.

The results of this scenario on the main risk factors facing San Felipe Resources in the Venezuelan market are summarized as follows.

Political, regulatory (improvement)

- Relative political stability through fiscal year 4, as martial law of late fiscal year 2 transitions to the puppet government in fiscal years 5–8.
- The oil and gas regulatory environment becomes simpler and more predictable; permitting delays and bureaucracy for oil and gas investments decrease.

- "Creeping nationalism" in production agreements continues, but oil company lobbying and company-sponsored infrastructure projects benefiting politicians and military officials keep this manageable over fiscal years 2–8.

Legal risk (worsening)

- Corrupt judiciary now controlled by the military with a two- to three-year period of "extra-constitutional" laws.

Tax/government take risk (improvement)

- All major oil and gas projects are considered "in the national interest" and are taxed at 34% of net income. A 30% royalty tax is applied.

Financial/macroeconomic risk (worsening)

- Prime lending rate: 40% in fiscal years 1 and 2; 30% thereafter.
- Exchange controls and FX policy: maintained.
- Inflation: 35% average.
- (Real) GDP growth: 1.1% average.
- No depth and little liquidity on the Bolsa de Valores. Little or no affordable financing available in local currency.

Labor risk (stable)

- Workers' rights to strike are restricted in the interests of "national security."
- More socialist system (low-paying job for life) of wages and benefits.

Corporate governance/transparency (stable—no change under this scenario)

Currency risk (stable)

- Military leaders continue to peg the currency to the dollar, while current account surplus shrinks with the drop in oil prices, thus spurring inflation.

Personal security of employees (improvement)

- Personal security and risk of property, plant, and equipment loss improve in the major cities and oil facilities.

Scenario II: "Leadership by Committee"

Oil prices maintain a new long-term equilibrium price of $60/bbl. Increasing frustration with the results of Chavez's Bolivarian revolution contributes to significant social unrest. Opposition parties (the Accion Democratica and the Social Christian Party of Venezuela) form a coalition government behind a charismatic businessman from Maracaibo, who defeats Chavez in the next election. This coalition government's first order of business is yet another revision of the constitution—fully dismantling Chavez's revolutionary order. Results of this scenario on the main risk factors facing San Felipe Resources in the Venezuelan market are summarized as follows.

Political/regulatory risk (significant improvement)

- After short-term unrest, political stability improves, as the coalition adopts the "big tent" philosophy of political inclusion of dissident groups.
- Several of the more controversial reforms of Chavez's government will be reversed. This is something even the divisive coalition agrees upon unanimously. The crime rate remains the same due to persistent corruption among the law enforcement officials. Personal security and risk of property, plant, and equipment loss marginally decrease over the medium term.

Legal risk (improvement)

- There will be a better implementation of three laws adopted by the government of Venezuela in the early 1990s: an anti-trust law (1992), an antidumping decree (1989), and a consumer protection law (1995).
- The bidding process of contracts offered by the state-run PDVSA will be more transparent.
- Venezuela's Criminal Environmental Law (CEL), which has been criticized as being too vague and for extending overly broad criminal liabilities, is bound to receive an overhaul.
- Bureaucratic obstacles may show some improvement; though with more special interests involved, the complexity may increase.

Tax/government take risk (improvement)

- Short term (< two years): Oil and gas will continue to be the major source of revenue for the country. Oil and gas players can expect to get a more favorable 30%–34% income tax rate. Moreover, tax credits may be provided to further boost investment.
- Long term (> three years): With the stabilization of the economy and a more diverse infrastructure (which will be the result of the government policies), Venezuela can start receiving reasonable revenues from other sectors. Some of the tax credits available for new oil and gas investments may be withdrawn (as they should be).

Financial/macroeconomic risk (significant improvement)

- With an improved investment climate, reversal of some of the controversial measures of Chavez, and a move toward a more stabilizing economic policy, the real GDP growth will turn positive by fiscal year 3 (to around 2.8%).

- Prices will stabilize as the floating exchange rate finds its new level, producing an inflation rate averaging 15% annually through fiscal year 3 (significantly lower than the current rates).

- Capital markets may start to show some improvements. Trading on the Venezuelan stock exchange is very thin and highly concentrated. The political uncertainty regarding the process of constitutional change inaugurated by Chavez is one of the main reasons. The new government can implement measures that could also reduce the capital flight that has soared over the last few years. In short, the market liquidity will go up significantly even with minimal reforms.

Labor risk (worsening)

- The coalition government will need to deal with an increasingly independent and resurgent labor movement. Workers' rights and wages will show improvement. This will result in more union demands, work stoppages, and strikes.

Corporate governance/transparency (stable)

- This will remain the same irrespective of the government that comes to power.

Personal security of employees (stable)

- The level of insecurity and crime in the cities stays the same. With improved macroeconomic conditions and stronger nonoil industrial sectors, there may be more employment. However, a squeeze on public services due to a drop in oil prices, and the general lack of organization of the new government, allow organized crime to thrive.

Scenario III: "Long Live the Cacique!"

This scenario's key theme is the extended rule of Hugo Chavez, who takes on the mantle of "Cacique." Often Latin American strongmen in Brazil and the Caribbean are referred to as *caciques*. A *cacique* is a tribal chief in Latin America, particularly of the Spanish West Indies and Brazil from the 16th century. Chavez's populist rhetoric, social programs, and support by the underclasses carries him through various reelections, until his tenure is as well established as that of Fidel Castro.

Political/regulatory risk (worsening)

- The current instability will continue as Chavez spends time and money consolidating his power base among the poor through subsidized food programs.

- The opposition, increasingly led by radical right wing groups, continues to try toppling the Chavez government by force.

- Growing impatience among the lower classes for tangible economic reforms could lead to a bloody revolt.
- Relations with the developed nations continue to deteriorate, in particular with the United States. Tensions with neighbors, particularly Colombia, Trinidad, and Guyana, increase.

Legal risk (worsening)

- Legal risk tends to increase, as the judiciary becomes less independent of the executive branch as long as Chavez is in power.

Tax/government take risk (worsening)

- Tax exemptions may be extended on the undeveloped industries like agriculture, tourism, construction, and telecommunications to lure foreign and private investors.
- Overdependence on tax revenue from the developed sectors, particularly the oil and gas industry, leads to an increase in income taxes from 34% to more than 50%, and royalty taxes are doubled for heavy oil projects.
- Expect ad hoc or temporary "windfall profits" taxes on foreign oil producers.

Financial/macroeconomic risk (worsening)

- GDP growth is set to be at an average of 1%.
- Inflation will be contained as time passes with an average decrease of 2% per year until fiscal year 3.
- Heavy domestic borrowing by the government will continue to crowd out the private investors and drive interest rates higher.

Labor risk (stable)

- Labor risk remains high as industrial accidents become more frequent and more severe at PDVSA's major terminals, refineries, and production facilities. Environmental disasters at tankers and offloading facilities provide NGOs an opportunity to join forces with organized labor. Chavez keeps labor under control and limits strikes through military force.

Corporate governance (stable)

- There will be no dramatic changes in the legal system nor in the diligence of anticorruption enforcement officials; therefore, current practices of extensive corporate bribery and corruption continue.

Currency risk (slight improvement)

- The fixed exchange rate remains as it is now (1$: 2165Bs) over the long term. Increasingly, this drives up inflation as imported goods increase, and interest rates remain high.

Personal security of employees (improvement)

- Chavez begins to suspend civil liberties as the level of street crime spirals higher, and this begins to affect his support among the lower classes. Eventually military and police forces clamp down on criminals and create a state of martial law that eliminates organized and petty crime.

A summary of the three scenarios along eight separate political risk indicators is shown in the attached summary (table 5–2).

Table 5–2. Summary of Venezuelan risk scenarios

Current and Projected Change in Risk Factors for San Felipe Resources
(Fiscal Years 1 to 5)

Risk Factor	Current Situation	Long Live the Cacique	Leadership by Committee	Return of the Puppet Rulers
Political/ Regulatory/		Worsening	Improvement	Improvement
Legal		Worsening	Improvement	Worsening
Tax/Government Take		Worsening	Unchanged	Improvement
Financial/ Macro Economic		Worsening	Significant Improvement	Worsening
Labor		Worsening	Worsening	Stable
Corporate Governance Transportation		Worsening	Stable	Stable
Currency		Improvement	Worsening	Stable
Personal Security of Employees		Improvement	Stable	Improvement

With these scenarios and the data from their trip to Venezuela, Barry and Elena were prepared to analyze and explain the political risk picture to Dave Anderson and any of the rest of SFR upper management. What they did not know was that Barry would be soon asked to take this one level higher: to the SFR board of directors.

Blessed assurance

Bart Jensen, the company's CFO, had called Barry into his office with some urgent concerns about the transparency of SFR's data and their assumptions regarding oil prices and the Venezuelan political risk scenario. What worried Bart the most was the level of documentation required behind the new enterprise risk management system. On the one hand, Bart had recently been overwhelmed with (and disgusted by) the amount of documentation required by his accounting auditors to support the Sarbanes-Oxley Act, Section 404 and Section 302 compliance. On the other hand, he was worried that he might not have enough documentation to shield himself from criminal liability under the Act. Bart did not want to even *think* about the personal nightmare of prosecution and the infamous "perp walk" in front of the cameras.

"Barry, as you know, we've just gone thorough a Sarbanes-Oxley compliance exercise with the external auditors," said Bart. "Although we came out okay, one of the things we learned was that our financial compliance activities are now taking twice as long as expected because we have to dig up evidence behind every accounting process flow diagram. Now, you're a member of the internal audit group, so the need for documentation or evidence is nothing new for you. But after getting beat up first by your group, and then by the external auditors, I am concerned about how much more documentation we will need in the future. For example, on this enterprise risk stuff, I really want you to tell me how much is enough documentation, and what do we need to do to be compliant?"

The last thing Barry wanted was for the CFO to throw the burden of defining how much documentation was enough onto his shoulders. In addition, Barry saw compliance as only one of the reasons for transparency through documentation. Beyond compliance, there were strategic reasons for requiring people to justify their assumptions, such as developing a deeper awareness of SFR's competitive positioning and the dynamics of the market. Finally, Barry believed that enterprise risk, transparency, and adequate documentation were organizational issues requiring a culture change. Ideally every senior manager would become an enterprise risk manager. So the real goal here was to get everyone in management to make a personal determination about how much data would be sufficient using a risk-based cost/benefit analysis. This enterprise risk assignment had truly given Barry a new perspective on corporate strategy and effective ways of running an oil and gas business. Barry was beginning to realize that when Dave Anderson gave him the enterprise risk assignment, it was not just to comply with the regulations, but to help him grow professionally.

"Well, Bart," responded Barry. "The first thing we considered in our enterprise risk approach was the materiality of various businesses and activities. The basic question is, How much would it cost for additional information vs. the benefit gained in terms of risk reduction? I'm talking about all kinds of risk reduction, including compliance, operational, strategic, technical, etc. Personally, I think there is no use in adding a whole bunch of paperwork by documenting something that is not likely to be important. But first you need to know what is important."

Barry continued, "For example, we found that within our RM&L (refining, marketing, and logistics) group, things such as managing gasoline stations were not as critical to the business value chain as we thought. Furthermore, we are already complying with the letter of the law here in terms of statutes. Overall, in this retail marketing business, the risks are much smaller than we imagined relative to the refining group, which, as you know, is our cash cow. So after documenting what is strictly required by the regulators, the first thing to do is apply a risk-based approach to documentation. In fact, with regards to documentation for Sarbanes-Oxley, it is actually the other way around. The SEC is *advising* us to apply a risk-based approach in order to comply with the regulation! Second, of those activities that we found to be critical to the future of our business and were quite risky, we asked ourselves, 'What are the drivers behind these risks?' Considering the price of oil, for example, do we know how to monitor the risks of a fall in crude prices?"

At this point, Bart, the CFO, shifted uncomfortably in his chair. He remembered his conversation the day before with Dave Anderson, the president, around their basic assumptions supporting the corporate oil price forecast. For Bart, the uncertainty of this crude oil price forecast created a mortal fear in him greater than that of regulatory noncompliance. This fear was because of the menacing tone of the questions raised by board member Karen James and the implied threats of that Russian corporate raider/troublemaker, Victor Komarovsky. Bart knew that they had no hedging strategy in place, and if there were a drop in prices, it would cause some serious cash flow problems at SFR. That could cost him his job.

"The ups and downs of commodity prices have always been part of our risk profile, it's a natural part of being an oil and gas company," Bart stated in his most confident tone of voice. "Of course, we can always improve on the way that we manage and report on this commodity price risk. What are you are doing in this area as part of your enterprise risk initiative?"

Barry distinctly noted the *you* and the not the *we* in Bart's question. The CFO had not yet bought into the ERM initiative.

"Well, we have first broken down the price of oil into its various drivers that we call key forces and driving factors," Barry answered. "Next we looked at both leading and lagging indicators behind each driving factor and found valid information sources for each indicator. Finally, we've begun to create a system for monitoring changes in these indicators by regularly updating the information from the sources."

"But how do you keep track of all this? What can you show me that acts as evidence of a system or a process?" questioned Bart.

At this point, Barry felt that he and Bart had traded careers, for it seemed that Bart was now the auditor and Barry the annoyed executive. But Barry adopted the patient, measured tone of voice that he, as an internal auditor, had listened to from San Felipe's executives so often over the years.

"That's a good question, Bart. We first used a decision analysis technique called a *fault tree* to discover and diagram out the key forces and drivers. For crude oil prices, we found them to include supply/demand fundamentals and (of course) a fear premium factor that is what in finance you might call the *convenience yield* factor. We then went one step further and diagrammed our information sources behind each indicator. Finally, we used this fault tree diagram as a specification for the algorithm, or the process flow, for creating what we call an expanded *enterprise risk register*.

"Now normally, as you probably know, a risk register is a tool for capturing, documenting, and communicating risks to the greater organization," Barry continued. "In its simplest form, it is no more than an Excel spreadsheet. For very small capital projects, our projects risk group has used a spreadsheet format like this one."

Barry then pulled out a printout of the Excel risk register format shown in figure 5–19.

Tracking Number	Title	Uncertainty, Threat or Opportunity?	Risk Description	Risk Breakdown Category (Political, Technical, etc)	Source	Likelihood	Consequence	Risk Level	Owner Assigned	Mitigation (Action)	Due Date

Fig. 5–19. Standard risk register (Microsoft Excel format)

"As you can see, it captures most of the information that would come out of a project risk workshop, or (as in the field of health and safety risk management) the results of a HAZID, or 'hazard identification' session," Barry added. "This is good as far as it goes. In terms of documentation, it is much better than meeting minutes for maintaining a record of risks. But when the project takes on any level of complexity, or you get beyond say 50 or 100 risks, and multiple users, it becomes unmanageable. In this case we prefer to use a simple database tool like MS Access, or a SQL database instead of Excel. A database has the advantage over a spreadsheet of allowing what software developers call 'a single version of truth.' This basically means that through a centralized system, there is one official version of the information that everyone accesses instead of dispersed spreadsheets sitting on each analyst's desktop. Going from spreadsheets to even the simplest of databases is a big step for many organizations, and there is often a fair amount of resistance. This is because people must give up the freedom to custom format their own desktop spreadsheet. However, having your risk register in a centralized database allows much better version control, restricted access of users by security level, wider sharing of information, and faster reporting capabilities. Now Bart, I know I'm starting to sound like a software vendor, but I have witnessed the advantages of using a database versus spreadsheets here at San Felipe Resources," said Barry.

"No, don't apologize," said Bart in a more conciliatory tone. "In the corporate finance group you wouldn't believe the uphill battle we've fought over the past few years to get our accountants to implement and use our SAP system instead of their spreadsheets. In the end, though, I am convinced we couldn't meet our reporting goals today without that new database system in place."

Barry knew he had finally struck a chord with Bart.

Barry continued with his explanation, adding, "Now, this is all fine and good, but it still doesn't stand up to much scrutiny. This is because the standard risk register is designed to capture only internally generated information. What we are talking about here is, what is behind those risks, i.e., the *external* information? To have a robust enterprise risk management system, we need to document the basis of our risk assumptions and capture it in the same database. Here is where the concept of the *expanded* risk register comes into play. The scope of the database is expanded through to the information sources. To illustrate, let me show you a comparison of the standard versus the expanded risk register scopes in the form of the fault tree diagram we discussed earlier."

Barry showed Bart an outline of the fault tree (fig. 5–20) that he and Elena had developed to document crude oil price risk analysis.

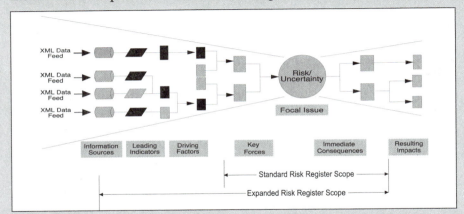

Fig. 5–20. Standard and expanded risk register

"Nice illustrations," said Bart. "They remind me of the binomial approach I've seen for asset valuations using real options. I can see how this is starting to hang together."

Gradually, Barry was moving Bart from a skeptic to a collaborator by appealing to the CFO's intellectual curiosity.

Barry continued, "This diagram shows the basic architecture of our expanded risk register along one risk 'vector,' i.e., crude oil prices. However, there is yet one more consideration required to make this truly a robust enterprise risk management tool: maintenance of timely external information. For this, we need to feed the database with fresh information as it becomes available. We could do this manually, but that introduces the possibility of a considerable number of data input errors. Besides, many of the information sources we use for our assumptions are available in electronic form. Once we've identified and qualified these data sources as reliable, we can have the information electronically fed directly into our expanded risk register database. For example, some of the best sources of data on economic growth projections come from a private market intelligence service in the UK called the EIU. The EIU gives us updated country economic growth projections, which are indicators of petroleum demand growth using electronic data feeds in RSS (Really Simple Syndication). Each of these data streams is coded using a software language called Extensible Markup Language or XML, that contains electronic labels (or metatags) attached to different categories of data within the stream. In this way, when the data comes into our expanded risk register, it knows by the metatag how to be routed to different fields in the risk register database."

"I think I understand the concept," said Bart, in a more animated tone. "It sounds a lot like what the SEC is trying to get us to do with our financial statements. They would like us to code all our filings, say our 10-Ks, 10-Qs, and now our 8-Ks, using a similar reporting software code called XBRL, or Extensible Business Reporting Language. At first, I thought this electronic coding stuff was going to be a real bureaucratic burden, but when I realized that all our competitors would be doing this as well, I saw some tremendous opportunities for benchmarking our results against the competition."

Barry could see it was time to go in with his closing arguments.

"Bart, for San Felipe, this is a significant advance in the area of information integrity," said Barry. "What an ERM information architecture does is create a transparent system that is not only auditable, but allows the analysts to document their assumptions behind the risks. It has the added benefit of improving awareness of the market drivers and the assumptions behind those drivers. To accomplish this, we need to use the database structure that accommodates numerical, text, graphics, and even PDF files. It should be relational, in that different types of information can be linked together for sorting, filtering, and analysis. Finally, it needs to be flexible enough to evolve with our needs. On the input side, we should be able to have multiple types of data entry templates, and on the output side, we need customized reports suited to the needs of different stakeholders."

"I see what you are saying, Barry," said Bart, "but this is starting to sound like another complex software implementation. We have been through two of these nightmare implementations over the past five years. The last one ended up as a $20 million write-off after our refinery managers revolted, and we were forced to abandon the whole program. We will not go through that again. I've already spent all my political capital for software implementations, Barry."

"I hear what you are saying, Bart," responded Barry, "so what I'm proposing is to keep this extremely simple at first. At this point, we are looking for a number of double and single hits rather than a home run. The IT department will laugh, but over the next three months, we plan to develop this as a pilot project with a team of no more than two or three people. Furthermore, to develop the concept and get something in place, we will not be buying some big, expensive, off-the-shelf database application. Instead, we will use the standard application that is already on everyone's desktop, Microsoft Access. Elena has already begun to develop a prototype of this expanded risk register to capture and analyze information behind two of our major sources of risk: the Venezuelan political situation and our crude oil prices. Over the next year, we will continue to refine this prototype in-house, and we have periodic upper management review points scheduled to make sure that we keep having the buy-in. It won't be perfect, and it won't be flashy, but it will be a successful start. Through continual improvement over the medium term, we can refine, deepen, and broaden the scope of the program to effectively cover the entire organization, including each of the company's major risks."

"Barry, what you are doing is more important than you realize," Bart said. "Understanding and documenting our assumptions around the Venezuela strategy and the oil price risk issue are crucial to our future as an independent oil company. Right now, we have some very powerful stakeholders who are beating down the door demanding evidence that we have a plan and some kind of system for making sure we understand our major risks, and that the information and assumptions behind those risks are accurate and validated. I'll be meeting with Dave Anderson this afternoon. I am going to get him to put you on the agenda for the executive committee meeting next Thursday. You need to prepare a 20-minute presentation on oil prices, as well as a review of the scenario approach you've been developing for Venezuela. I'll send you the meeting notice before noon today."

Apparently the executive committee was dealing with some short-term crisis for which Barry's work would be useful. Barry wondered to himself what it could all mean.

Coup de grâce: the big day

The day had arrived for Barry to present the results of SFR's Venezuelan political risk analysis, as well as the crude oil price risk analysis to Dave Anderson, Bart Jensen, and the rest of the SFR executive committee. Barry had to admit that he was a bit nervous. He had done his homework, and Jack Montgomery had coached him on the finer points of scenario presentation, but still, some of the information he would deliver would stir up a significant discussion about the strategy and future direction of the emerging oil (EO) segment at SFR. He was concerned about being caught in the crossfire of the rivalries between different members of the executive committee.

Barry had decided last week that the most effective way to present the political risk scenarios would be to use a "storyboard" approach. Creating storyboards to illustrate hypothetical situations was a presentation technique he had used a few years earlier to explain the company's new management system to the directors and maintenance managers at seven different SFR refineries across the country. Barry recalled that the storyboarding approach had been developed in the film industry in the 1930s and 1940s as a means of visualizing a movie's script, characters, and scenery prior to commitment of major funds toward the production. As with its film industry counterpart, business storyboards often involve characters and plot development. For business management presentations, the storyboard can be a visual representation using a series of "boards" or flip charts depicting what could happen in a business-related scenario.

Explaining scenarios in a short period of time can be quite a challenge, as it requires the facilitator to be a storyteller, allowing the audience to visualize the scene. To do this, the presenter must first "set the stage" with the known facts and then attempt to draw people out of their individual frames of reference and lead them to look at a situation with different eyes. This is not easy. For Barry, the approach had proved quite successful at the refinery sites because it engaged the entire group of managers in fairly extensive discussions about the implementation of the new system. However, both the use of scenarios and the storyboard approach were risky precisely because in order to work well, they demand that the audience follow the plot. For example, Barry could remember a story his friend Jack Montgomery had relayed to him where the approach had not worked as well as planned. It was during two class exercises of a course in scenario building Jack had once taught to a group of SFR employees. The first exercise involved division of the class into groups of four or five young engineering managers. Each group was tasked with creating a skit with characters and a plot based on a historical event of their choosing. The results of this first exercise were impressive. The skits had unleashed a flood of creative thinking, and the well-developed, humorous skits surprised even a seasoned scenario builder like Jack.

"I was really getting excited to see how these engineers began to think like executives, an important strategic skill. They had tapped into the creative process of the right side of the brain to dream up the plot and characters while using their (left-brained) rational skills to plan the process, write it down into a sequential series of events, and deliver a finished product. It was beautiful," said Jack. "Unfortunately, that mountaintop experience of the first class exercise only set me up to later plunge into the valley of despair of the second class exercise."

In this second case, instead of a fictional skit, the scenarios were to be centered around a "focal issue," a real decision involving the possible construction of a new refinery. The students stayed in the same groups of four or five and tried to develop their scenarios in the same way as with the historical skits. This time the results were very disappointing. What Jack observed was that once the engineers began to consider a *real* decision where each had technical expertise and experience, they jumped to the conclusion that a conventional refinery would definitely be built. Thus, their "scenarios" ended up being nothing more than variations on the major equipment layout and plant throughput for the new refinery. The reality of the situation had blinded them to the possibility that under some economic conditions, a new refinery would not be built.

Jack's conclusion was that the first exercise with a fictional plot allowed the students to *suspend disbelief* because they were already dealing in the world of fiction. On the other hand, in the second exercise, the reality of the situation overwhelmed the creative thinking process and they were unable to think about true "scenarios." Unfortunately for Barry's scenario explanation to the executive board, SFR's current investments in Venezuela were not fiction; they were very real. This made his upcoming presentation to the executive committee perilously close to Jack's second class exercise.

That morning when Dave Anderson arrived, many of the company's key players were assembled in the conference room: the vice presidents of International E&P and Major Projects, the company's legal counsel, the PR director, and even his old buddy, Jack Montgomery. Nancy distributed the agenda, and Bart Jensen, the CFO, chaired the meeting.

"As many of you know, we've been questioned by one of our board members, Karen Archer, as well as one of our major shareholders about political risk related to our investments in Venezuela. On top of this, we've heard that Karen and a minority shareholder are concerned about the level of controls around our assumptions about the overall crude oil markets. We've said that strategically, our EO segment represents the future of the company, but aside from the small holdings we have in the Rockies, our heavy crude production in El Tigre, Venezuela, is our EO segment. We need to come to some type of decision about whether we should stay or we should go…and that's why we're here," said Bart.

Dave then interjected, "I want to clarify a bit of what Bart is saying. We are **not** moving away from emerging oil, but we need to decide pretty quickly what the opportunities and threats are, what our plan is, and how we are going to communicate this to the board and to the street. I know that some of you have very strong opinions about doing business in Venezuela. But we can't make decisions based on opinions. That is why I've asked Barry to take a look at the political risk situation in a structured, organized manner. Barry?"

Barry's palms were sweating in this emotionally charged environment. The entire executive committee was looking to him for the answer. He could see the whites of their eyes, but he couldn't gauge the sentiment around the table that morning about what each was expecting to hear. He only had one choice. In the words of Admiral Farragut, "Damn the torpedoes. Full speed ahead!"

"Ladies and gentlemen, what I'm going to tell you this morning will not be a forecast, but rather a series of alternative views, or scenarios, backed up by our market research over the past month. As I talk, I am going to request only one thing of you—that you suspend disbelief until I finish explaining the scenarios."

Out of the corner of his eye, Barry caught a sly smile growing over the face of his friend and scenario mentor, Jack Montgomery.

For the next 15 minutes of his presentation, Barry set the stage by briefly reviewing the "focal issue," or decision of whether SFR should stay in Venezuela. He first presented the facts and key forces behind SFR's current situation in Venezuela such as the supply and demand for Venezuelan heavy crude oil over SFR's fiscal years 1 to 5.

- On the supply side was the Venezuelan Orinoco belt, represented a potentially huge, undepleted source of proven, nearly developed reserves. SFR operated two conventional production sites in the eastern part of the country near Maturín, and one heavy oil project in El Tigre in joint venture with PDVSA and a European partner. Each conventional field produces 40,000 barrels per day (bpd), and the heavy oil project, when fully developed, could result in at least 200,000 bpd over the next five years. There were few places in the world that offered SFR the chance for such steady, high-volume production.

- Then there was the issue of the product quality. Venezuela produces significant quantities of crude oil of between 10° API and 22° API—the heavy stuff. In addition to Venezuela, Russia and Canada also had a some significant heavy oil reserves. Traditionally the economics of refining this crude has made development difficult. However, with improved refining and coking capacity at many of the world's refineries, heavy crudes were no longer the poor step-sister to the world's better-known light and medium weight crudes, such as Bonny Light, West Texas Intermediate, and Brent. Today there is a brisk business buying some of the heavier crudes, such as Venezuela's Orinoco and Mexico's Maya crude, at a discount to WTI for example, and then using this new refining and blending capacity to "capture the spread."

- On the demand side, the capability of the world's refineries to process Venezuelan heavy crude was improving every day. The Chinese and Indians, with their new refineries, were glad to take this previously less desirable product. For any oil and gas company like SFR, having access to a steady supply of heavy crude oil could position them to secure long-term, off-take contracts and a steady cash flow to buffer the company's capital expansion program against the wild swings in commodity prices on the spot market.

Beyond the focal issue, facts, and key forces were the two major sources of uncertainty: the price of crude oil and the continuance of Hugo Chavez as the country's president. Finally, a key concern of the investor community and the board was the "all your eggs in one basket" strategy that SFR had undertaken. At this point, a thought came to Barry's mind. In a way, Bart Jensen was right in his opening remarks. By so heavily investing in Venezuela, they had made the success of their entire EO effort dependent upon the politics of that one country. It was a shame that SFR had not diversified its EO holdings. Barry wondered if the executive committee had ever thought about other opportunities for heavy crude development.

With this background, Barry began to describe the three Venezuelan scenarios he and Elena had developed. In his best oratorical style and using the storyboard approach, Barry verbally developed each scenario. He successively unveiled the predrawn graphics shown in figure 5–21 on 3' X 3' panels covered with white butcher paper.

Fig. 5–21. Three Venezuelan scenarios

From a review of the variables around each scenario, Barry led the group to conclude the following:

- Contrary to other E&P locations in places such as Nigeria and the Ivory Coast, where the levels of personal security of employees, corruption, and transparency were rapidly degenerating, in Venezuela these were likely to remain unchanged.

- The wild cards in any scenario were the changes in the corporate tax burden, the increase in royalties, and the changes in the country's legal protections and macroeconomic situation. These financial, commercial, and regulatory factors might improve, but probably not without a drop in oil prices, a change in government, and significant macroeconomic problems for the country in the short term.

- Against this backdrop were the predetermined elements of continued economic growth in China and India, and with it, steady growth in the demand for oil.

To make the situation more interactive, Barry began to prod the committee members with questions concerning the various outcomes for SFR under the most unfavorable conditions.

"Under more than one of these scenarios, we might be forced to sell some of our holdings to the Venezuelan government. In this case, how much do you think we could be left with, and more importantly, would it be worth our while to continue in the partnership?" questioned Barry.

"I could easily see them requiring up to 40%, plus demanding 'golden shares,' like we've seen happen to one of our competitor's refineries in Zimbabwe," said Linda Morris, SFR's corporate counsel.

At the refinery partnership, golden shares had given the government of Zimbabwe veto rights on operational decisions. The effect was that every management proposal became politicized, from the amount of community development obligations down to how many gardeners and drivers would be on the company payroll.

"I could imagine them requiring 70% outright, thus forcing us to reduce our share down to as little as 30%," said Art Joplin, the vice president of Major Projects.

"Well, then, let's look at what 30% might mean," interjected Barry. "Bart, what do you think about the commercial ramifications of a 30% share?"

"Well, first of all this would mean a reserves write-down—very bad for our stock price. The reduced share would also limit our chances of expanding the off-take agreements we have with Exxon and Shell in Lake Charles. But even if a forced divestiture were to happen, SFR's per-barrel services fee revenues on the resulting 72,000 bpd would still be substantial over the next five years. With these types of steady revenues, we might want to think carefully about pulling out of the country completely," stated Bart hesitantly.

All the while, Dave Anderson, the company president, was sitting back listening. He was using the John F. Kennedy approach to executive management: allow expert opinion to flourish in a free form discussion and then pounce in at the end with a summary and an executive decision.

"The other key uncertainty in all this is the price of oil," stated Barry.

"I am wondering what we can do about that," jumped in Bart, rather slyly looking over to Dave Anderson. "Or better yet, what can you tell us, Barry, about how comfortable we are with our understanding of crude oil markets?"

Now, for the first time since they had begun to work together, Barry felt that he and Bart were on the same team. Bart had expertly set Barry up for the final blow, the *coup de grâce*, that would show that they really had done their homework on not only the Venezuelan issue, but on their crude oil price assumptions as well. Beyond these immediate issues, however, Barry briefly explained how this methodology formed the basis for the overall SFR information integrity management system as he had done in Bart's office a few days earlier. He described how his team had modeled the crude oil markets and applied a rigorous approach to finding and qualifying credible information sources and validating external data. He then described the electronic information system they were setting up, including the expanded risk register concept, and how the whole process would be periodically updated with new electronic feeds from the qualified sources.

Dave Anderson was beaming with pride. Bart Jensen was relieved. The rest of the management team was quite impressed with how Barry had discovered that reliable external information and an organized way of analyzing it were the foundation of a robust enterprise risk management system.

"Given this analysis of the crude oil markets and the Venezuelan political situation, I'd like to ask you, Barry, what you think we should do with our emerging oil division," said Dave Anderson.

All eyes were trained on Barry, and the air was filled with a palpable tension. Everyone knew that the future of SFR could hinge on what Barry was about to say.

"We need to take a portfolio approach to emerging oil rather than focusing all our investment in Venezuela. We should partially divest in Venco by selling half of our ownership to our European partner over the next few months. In this way, we can become the minority partner now, before it becomes evident to everyone in the industry that the Venezuelan government is going to take control and our holding is devalued. With commodity prices at their currently high levels, we could probably get a pretty good premium for the shares. We can still stay in heavy oil, but we will be diversifying. There are other heavy oil plays we should consider around the world, for example, in northern Alberta. We should take the proceeds from the share sale in Venezuela and invest in a Canadian start-up partnership with Asian investors, thus ensuring stable, long-term off-take agreements. Not only is this a prudent business move, but it should play well on the street and with the board," said Barry confidently.

"I have to agree with Barry. The portfolio approach spreads our political risk, investing with an Asian partner mitigates some of the commercial risk, and it is clear that we have solid information to support our decision," said the CFO.

"We've always had a good experience whenever we've dealt with the Canadians from Alberta. They tend to be good people, real down-to-earth straight shooters," said the vice president of E&P.

"Well, Barry, you've done a great job of helping us get our heads around a complex issue. We are going to take your recommendation and go ahead with the divestiture in Venezuela and the investment in Canada," said Dave. "Furthermore, this new approach is just the silver bullet we needed to keep Victor Komarovsky at bay and ease the concerns of our largest shareholder, Bruce Wonderlein, and a powerful board member, Karen James."

At the mention of Victor Komarovsky, there was a sudden hush over the room. For at that point, Barry, Jack, and the entire executive committee realized that without Barry's information integrity system and the ensuing strategy recommendations, SFR would have been perilously close to a takeover by one of the most feared corporate raiders in the energy industry.

Barry went home that night exhausted but relieved. Certainly he had his work cut out for him in implementing the SFR enterprise risk management system over the next 18 months, but when he got home, all he could feel was relief. He poured a Johnny Walker Black Label and soda, the national cocktail of the Bolivarian Republic of Venezuela. As he sipped his drink, drifting off into a dream, he imagined himself the victorious bullfighter in Georges Bizet's famous opera *Carmen*, waving to the crowd and riding triumphantly on the shoulders of Bart Jensen, Dave Anderson, and his archrival, Carlos del Sordo. All the while from the spectators in the stands came the cries of "*¡Bravo! ¡Bravo!*" And from a distance, Barry could see the figure of Elena Alvarez in full 18th-century Spanish attire approaching his procession on a white Andalusian stallion. Majestically, she joined Barry and the executive committee on the final victory lap around the bullring to the call of trumpets and the roaring approval of the crowd.

Disposition: Parting Shots

1. San Felipe Resources management was threatened by activist shareholders but saved by its diligent pursuit of reliable information and a systematic approach to risk management. Over the coming years, what are the possible social, technological, economic, environmental, or political (STEEP) drivers that could transform shareholder activism into a major threat to executive management and boards of directors at publicly traded companies?

2. How do the rise in resource nationalism and the growing power of the environmental movement affect the competitive advantage of investor-owned oil companies (IOCs) relative to private companies and national oil companies in the 21st century? Aside from superior technology, what advantages do the IOCs have?

3. Is it possible to think that someone could come out of the blue and "upset the apple cart" in the international oil and gas industry? Could they do so using a new market-centric approach similar to how Apple and Dell revolutionized the computer hardware industry and how Southwest Airlines and Virgin Atlantic changed air transport?

4. How quickly are the Russian "oligarchs" likely to become key actors in the international mergers and acquisitions in the West, much as the Saudis were in the 1970s and the Japanese in the 1980s?

5. In the mid-1980s, Michael Porter wrote about IT as a source of competitive advantage. What he really wanted to show was how IT could enable people to use information more effectively to create either a cost advantage or a differentiated product. What he did not recognize was the basic inability of companies to gather information and use it strategically. The IT as we know it has morphed since 1985 into a dizzying array of hardware and software that has taken on a life of its own as an industry. The hardware and software will never drive a change in people's ability to think. Somehow along the way, we have forgotten that solid strategy, market intelligence, and analysis come first, and that hardware and software are only enablers, not creators of business success.

References

1. Schwartz, P. 1991. *The Art of the Long View*. New York: Doubleday. p. 3.

2. Ibid.

3. Bressand, A. 2005. *Shell Global Scenarios to 2025—The Future Business Environment: Trends, Trade-offs and Choices*. Royal Dutch Shell. www.shell.com

4. Global Risk Network. 2007. *Global Risks 2007*. Geneva: World Economic Forum. (January). www.weforum.org

5. Boulos, A. 2003. *Assessing Political Risk*. Presented at the 2003 North American Prospect Expo (NAPE), Houston, TX, January 28. Chapter 3, section 2. p. 15. Supplement to the IPAA *International Primer*, presented at the 2002 NAPE. http://www.ipaa.org/issues/international/PoliticalRisk.pdf

6. Construction Industry Institute. 2003. *International Project Risk Assessment*. Risk Assessment for International Projects Project Team. Implementation Resource 181-2. (October). http://construction-institute.org/catalog.htm

7. Day, A. L. 2003. *Mastering Risk Modelling: A Practical Guide to Modelling Uncertainty with Excel*. UK: Pearson Education Limited.

8. U.S. Energy Information Administration. 2002. *EIA Standards Manual*. Washington, D.C.: EIA. (September 29). http://www.eia.doe.gov/smg/Standard.pdf

9. International Standards Organization. 2001. *Guidelines for Quality Management System Documentation*. ISO/TR10013: 2001(E). Geneva: International Standards Organization.

10. Ibid. p. 35.

11. Det Norske Veritas. 2000. *Recommended Practice DNV-RP-A201. Standard Documentation Types*. (November). Høvik, Norway: Det Norske Veritas. http://www.dnv.com.

12. Det Norske Veritas. 2001. *Recommended Practice DNV-RP-A202. Documentation of Offshore Projects*. (January). Høvik, Norway: Det Norske Veritas. http://ww.dnv.com

13. HM Treasury of the United Kingdom. 2003. *The Green Book*. London: Office of Government Commerce, HM Treasury of the United Kingdom. http://www.ogc.gov.uk/documentation_and_templates_risk_log_risk_register.asp

14. Ibid.

15. Noetix Corporation. *Dashboard Development and Deployment: A Methodology for Success*. Redmond, VA: Noetix Corporation. http://www.noetix.com/Solutions/Dashboard/?ref=HPBanner

16. Choo, C. W. 2001. Environmental scanning as information seeking and organizational learning. *Information Research*. 7 (1).

17. Wynne, B. 2004. Public dialogues with science: some complications from the case of nanotechnology. Presentation for the British Association of Advancement of Science, Science-Communication Conference, May 24–25.

18. Choo, C. W. 2001.

19. Aguilar, F. J. 1967. *Scanning the Business Environment*. New York: Macmillan.

20. Morrison, J. L. 1992. Environmental scanning. In M. A. Whitely, J. D. Porter, and R. H. Fenske, eds. *A Primer for New Institutional Researchers*. Tallahassee, FL: The Association for Institutional Research. pp. 86–99.

21. Schwartz, P. 1991.

The 21st Century Energy Merchant and the Alpha Advantage

6

There is a commonly held idea regarding animal psychology that certain dogs and wolves will display dominant character traits (termed *alpha behavior*) that differentiate them from other canines, making them natural leaders of their pack. Prior to the establishment of a pack leader, wolves in the wild display confusion and uncertainty—a crisis of confidence. However, once the alpha wolf is established, the rest of the pack falls in line, and may even take on a new direction. Nearing the end of the first decade of this century, the energy industry is facing a stakeholder crisis of confidence. Is it possible that a new wolf will emerge as the energy merchant of the 21st century?

Turning to finance, there is another concept of alpha that is worth considering. It is the financial measurement of an asset's (or a portfolio's) excess returns over those expected by the capital asset pricing model (CAPM). The ideas behind CAPM were originally presented by Nobel prize winner William Sharpe in the 1960s.[1] The model describes how the risk of an individual asset can be measured and compared to a broader universe of assets in the market through measured historical performance above a benchmark "risk-free" rate. CAPM also assumes market efficiency. In an interview in 1998 for the Dow Jones publication, *Asset Management*, Sharpe stated that CAPM means "higher expected returns go with the greater risk of doing badly in bad times."[2] By extension, with efficient markets, he is saying that there is no way to beat the system other than to diversify one's holdings—no way to pick winning horses, no free lunches. Given this purist view, is it possible that alpha in this sense could exist? Many hedge fund managers say yes, but few have the magic recipe or "the secret sauce."

Although CAPM is regarded as one of the fundamental frameworks for understanding financial risk, there is constant debate in financial circles about whether CAPM actually works. This debate exists because (not surprisingly) markets do not work 100% efficiently. There may also be some questioning of CAPM related to prospect theory as proposed by Nobel prize winners Kahneman and Tversky, who have shown that people (and perhaps groups of people, or even markets) will not behave *rationally* when it comes to risk.[3] Thus, the opportunities afforded by inefficiencies and nonrational behavior could provide a way to beat the system. Now, finance academics and economists will claim that consistent achievement of excess returns (or alpha behavior) is impossible because inefficiencies in the market are quickly exploited by all market participants and are thus fleeting. But if this opportunistic behavior were somehow maintained through systematically superior information, could it provide for the creation of the elusive alpha energy company?

What these two uses of the term *alpha* have in common is that they signal something different or set apart from the rest. The first is the wolf behavior of going first and leading by example. The second is the practice of a consistently taking advantage of market inefficiencies using reliable information. Of course, leadership and competitive advantage through better information is hardly a new concept. For more than 25 years, renowned management expert Michael Porter has promoted the concept that corporate strategy using better market intelligence and information systems differentiates leading from lagging financial performers. His five forces of industry attractiveness laid the basis for enterprise risk management by identifying the sources of threats and opportunities facing modern companies. His two forms of sustainable competitive advantage, cost leadership and enhanced differentiation, continue to be valid. What is different today is the method (or strategic vehicle) for differentiation. This new strategic vehicle, or the modified Porter model for the energy industry, leverages reliable information in support of enterprise risk management for a sustained competitive advantage, as presented in figure 6–1.

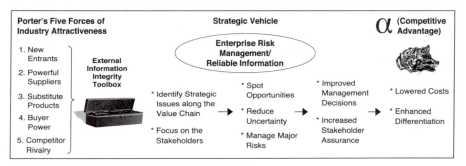

Fig. 6–1. Modified Porter model for energy industry competitive advantage

It is this leveraging of reliable information in support of enterprise risk management that characterizes the new lead energy wolf, the energy merchant of the 21st century. Among the most strategically critical types of information involves understanding of the stakeholders' needs.

The needs of each stakeholder are aligned with their role in the control and management of the company's activities. For example, investors, creditors, and regulators generally have a more passive, *oversight* role in the management of the company. The role of these company overseers differs from that of a manager. Generally they do not have inside knowledge of the day-to-day workings and thus rely on their appointed agents or on law enforcement to protect their interests. Even so, overseers sometimes see the need to monitor financial ratios and carry out spot checks and audits to ensure that their interests are being served. Another group of stakeholders includes board members, external analysts, and external auditors, who are responsible for *governance*. Theirs is more of a watchdog function than the oversight role of investors, creditors, and regulators. They help to ensure that the company operates within an acceptable legal and ethical framework. Board members also have a specific fiduciary responsibility to be the caretakers of shareholders' (not upper management's) interests. In this respect, board members sometimes are forced to step in and mandate a course correction when senior management has a risk tolerance or a strategy that deviates from what they believe to be in the interest of good corporate governance or adequate internal controls. The recent wave of proxy fights and lawsuits from institutional investors illustrates what can happen when board members do not do their job and fail to meet the needs of *their* customer—the shareholder. Finally, establishing business strategy and creating an organization structure is the role of the company's upper management, and implementation is the responsibility of middle management and those they supervise.

In summary, those responsible for oversight, governance, strategy, management, and implementation each have their associated stakeholders who are increasingly expecting reliable information and more effective enterprise risk management. To satisfy their customer needs and support the next higher level in the hierarchy, each group can use the tools, techniques, and methods I have described in this book. The appropriate tools for each level are illustrated as icons beneath the "Information Integrity Application" column heading in the pyramid diagram in figure 6–2.

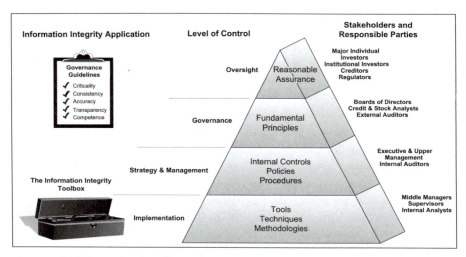

Fig. 6–2. The information due diligence pyramid

For those parties to the right of the pyramid in oversight and governance roles, the information integrity governance guidelines (assessment tool 2) provide a checklist of questions to determine the degree of integrity behind the information used in the company's forecasts. The 20-question governance guideline checklist spans the five categories of information integrity: criticality, consistency, competence, accuracy, and transparency. A failing score (< 60%) on the answers to these questions should cause boards of directors and others responsible for oversight to seriously question the reliability of information coming from the company's management.

For those responsible for strategy, management, and implementation, as shown in figure 6–1, systematic use of the tools presented in the information integrity toolbox will ensure that a passing score is obtained from application of the information integrity guidelines, thus providing adequate stakeholder assurance of the reliability of the information. An overview of all the qualitative and quantitative tools by information integrity phase (discovery, assessment, and disposition) and their application to each of the five fundamentals is shown in figure 6–3.

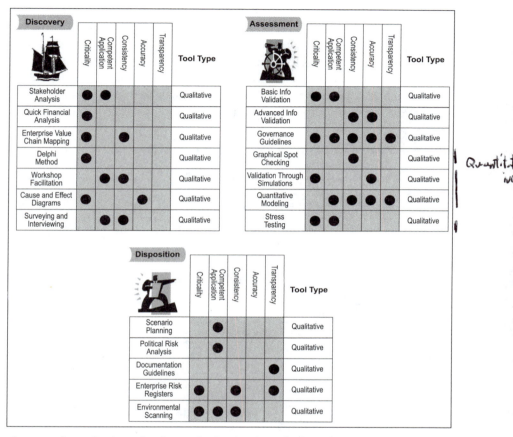

Discovery	Criticality	Competent Application	Consistency	Accuracy	Transparency	Tool Type
Stakeholder Analysis	●	●				Qualitative
Quick Financial Analysis	●					Qualitative
Enterprise Value Chain Mapping	●		●			Qualitative
Delphi Method	●					Qualitative
Workshop Facilitation		●	●			Qualitative
Cause and Effect Diagrams	●			●		Qualitative
Surveying and Interviewing		●	●			Qualitative

Assessment	Criticality	Competent Application	Consistency	Accuracy	Transparency	Tool Type
Basic Info Validation	●	●				Qualitative
Advanced Info Validation			●	●		Qualitative
Governance Guidelines	●	●	●	●	●	Qualitative
Graphical Spot Checking			●			Qualitative
Validation Through Simulations	●			●		Qualitative
Quantitative Modeling		●	●	●	●	Qualitative
Stress Testing	●	●				Qualitative

Quantit[...]ive [handwritten annotation]

Disposition	Criticality	Competent Application	Consistency	Accuracy	Transparency	Tool Type
Scenario Planning		●				Qualitative
Political Risk Analysis		●				Qualitative
Documentation Guidelines				●		Qualitative
Enterprise Risk Registers	●		●	●		Qualitative
Environmental Scanning	●	●	●			Qualitative

Fig. 6–3. Information integrity phases, fundamentals, and supporting qualitative and quantitative tools

An example of how a sampling of these tools would be applied in practice follows next.

"Feeding and care" of the stakeholders

We have mentioned the energy merchant of the 21st century as the alpha wolf, the oil and gas player that begins to lead the pack in this new era. From where will this new energy wolf come, and what will be its characteristics? First, this company will be increasingly outward focused and customer oriented. We must remember that the powerful "customers" for an oil and gas company are not retail consumers but rather the other stakeholders, ranging from regulators to environmentalists, board members, and stock analysts. These are the stakeholders who inhabit the new corporate landscape, and as mentioned in chapter 1, they are growing increasingly restless. To truly understand who they are and what they want, a stakeholder analysis (discovery tool 1) is useful for listing, prioritizing, and discovering their needs on the basis of the three stakeholder dimensions of attitude, sensitivity, and power. Table 6–1 below shows a sample listing of stakeholders resulting from a petroleum company stakeholder analysis.

Table 6–1. Petroleum company stakeholder analysis results

Stakeholder	Interests	Attitude	Sensitivity to Uncertainties	Power	Assurance Strategy
Board of directors	Corporate governance, legal, liability, financial results	Positive	Medium	High	Meet or exceed needs
SEC	Disclosure, financial (regulatory) compliance	Skeptical	Medium	Medium	Comply
Other regulators	Regulatory compliance, public welfare	Indifferent	Medium	Medium	Comply
Stock analysts	Short-term earnings, dividends, valuations, reputation	Positive	Medium	High	Meet or exceed needs
Bond rating agency	Liquidity, debt service, capacity	Negative	High	High	Focus on superior performance
Auditors	Compliance	Skeptical	High	Medium	Understand and meet needs
Institutional investors	Future earnings, dividends, valuations, reputation	Positive	High	High	Focus on superior performance
Individual investors	Share price growth, dividends, disclosure	Positive	Medium	Low	Status quo
Environmental NGOs	Air, water, land, pollution, "responsible care," minimal growth	Negative	Low	Low	Status quo, but monitor carefully
Host country government(s)	Legal compliance, investment, local content	Skeptical	High	High	Focus on superior performance
National oil companies (NOCs)	Technology, resource control, tax generation, social programs	Positive	Medium	High	Meet or exceed needs
Partners	Return on investment, reputation	Positive	High	Medium	Understand and meet needs
Employees	Safety, security, courtesy, job satisfaction, pay, benefits	Positive	Medium	Low	Status quo
Banks	Payment record, liquidity, collateral	Indifferent	High	Medium	Understand and meet needs
Local communities	Employment, security, safety, education, infrastructure, property rights	Skeptical	High	Low	Understand and meet needs
Local labor	Pay, benefits, safety, working conditions	Negative	High	Medium	Understand and meet needs
Politicians	Patronage to constituencies	Positive	Medium	High	Focus on superior performance

Once these stakeholders are identified, an in-depth understanding of their needs is obtained using market research techniques described in the section "Discovery Tool 7: Selected Surveying and Interviewing Techniques." Innovative approaches and development of new services would cause a step change in managing how the needs of these powerful stakeholders are met. From the consumer products arena comes an intriguing example of just such an approach to understanding customer needs and developing new solutions. Called the *lead user* concept, this approach to developing new products to satisfy customer needs is being used by 3M, the global manufacturer of consumer and industrial products.

3M's Deep Satisfaction of Customer Needs

An example of deeply understanding customer needs comes from the innovative, technology driven manufacturer, 3M Corporation, showing how new product development and customer needs satisfaction are taken to a new level. In collaboration with the prominent MIT business innovations professor Eric Von Hippel, 3M has figured out how to harness the creative energy of the *customers' own employees.*[4] 3M has convinced those customers to turn over new product ideas to 3M for commercialization, instead of relying solely on its own new ideas for new products. 3M encourages its customers' employees to develop the new ideas, then it shepherds them through the product development cycle and commercializes the products for its benefit. It calls this approach the *lead user* concept.

The way it works is that 3M first identifies leading edge customers—those who are the top companies in their respective fields. Because of their leading company reputation, these customers will often have attracted the brightest and most creative employees in their industry. 3M further identifies what the management author Tom Peters once called "skunk works," those small in-house creative teams of individuals within the customer's shop who are working on unauthorized but tolerated solutions to internal problems. It then convinces the customer to allow 3M to collaborate with these teams to capture, document, and prototype these new solutions. The distinguishing factor between Peters' skunk works products and 3M's lead user products is that 3M is not looking to steal from the customer's *own* new products development pipeline. Instead, it wants to take the innovative, but at times unorthodox or half-baked, solutions to *internal customer problems* that the customers do not intend to sell and market themselves, and commercialize them under the 3M banner.

How 3M gets its customers to agree to this is a case study in itself. It involves considerable executive-level support at both companies and tight intellectual property rights agreements. However, it is a fascinating example of how one company is developing close, trusting relationships that allow its customer needs to be uniquely met. One important element of success of this program is the intensive amounts of nonpaid time and resources that 3M (and the customer) are willing to invest in researching, talking, and working together toward new ideas to solve the customer's problems. Are there parallels here in the energy industry for how customer and stakeholder needs could be innovatively satisfied?

It is this type of innovative thinking about the satisfaction of stakeholder needs that will characterize the new energy wolf as a competitor. For example, could it be that the oil and gas company of the future will embed its employees into key stakeholder organizations (i.e., seconded employees) to more deeply understand how to satisfy their needs? In Japan, this seconding of employees into customer organizations and regulatory agencies is already a well-established practice. More and more, I expect to see leading multinational energy companies trying this with their customers as well.

To link customer needs and opportunities together with the company's internal environment, a solid understanding of the enterprise value chain is useful. For example, an analysis of an exploration and production company's value chain using enterprise value chain mapping (discovery tool 2) would show that access to new acreage containing proved reserves is a key driver of success. However, securing this new acreage requires more than overcoming technological or economic challenges. It requires listening to the voice of the customers (i.e., the stakeholders). However, when listening to earnings calls and analyst guidance by oil and gas company executives, a great deal of talk is focused on the geological, technical, and economic challenges relating to finding and developing reserves. Very little time is spent on opportunities based upon social, environmental, and political factors.

Beyond technical and economic threats and opportunities, there are macro trends affecting the social, environmental, and political aspects of finding and developing reserves that oil and gas exploration and production companies will increasingly need to deal with on a corporate or enterprise level. For example, the rise in resource nationalism and the strength of national oil companies (NOCs) as competitors outside their country of origin is an important long-term trend. The alignment of oil producing and consuming countries into non-OPEC political blocs is another trend. A third trend is the global climate change movement, which has gained mainstream support outside the confines of the traditional environmental NGOs. Identifying similar trends and spotting opportunities from more than simply a technical and economic perspective, using environmental scanning (disposition tool 5), is becoming an important core competence. The ability to spot multivariate or multidimensional opportunities will be an important characteristic of the new energy wolf. Environmental scanning is an enabling technology for this ability.

Sustained competitive advantage

We continue our previous consideration of national oil companies as stakeholders. First we assume that access to acreage is a significant value driver for investor-owned oil and gas companies (IOCs) because it drives reserve replacement and the creation of shareholder value. The world's largest untapped reserves are outside the home country markets of the major and independent IOCs. NOCs today control more than 60% of the world's oil and gas resources. Politicians from countries with large oil and gas reserves, from Russia to Venezuela, are restricting IOC ownership of natural resources. Around the world, resource nationalism with respect to hydrocarbons is on the rise. This creates a new challenge for reserve replacement and the creation of shareholder value for the IOCs.

For most of the 20th century, technological know-how, project management skills, and the ability to supply financing have allowed the IOCs to be in the driver's seat with respect to much of the crude oil value chain worldwide. Of course, financing and technology continue to be important catalysts for new field developments. But as commodity prices increase and exploration and production technology becomes available through the worldwide oil and gas supplier base, financing and technology are less of a differentiator than in the past. NOCs may not have state-of-the-art technology or unlimited capital, but they still control the resource. Today the balance of power between the IOC and the NOC has changed, with the latter emerging as a significant competitive force not only in their respective domestic markets but outside their countries of origin. This trend can be considered a threat or an opportunity depending upon how the IOCs view the NOCs as new partners, competitors, and stakeholders.

A careful analysis of the NOC as a stakeholder should reveal new ways that our energy wolf will differentiate itself in the 21st century to gain access to acreage where others cannot. In contrast to requiring financing, technology, and project management expertise, the NOC needs stem increasingly from the inherent commercial and administrative weaknesses of their native country governments, societies, educational systems, and cultures. Some of these countries have been developing their abundant natural resources for more than 50 years, yet have been unable to pull the majority of their citizens up from the depths of ignorance, disease, or poverty. These nontechnical problems (not related to project finance) result in continued political and social unrest. Over the life of a 30- to 40-year field development project, this unrest creates the political risks of sabotage and expropriation of assets for the IOCs. Unfortunately, neither the NOCs nor their governments are capable of satisfying these social and societal needs alone. They need outside expertise. Thus as a strategy for market dominance, the new energy wolf will actively take up this responsibility, effectively becoming one of the prime agents for long-term social and physical infrastructure development in these countries. Is this the appropriate role for a nongovernmental, foreign-headquartered multinational company? It depends upon how important this IOC considers access to new acreage and reserve replacement.

There are those who will argue that the development of host country infrastructure by multinationals is not new. It is argued that social offsets and community infrastructure development have always been part of the multinational's social responsibility when doing business in developing countries. To a degree, this is true. The invested capital compared with the resulting benefits to the local communities has at times been remarkable. A recent example is the Bioko Island Malaria Control Project (BIMCP) promoted by Marathon Oil, its partners, and the government of Equatorial Guinea, paralleling their natural gas developments there.[5] While commendable and certainly valuable to the community, from an enterprise risk perspective, the question should be, how much regulatory risk advantage does this effort gain with the powerful stakeholders who award permits and concessions? If I were the CFO of Marathon, Janet Clark, I would want to know how much reducing malaria in Equatorial Guinea acts as a hedge against expropriation of assets over the 30- to 40-year field life. These are the types of important questions that the energy wolf will have answered before investing in social programs and infrastructure development. Nevertheless, we expect that our wolf will look at social programs and infrastructure development (wherever it operates) not as an obligation, but as a strategy for competitive advantage.

Another scenario where a powerful stakeholder creates a threat to an oil and gas company's cost competitiveness is when a credit rating agency questions the reliability of information supporting the company's cash flow projections. As mentioned in chapter 2, the credit rating agencies Standard & Poor's (S&P's) and Moody's have poured significant effort into improving their ability to understand not only what is shown on a company's financial statements, but how a company manages its business risks. As explained previously, S&P's new business risk assessment procedure, called *PIM* (policy, infrastructure, and methodology), has a specific requirement for its rated companies to "ensure that there are processes in place to verify inputs to pricing models, assumptions made, and methods employed for verification."[7] What if they were to perform an assessment of the oil and gas company in question and found there to be no process in place to verify inputs and assumptions? This lack of assurance would certainly affect their view of the future liquidity of the oil and gas producer. The result could be that the agency would put the company on credit watch followed by a downgrade in its credit rating. Ultimately, this could increase expenses both by triggering interest rate hikes based on embedded covenants in the company's loan agreements as well as increasing the cost of issuing new bonds. Under this scenario, the lack of evidence of a validation process leads to decreased cost competitiveness.

Yet another scenario involving a stakeholder threat is from the environmental NGO that actively targets exploration activities of particular oil and gas producers. Today this activism is more than an annoyance to oil and gas producers and has escalated to the point where multibillion-dollar developments are being threatened on environmental grounds. The World Wildlife Fund, for example, has been particularly effective in organizing local communities and environmental regulators against exploration due to fears of the disruption of whale habitats in Arctic waters. Efforts from environmental groups have caused disruptions for Royal Dutch Shell on its Sakhalin II project, as well as for its exploration in the Beaufort Sea.[6] Environmental groups can no longer just be "controlled" as minor pests. Due to their increasing stakeholder power and sensitivity, they need to be studied and engaged. Some would even say they have earned their way to the bargaining table! The upper management of our energy wolf will understand and manage the concerns, motivations, and organization of its environmental stakeholders as thoroughly as it understands those of its investors.

The energy merchant of the 21st century is not called a *wolf* for nothing. There is no trickery or lack of transparency here, just a relentless focus on the customer (i.e., the stakeholder). The goal is to secure commercial advantage by legally and ethically satisfying the needs of the powerful stakeholders, whether they are NOCs, host country governments, credit rating agencies, or environmental groups. The tools in this book provide an IOC with the vehicle to move ahead of the pack.

Conclusions

As we have argued, from a strategic standpoint, one of the keys to success for tomorrow's energy wolf will be understanding and satisfying the needs of its stakeholders through the application of the tools, techniques, and methodologies presented in this book. Successful implementation of enterprise risk management (ERM) will extend beyond simply ensuring that financial statements are not fraudulent or that health, safety, and environmental regulations are complied with. To be successful, ERM should be viewed as strategic opportunity spotting, as opposed to defensive tactics. Finally, to discover the energy wolves who will be the leading energy merchants of the 21st century, stakeholders should look for a robust information integrity process and application of a toolbox. This toolbox must demonstrate evidence of criticality, consistency, competence, accuracy, and transparency behind the data. It is this systematic approach to the reliability of information that creates the *alpha* (or sustainable competitive) advantage.

References

1. Sharpe, W. 1964. Capital asset prices: a theory of market equilibrium under conditions of risk. *The Journal of Finance*. 19 (3): 425–442.

2. Burton, Jonathan. 1998. Revisiting the capital asset pricing model. Interview with William Sharpe. *Dow-Jones Asset Management*. May/June. pp. 20–28.

3. Kahneman, D., and A. Taversky. 1979. Prospect theory: an analysis of decision under risk. *Econometrica*. (March). 47 (2): 263.

4. von Hippel, E., and M. Sonnack. 1999. Breakthroughs to order at 3M. MIT-SSM Working Paper. January. http://web.mit.edu/evhippel/www/papers/3M%20Breakthrough%20 Art.pdf

5. Marathon Oil Company. 2006. Social responsibility Equatorial Guinea malaria control project. *Marathon Facts*. (September). http://www.marathon.com/content/documents/fact_sheets/fact_sheet_malaria_september_2006.pdf

6. Gullo, K., and T. Hopfinger. 2007. Shell's Alaska drilling project halted by court (update2). *Bloomberg.com*. (July 20). http://www.bloomberg.com/apps/news?pid=newsarchive&sid=a6JWfXjfp9Xc

7. Samanta, P., Azarks, T., Martinez, J., Nov. 2005. *Enterprise Risk Management for Financial Institutions: Rating Criteria and Best Practices*. New York: Standard & Poor's.

Acronyms and Abbreviations

APT	arbitrage pricing theory
AICPA	American Institute of Certified Public Accountants
bpd	barrels per day
BIMCP	Bioko Island Malaria Control Project
CAPM	capital asset pricing model
CCRO	Committee of Chief Risk Officers
COSO	Committee of Sponsoring Organizations of the Treadway Commission
EBITDA	earnings before interest and taxes, amortization, and depreciation
EFQM	European Foundation for Quality Management
EIU	Economist Intelligence Unit
ERM	enterprise risk management
EUR	estimated ultimate recovery
GARCH	generalized autoregressive conditional heteroscedasticity (model)
IOOC	investor-owned oil company
IPAA	Independent Petroleum Association of America

IQRS	International Quality Rating System
ISRS	International Safety Rating System
JODI	Joint Oil Industry Data Initiative (coordinated by OPEC)
MSCI	Morgan Stanley Capital International (world stock index)
NGO	nongovernmental organization
NOC	national oil company
NSRO	Nationally Recognized Statistical Rating Organization
OPEC	Organization of Petroleum Exporting Countries
PDVSA	Petróleos de Venezuela S.A.
PERD	plant and equipment reliability (database)
PIM	policy, infrastructure, and methodology (framework)
RSS	Really Simple Syndication
SMOG	standardized measure of discounted future cash flows
SPE	special purpose entity
STEEP	social, technological, economic, environmental, and political
TQM	total quality movement
XBRL	Extensible Business Reporting Language
XML	Extensible Markup Language

Index

E

I

Q

qualitative, 96
Quality Toolbox (Tague), 102, 146
quantitative modeling, 156, 157–162
  consistency in, 160–162
  ERM and, 162
quarterly business risk
  management workshop, 84
questionnaires, 90–91
  administering, 91
  testing, 105–106
quick financial analysis, 65, 66–70, 75
quick look, 65, 66–68
  at balance sheets, 67–68
  at cash flows, 68
  at income statements, 66–67

R

RAND Corporation, 87
rational, 254
RDI Consulting, 6
reasonable assurance, 10–12, 130,
  181–182
reasonable certainty, 52, 181, 182
rectangles, 95
reference data sets, 146
refining, marketing, and logistics
  (RM&L), 108, 111
relations diagram, 93
reliability of information, 34, 43, 182
  external, 50–53
reliant, 16
Repsol, 45, 46
research instruments, 102
residuals, 169
Respol YPF, 20
responsibilities, establishing, 60

Reuters, 139
revenue model output, 158
review, 59
rising stars, 112
@Risk, 153, 154, 156
risk analysis, 41
risk assessment, 58
risk dashboard, 217
risk decomposition, 171
risk factors, standard financial
  statement disclosures, 69
risk governance, 41
risk identification, 58, 222
risk infrastructure, 41
risk logs, 211
risk management, 1–12, 41
  on corporate level, 215
risk matrices, 213
risk profile, 112
risk quantification, 41
risk registers, 9, 211–217
  databases, 213
  in ERM, 216
  expanded risk, 215, 238
  input, 212
  in Microsoft Excel, 214
  process, 213–216
  standard, 215, 237, 238
risk response and control
  activities, 60, 191
risk terminology, 165
risk treatment, 58, 60
RM&L, 108, 111
robust model development, 161–162
roles, establishing, 60
Royal Dutch Shell, 20, 263
RSS feeds, 215, 239
Russel Reynolds Associates, 38, 41
Ryder Scott Company, 46, 149, 150

S

Sakhalin II, 263
Sampling, Monte Carlo, xv, 10, 58, 74, 94, 112, 153, 154
San Felipe Resources (SFR), xix, 64, 107–125, 126, 174–187, 224, 225–248
    conceptual model for crude oil price behavior, 183
    memorandum, 122, 228
    price decks, 183
    value chain, 112
Sandia National Laboratories, 226
Sarbanes-Oxley Act, 9, 16, 37, 45, 71, 108, 177, 191, 208, 234, 235
Saudi Arabia, 21, 100
Saudi Aramco, 22
Scanning in the Business Environment (Aguilar), 220
scatter plot examples, 145, 148
scenario analysis, 165, 192
scenario building, 197
    steps, 198
scenario development, 196
    process, 227
scenario planning, 194–200
    development, 196
    elements of good, 196
    ERM application, 199
    highlighting, 195
scenarios, 166
Schwartz, Peter, 194, 196, 204, 224, 226
scribes, 83
searchability, 8–10
searching, 220, 221
SEC, 51, 64, 65, 69, 235
secondary data validation process, 208
secondary sources, 137
Section 404, 51
security, 8–10

sensitivity, 5–6
    multiple, 166
    stakeholder, 79
SER, 166
SFR, xix, 64, 107–125, 126, 174–187, 224, 225–248
    conceptual model for crude oil price behavior, 183
    memorandum, 122, 228
    price decks, 183
    value chain, 112
shapes for information integrity, 94
Sharpe, William, 253
Shell, 16, 20, 45, 46, 199, 246
Shell Global Scenarios to 2025, 199
significant assumptions, 17, 44
Simmons, Matthew, 21, 22
simulation, 143–144
    inputs in, 155–156
    outputs in, 155–156
    validation through, 153–156
single event risk (SER), 166
Skilling, Jeff, 18
Smith, Sarah Harrison, 139, 142
SMOG, 45
Social Christian Party, 229
Society of Petroleum Engineers (SPE), 21, 46, 143, 160, 177
soundness standards, 28
Southern Company, 29
spark spreads, 31
SPE, 21, 46, 143, 160, 177
special purpose entities (SPEs), 79
SPEs, 79
spreadsheet models, 154
SQL, 237
stakeholder analysis, 76–82
    acting on, 80–81
    ERM and, 77
    petroleum company, 258
    process, 78–81
    workshop template, 80

W

X

Y

Z